*The Social Anxieties
of Progressive Reform*

The American Social Experience
SERIES

General Editor:
JAMES KIRBY MARTIN

Editors:
PAULA S. FASS, STEVEN H. MINTZ,
CARL PRINCE, JAMES W. REED & PETER N. STEARNS

1. *The March to the Sea and Beyond: Sherman's Troops in the Savannah and Carolinas Campaigns*
   JOSEPH T. GLATTHAAR

2. *Childbearing in American Society: 1650–1850*
   CATHERINE M. SCHOLTEN

3. *The Origins of Behaviorism: American Psychology, 1870–1920*
   JOHN M. O'DONNELL

4. *New York City Cartmen, 1667–1850*
   GRAHAM RUSSELL HODGES

5. *From Equal Suffrage to Equal Rights: Alice Paul and the National Woman's Party, 1910–1928*
   CHRISTINE A. LUNARDINI

6. *Mr. Jefferson's Army: Political and Social Reform of the Military Establishment, 1801–1809*
   THEODORE J. CRACKEL

7. *"A Peculiar People": Slave Religion and Community-Culture among the Gullahs*
   MARGARET WASHINGTON CREEL

8. *"A Mixed Multitude": The Struggle for Toleration in Colonial Pennsylvania*
   SALLY SCHWARTZ

9. *Women, Work, and Fertility, 1900–1986*
   SUSAN HOUSEHOLDER VAN HORN

10. Liberty, Virtue, and Progress: Northerners and
Their War for the Union
EARL J. HESS

11. Lewis M. Terman: Pioneer in Psychological Testing
HENRY L. MINTON

12. Schools as Sorters: Lewis M. Terman, Applied Psychology,
and the Intelligence Testing Movement, 1890–1930
PAUL DAVIS CHAPMAN

13. Free Love: Marriage and Middle-Class Radicalism in America, 1825–1860
JOHN C. SPURLOCK

14. Jealousy: The Evolution of an Emotion in American History
PETER N. STEARNS

15. The Nurturing Neighborhood: The Brownsville Boys Club and
Jewish Community in Urban America, 1940–1990
GERALD SORIN

16. War in America to 1775: Before Yankee Doodle
JOHN MORGAN DEDERER

17. An American Vision: Far Western Landscape and
National Culture, 1820–1920
ANNE FARRAR HYDE

18. Frederick Law Olmsted: The Passion of a Public Artist
MELVIN KALFUS

19. Medical Malpractice in Nineteenth-Century America:
Origins and Legacy
KENNETH ALLEN DE VILLE

20. Dancing in Chains: The Youth of William Dean Howells
RODNEY D. OLSEN

21. Breaking the Bonds: Marital Discord in Pennsylvania, 1730–1830
MERRIL D. SMITH

22. In the Web of Class: Delinquents and Reformers in Boston, 1810s–1830s
ERIC C. SCHNEIDER

23. *Army of Manifest Destiny: The American Soldier in the
Mexican War, 1846–1848*
JAMES M. MCCAFFREY

24. *The Dutch-American Farm*
DAVID STEVEN COHEN

25. *Independent Intellectuals in the United States, 1910–1945*
STEVEN BIEL

26. *The Modern Christmas in America: A Cultural History of Gift Giving*
WILLIAM B. WAITS

27. *The First Sexual Revolution: The Emergence of
Male Heterosexuality in Modern America*
KEVIN WHITE

28. *Bad Habits: Drinking, Smoking, Taking Drugs, Gambling,
Sexual Misbehavior, and Swearing in American History*
JOHN C. BURNHAM

29. *General Richard Montgomery and the American Revolution:
From Redcoat to Rebel*
HAL T. SHELTON

30. *From Congregation Town to Industrial City: Culture and Social Change
in a Southern Community*
MICHAEL SHIRLEY

31. *The Social Anxieties of Progressive Reform: Atlantic City, 1854–1920*
MARTIN PAULSSON

The Social Anxieties of Progressive Reform

Atlantic City, 1854–1920

MARTIN PAULSSON

NEW YORK UNIVERSITY PRESS
New York and London

NEW YORK UNIVERSITY PRESS
New York and London

Copyright © 1994 by New York University

All rights reserved

Library of Congress Cataloging-in-Publication Data
Paulsson, Martin.
The social anxieties of progressive reform : Atlantic City, 1854–1920 / Martin Paulsson.
p.   cm.—(The American social experience)
Revision of the author's thesis (Ph.D.)—Rutgers—The State University.
Includes bibliographical references and index.
ISBN: 978-0-8147-6643-9
1. Atlantic City (N.J.)—Politics and government.   2. Atlantic City (N.J.)—Social conditions.   3. Kuehnle, Louis, d. 1934.   4. Progressivism (United States politics)   I. Title. II. Series.
F144.A8P28   1994
974.9′85041—dc20   93-47416

New York University Press books are printed on acid-free paper, and their binding materials are chosen for strength and durability.

Manufactured in the United States of America

10   9   8   7   6   5   4   3   2   1

To Eleanor Miller Paulsson

Contents

	List of Illustrations	xiii
	Acknowledgments	xv
ONE	The Kuehnle Myth	1
TWO	From Pitney's Folly to World's Playground	14
THREE	The Robbery of the Sabbath	57
FOUR	Low Resorts	87
FIVE	A Saturnalia of Vice	116
SIX	The Reason: The Rise and Fall of Boss Kuehnle	141
SEVEN	Pharisees and Hypocrites	179
	Notes	201
	Bibliography	233
	Index	241

Illustrations

Atlantic City in 1905   44

The following illustrations appear as an insert after p. 110

Absecon Island, 1890s

The Founding Triumvirate: Jonathan Pitney; Samuel Richards; Richard Osborne

The *Roanoke*, the Camden and Atlantic's First Engine

Atlantic City Hotels, 1857

Beachfront at Virginia Avenue, 1866 and 1896

The Boardwalk, 1867, 1870, 1885, and 1895

Seabathing, 1867; A Beach Scene, 1886; Woman on the Beach, 1914; and Woman Bathing, 1904

The Beach, 1895 and 1915

Schaufler's Hotel, 1885

The Extra Dry Cafe, 1900

Kuehnle's Hotel, 1900

Louis Kuehnle

Louis Kuehnle

Chalfonte House and Chalfonte-Haddon Hall

The Traymore Hotel

Atlantic City, 1912

Black Excursionists, 1895

Unsigned Postcard, 1908

Harry Bacharach

The Kuehnle Fortress under Siege

Louis Kuehnle

William Riddle

Louis Kuehnle with Dog   166

Cartoon of African-American Voters   168

Acknowledgments

A public school teacher does not write a doctoral dissertation without incurring significant personal debts to mentors, colleagues, friends, and family. My committee from the Rutgers Graduate History Faculty, Professors David Oshinsky, Richard L. McCormick, and James Reed, persevered with this project over a long period of time and gave me unfailing advice and encouragement. Professor Angus Gillespie offered valuable comment and criticism. Each member of my committee extended himself well beyond what was required and deserves credit for the completion of this study. Its errors and failings are entirely my own.

Professors John Karras and Daniel Crofts of Trenton State College, Professor Maxine Lurie of Rutgers University, and George and Nancy Tapper read large portions of my preliminary text and helped bring a semblance of order to a potentially chaotic study. During the course of my work I was fortunate to have made the acquaintance of historians Alan Dawley, Arthur Link, Clement Price, and John Reynolds, each of whom lent a sympathetic ear as I wrestled with the problems of Progressive reform and suggested sources and approaches that were helpful.

Niko Pfund of New York University Press provided timely assistance in making the manuscript into a book, including introducing me to assistant editor Jennifer Hammer, who, by phone and letter, helped demystify the science of word processing. I owe a special debt to Jim Reed, who has been with this project from beginning to end. During the final stages, he gave me a great deal of assistance, but little sympathy, as he had done manuscripts on a typewriter.

I did much of the research during two sabbaticals granted by my principal employer, the Lawrence Township Public Schools. My superiors, colleagues, friends, and students at Lawrence High School and Trenton State College were both indulgent and supportive of my effort. Ruth Bills, Virginia Bogart, James Csogi, Samuel Floyd, Joanna Gerwell, Barry Gleim, Onee Hertzog, Jeffrey Kirswell, Sue Miller, Andrea Odinov, Walter Radomski, Stanley Rose, Stephanie Rose, Mark Rowe, Michael Saetta, Magdalena Sobieszczyk, Gale Tapper, Anthony Watson, and especially Joanne Manto, Marilyn Roman, and Patricia Wooley, provided support and assistance along the way for which I am grateful.

Librarians, archivists, and other friends of history are the unsung contributors to every dissertation. Elizabeth Barker of the New Jersey State Library and Richard Matthews and Carol Miklovis of Trenton State College were very helpful in locating obscure sources. A grant from the New Jersey Historical Commission aided in getting the research underway, and research director Howard Green contributed his own knowledge of the New Jersey sources on Progressivism. The personal collections of A. Tobias Grace and Howard Kyle contained useful treasures, which they generously shared along with their time and effort. The volunteer staff of the Atlantic County Historical Society, especially the director, Betty Ehrhart; Marie Boyd of the Heston Room at the Atlantic City Public Library; and the staff of the Southern New Jersey Methodist Conference at the Pennington School were congenial and helpful hosts as I made my way through local sources.

My deepest debt is to my family. My wife Paula and my children Albert and Mary managed to preserve the amenities of family life while I was cloistered in my room. My sister Lynda, and Jim and Mary Russo, supported me in a number of ways. Finally, and most importantly, there is my mother, Eleanor Miller Paulsson, whose idea this was in the first place. Her love of books and interest in the topic were a constant inspiration. This work is dedicated to her. I can only hope she approves.

*The Social Anxieties
of Progressive Reform*

CHAPTER ONE

The Kuehnle Myth

The arrest of Mayor James Usry for bribery in July 1989 was to an *Atlantic City Press* reporter merely the latest episode in an "unending tale of corruption" that began in Atlantic City before the turn of the century. In 1984 Usry's predecessor, Michael Matthews, pled guilty to accepting bribes, and federal investigators revealed that he had connections to organized crime. Usry was the eighth mayor of Atlantic City to have been arrested or indicted by state or federal authorities since 1909, and there is a good deal more in the history of the resort that justified the reporter's assertion that "corruption was built into the town's very streets and sewers." At this writing, Usry has not been convicted of anything. Yet, given the incessant cycles of scandal and reform in Atlantic City, it is not surprising that a local citizen reacted to Usry's arrest by wondering if there were something in the air or the water of Absecon Island that predisposed the city to vice, municipal corruption, and boss rule.[1]

The period prior to the advent of legalized casinos in 1976 is known as "The Republican Boss Era of Atlantic City." One writer observed that "no Big Bill Thompson, Huey Long, or Boss Crump was more corrupt or exercised more political control than the three bosses who successively ruled this tiny island during this period.[2] The "bosses," in order, were "Commodore" Louis Kuehnle (1900–1914), Enoch L. "Nucky" Johnson (1916–1941), and state senator Frank S. "Hap" Farley (1941–1971). That era ended with Farley's defeat for reelection in 1971.

According to a view that has gained wide currency both within and outside Atlantic City, Farley fell heir to a political machine forged around 1900 by Louis Kuehnle, the first of the "all powerful bosses" to rule the city. Kuehnle was sentenced to state prison for grafting in 1912 during the administration of Governor Woodrow Wilson, an event that figured significantly in Wilson's presidential campaign. His downfall was the result of a reform movement that took place between 1908 and 1912. This study analyzes that reform movement.

The *Philadelphia Evening Times* saw Kuehnle's sentence as "welcome news." Atlantic City's politics "smelt as vile as the mud flats on its own thoroughfare" (the creek that separated the island from the meadows), and if Kuehnle could be brought down, "why, there's hope for us." According to the *Philadelphia North American*, "the genial, open-handed Commodore was perhaps the most powerful political boss a city ever had. He controlled not only its politics, but its legitimate business."[3] An editorial in the *New York Sun* exclaimed: "If you were to take all the power exercised by Boss Tweed, the Philadelphia gang, the Pittsburgh Ring, Abe Ruef in San Francisco, and Tammany Hall, and concentrate it on one man, you would still fall a little short of Kuehnle's clutch on Atlantic City."[4] Speaking at the Traymore Hotel in November 1911, Governor Woodrow Wilson found the city living under a "reign of terror." "There are policemen at the door," said Wilson, "who would lay hands on me if they dared. . . . It is a question of emancipation from everything that is disgraceful and rotten."[5]

Less than a year later, Wilson would also exclaim privately that New York was "rotten to the core," but to him, and to a host of Progressive reformers, particularly evangelicals, the rawness of commercial vice, election frauds, and municipal corruption in Atlantic City transcended the evils they had discovered in even the worst of other cities. Black votes sustained a Republican machine so powerful as to render the laws of the state a virtual nullity on the island. The city swarmed with prostitutes and was controlled by a shadow government of gamblers and saloon keepers. Registration lists were padded, ballot boxes stuffed, and black repeaters openly sold their votes on the street corners at the going rate of two dollars. Kuehnle controlled the mayor, city council, the police department, and the sheriff's office. Reformers were terrorized. County grand juries, stacked with party stalwarts, refused to indict lawbreakers, and Kuehnle and his henchmen looted the city with impunity until the Wilson administration broke the machine in 1911. To the *Philadelphia*

North American, "Kuehnleism" was "the menace of political domination through terrorism and vice."[6] This is the essence of the Kuehnle myth.

Beginning in 1908, when reformers commenced a political battle for control of the city, stories of the resort dominated by a powerful and corrupt Republican machine resting on black votes found wide credibility among a reading public inundated with muckraking accounts of city bosses grown fat from municipal graft and the protection of vice lords. This facile picture has endured for eighty years, and has seduced contemporary journalists, and even scholars.

Myths are not made out of whole cloth. By 1911 much in outward appearances seemed to confirm this view, especially the existence of a large bloc of black Republican voters who made convenient targets for political reformers. Atlantic City's reputation for wickedness during the Progressive era derived more from commercial vice than from municipal corruption, and, to be sure, the resort has had its share, and perhaps more, of gamblers and prostitutes since 1890. But what may have been true of the Johnson and Farley years was much less in evidence during this period. Kuehnle was indeed an influential citizen and, for a time, the titular head of the Republican organization. But at no time, between 1900 and 1912, did either he or that organization control the city or dictate its policies.

The first serious effort to "clean up Atlantic City" began at a time when the control of amusements and commercial vice was tighter than it had ever been. By 1908 the city was governed by the "liberal policy," a system of strategic censorship designed to assuage evangelical objections to the city's violation of New Jersey's strict Sunday laws and to mute class conflict among visitors and residents. Since 1902 the liberal policy had undergone several revisions as concessions to Protestant clergymen and wealthy Boardwalk hotel owners, themselves mostly Republicans, and the groups who formed the nucleus of the reform movement. By 1908, in matters most important to its economic and social well being, the city was governed not by a machine, but by a compact. The liberal policy, in effect, sanctioned Sunday drinking as well as gambling and prostitution, under certain controls, but it closed the amusements on Sunday, eliminated the grosser manifestations of social disorder, and it also segregated blacks from the beach and the Boardwalk. If the liberal policy was neither legal nor especially moral, it represented a compromise among all of the diverse interests that made up the community, save, of course, the black Northside. It also found acceptance among the thousands of working-, middle-, and upper-class visitors who regularly patronized the resort and gave it a period of unprecedented prosperity.

How then do we explain a reform movement in which Woodrow Wilson bent the entire machinery of state government to the destruction of Kuehnle and the local Republican organization, a movement that convulsed and polarized the city for four years and produced over two hundred indictments against city and county officials and local citizens for gambling, excise violations, election fraud, bribery, extortion, and graft? The laws of New Jersey were indeed broken, and part of the explanation, as reformers correctly perceived, lay in the loose moral ambience of commercial resorts and the tendency of some recreational entrepreneurs to provide amusements that were unsanctioned by the larger society. But lawlessness and greed do not begin to explain Progressive reform in Atlantic City.

For at least a generation, historians have argued convincingly that the visions of social justice and public rectitude that have shaped American politics have been conditioned primarily, though not exclusively, by the ethnocultural identities of citizens. Nativism, racism, and concern over the erosion of traditional institutions of authority, particularly the church and the family, have constituted the real fault lines of American society.[7] This interpretation applies with added force to the study of urban reform movements during the industrial era, a period when large numbers of Southern blacks and Catholic and Jewish Europeans changed the face of Northern cities, when the disruption of traditional patterns of work and leisure profoundly altered the relationships between men and women, and when the anonymity of urban life held out the lure of increased personal and sexual freedom for Americans of all social and economic classes. For all of the modern hygiene, medicine, technology, and social science that both secular and evangelical Progressives had come to embrace, one of the simple truths, and, indeed, the human tragedy of Progressive reform, is that, at least as often as not, it found itself sharply at odds with the reality of human behavior in industrial society.

The development of the commercial resort industry during the last half of the nineteenth century meant that leisure activities would increasingly take place apart from the traditional constraints of community, church, and family. What we now call "lifestyle" underwent a profound transformation, one that is still underway. Since the 1870s Atlantic City has hosted thousands of visitors, each of whom would draw his or her own line between vice and innocent pleasure. Despite its elitist pretensions, the lifeblood of the city's economy had always been the middle and lower classes who sought in its breezes and amusements a brief respite from the grime and monotony of the industrial world.

This cultural revolution was rooted in the secular diversions of the working classes and found its purest expression in commercial recreation. Such things as baseball and mechanical amusements were beginning to gain wide acceptance during the 1880s. During the 1890s vaudeville, dancing, and popular music, and later, motion pictures attracted large crowds. Of course, during this period, the saloon, as well, came into its own as a recreational institution. Many secular Progressives such as Jane Addams, but more especially, evangelicals, cast a jaundiced eye at the new forms of leisure, seeing in them a disintegration of standards and social order. Their cultural hegemony was slipping away to a class of recreational entrepreneurs who were quick to seize the profits of mass culture. Worse yet, their own children were not immune. The lure of secular amusement was pervasive, and nowhere was this more evident than in Atlantic City.[8]

Coming to terms with the new social order was easier for some Protestant elites than for others. Bicycling, baseball, football, and prizefighting were the rage in the 1890s, as were ragtime and the cakewalk which sprang from the syncopated rhythms of the black South. Sports and popular music were seen as expressions of the vigor and virility of American society, what Theodore Roosevelt praised as "the strenuous life." In this culture of youth, men became more masculine and women "more manly."[9] In 1895 *Scribner's* spoke approvingly of the "summer girl" (aged 17 to 23) who "invariably wishes to go where it is gay. Her idea of enjoyment does not admit to domesticity and peaceful relaxation. She craves to be actively amused, if not blissfully excited." It concluded its analysis of the "summer problem" by adding: "It speaks well for the intelligence and unselfishness of middle-aged parents and guardians in this country that they so promptly recognize the legitimate claims of youth."[10] The crowds of middle- and upper-class patrons who thronged the Boardwalk amusements in Atlantic City provide evidence enough that the popular forms of commercial recreation had captured broad segments of middle- and upper-class America.

To many Protestant clerics, commercial resorts, even in their most innocent aspects, presented a continual public spectacle of sin and social disorder. This could be true of any day in Atlantic City where such things as mixed bathing and drinking and dancing to the strains of popular music excited the worst fears of evangelicals. But it was especially true of resort Sundays, when the crowds were largest, and the seeming indifference of the people to the sanctity of the Sabbath and the laws of the state confirmed the evangelical view that commercial recreation had legitimized the worst manifestations of industrial society.

In 1891 Josiah Strong wrote: "Most foreigners bring with them continental ideas of the Sabbath, and the result is sadly manifest in all our cities where it is being transformed from a holy day into a holiday. But by far the most effective instrumentality for debauching popular morals is the liquor traffic, and this is chiefly carried on by foreigners."[11] The image of the city, the immigrant, and the saloon as instruments of public debauchery is a well-explored theme, long familiar to students of *fin de siècle* America. Less familiar, and less understood, is the issue of Sabbath observance, a facet of evangelical reform that impinged as heavily on the cities as did Prohibition. "There is, perhaps, no better index of general morality than Sabbath observance," warned Strong, "and everybody knows that there has been a great increase of Sabbath desecration in (the past) twenty years."[12]

Beginning with the formation of the National Reform League in Ohio in 1863, the movement to preserve the Christian Sunday steadily gathered strength in the United States and reached the peak of its influence during the Progressive era. During the 1870s and 1880s, states and municipalities throughout the country passed stringent Sunday closing laws in response to the growing influence of the Sabbatarian movement. Widespread defiance of Sunday restrictions generated intense social and political conflicts, particularly in urban areas, and sharply accentuated the growing social chasm between the Protestant churches and the masses of the American people.

Historians of urban reform and Prohibition have not ignored Sabbatarianism. In most accounts, they faithfully include Sabbath desecration in the litany of protests made by the Strongs of the era. Often there is a paragraph or two, or perhaps a footnote, attributing the movement to class and ethnic tensions. More traditional approaches either dismiss Sabbatarianism as a vestige of Puritanism or see Sabbatarian conflicts as evidence of the widening urban/rural dichotomy in American society after the Civil War or as modern antagonism toward the quaint strictures of Victorian morality. But Victoria herself was known to take a drink and had little patience with Sabbatarian reformers.[13] What is lacking is the recognition of the power and pervasiveness of modern Sabbatarianism

ism and the moral ambivalence among Protestants themselves over the Sunday issue. No less important is the ambivalence of the state and federal courts and the resulting legal and social complexities arising from the attempts of state and local authorities to enforce Sunday restrictions, which, by 1890, were in place in practically every state.

One historian, in a study of the American work ethic, attributed Sabbatarian conflict to changing attitudes toward leisure and recreation and to the shortening of the industrial workweek.

> The Sabbath controversy stood for more than the legitimacy of a Sunday ballgame. Sabbatarianism had been a fighting, defining point for English Puritans, and the stiff and proper regime of serious thoughts and disciplinary self-denials had formed a central part of the experience of generations of churchgoing Northern families. Nothing more clearly symbolized the injunctions to duty and self-discipline, the obligations of careful, watchful control of self and time that were at the heart of the Protestant Reformation.[14]

Sabbatarians battled the forces of commercialized recreation throughout the Progressive era, but "the old rigid rhythms of the Protestant Sabbath were no match for the influx of new amusements." Politically, they were successful; Sabbath restrictions were a fact of life in every Northern state. But by 1920 the laws were a dead letter, undermined by the habits of industrial society.

The only comprehensive and scholarly treatment of American Sabbatarianism is Winton Solberg's *Redeem the Time*, which traces the movement from its Puritan beginnings in Elizabethan England to the Great Awakening in the 1730s and 1740s. "No phase of our early history," said Solberg, "exhibits a greater discrepancy between the importance of the subject to contemporaries and the indifference to it of most historians." Originally intending to use Sabbath observance as an index of religious pluralism in the United States after 1800, he found the subject "highly significant in its own right." The intended chapter on Sabbatarianism became a book.[15]

Looking ahead to another volume, he suggested that "after 1740 the periods of greatest significance in the history of Sabbatarianism were in the late eighteenth century and the decades from the 1820s to the 1880s."[16] During the 1780s and 1790s Sabbath restrictions were codified by the states, and the 1820s witnessed a strong nationwide effort to stop the Sunday mails. My own research indicates that the power and influence of the movement was only beginning to be felt in the United States by the 1880s, that it crested in New Jersey in 1909, and that it was a significant and perplexing factor in urban reform movements during the Progressive era, and not just in commercial resorts.

The conflict over Sabbath observance came to a head in New Jersey in 1908 when Governor John Franklin Fort appointed the Crimes and Excise Commissions to investigate law enforcement and the liquor traffic. The commissions conducted hearings and investigations and produced reams of evidence on social conditions and levels of commercial vice in each county and in practically every city of the state. They also documented the determined decade-long struggles of church-based law and order leagues to close the bars on Sunday and the stiff opposition they encountered from police and local officials and from a wide range of citizens' groups who held that Sunday drinking was a matter of personal liberty. When the mayor of Atlantic City ignored a direct order from the governor to close the bars on Sunday, the conflict reached a crisis. The irate Fort declared the city a "Saturnalia of Vice" and threatened to call out the militia to enforce the Sunday laws.

Fort's Saturnalia proclamation had a devastating effect on Atlantic City. It destroyed the liberal policy and generated an intense political conflict among factions of the local Republican organization. But the events of 1908 only partially explain the origins of the reform movement. The term "Kuehnleism" conjured a hydra of evils that were anathema to evangelicals and secular Progressives alike. If we need nine serpents to satisfy the metaphor, we have gambling, prostitution, the liquor traffic, graft, materialism, election frauds, race suicide, the decline of religiosity—or at least of moral standards—and the desecration of the Sabbath, the last of which was symbolic of all the rest.

But each of these evoked primary responses among diverse social, religious, economic, ethnic, and political groups with the result that, by 1911, Kuehnle, "the machine," and Atlantic City itself confronted an array of related but distinct hostile forces. The efforts of this diverse legion of reformers were legitimized by a host of muckraking journalists, much to the detriment of the city's image.

To describe the forces of reform is to paint only half of the picture. What of the counterforces? If the study of Progressive reform is to have meaning in terms of what it reveals about American society and its institutions, we must deal in similar depth with the "objects" of reform, in this case with the boss, the machine, and the underclass.

Progressives never won an election in Atlantic City, a fact explained by reformers in typical fashion. The resort, like its parent city, the Philadelphia of Lincoln Steffens, was "corrupt and contented," a condition invariably reduced to the phrase "the easy purchasability of black votes." Kuehnle was a diabolically appealing figure, a shrewd practitioner of the wisdom of George Washington Plunkett. Words like "boss" and "machine" constituted a brusque dismissal of urban political organizations as creatures of venality who preyed upon and perpetuated the poverty and degradation of their constituents. A Newark jeremiah saw an election defeat of resort Progressives in 1911 as evidence that the residents were content to wallow in their own filth and predicted that they would soon get their comeuppance. Decent people would stay away, and the city would wither and die.[17]

But decent people did not stay away. They came in increasing numbers. For Progressives, this posed an interesting intellectual dilemma, the Atlantic City version of the age-old Paradox of Democracy. If indeed the city dispensed wickedness, what could they say of its consumers, who, by their own evidence, consisted of a broad spectrum of American society? Evangelicals had a ready explanation: Americans had lost their soul. To secular Progressives, wedded, in principle, to freedom and democracy, the explanation was not so simple.

Laying the cornerstone of a new YMCA building in Atlantic City in July 1912, Woodrow Wilson offered the following: "One of the great dangers of Atlantic City is that so many men come here. They know that they are a great distance from their homes and believe that there are no home folks here to watch them. They are too apt to adjourn their morals and have a fling. If they would only realize that if they thought the people at home were down, they would keep steady and would realize what homes mean to them."[18] Wilson went on to praise the YMCA as an instrument of "moral sanitation" and a "means for purifying man." For Wilson the Progressive, the answer lay in education; for Wilson the Presbyterian, in moral uplift. But what if the students failed to "keep steady"? The YMCA building still stood in 1992, but housed a drug rehabilitation program.

Jane Addams wrestled with this dilemma, as did Herbert Croly, Walter Lippmann, and Louis Brandeis. From another perspective, so did William Jennings Bryan and Eugene Victor Debs. Why could people not see the self and societal destructiveness of their own behavior, or why couldn't workers bury the differences between native and immigrant and black and white and recognize that the obstacles to social progress lay in the arrogation of wealth and power by industrial capitalists? For some reason, "the people" never quite behaved as they should, even when rigorously instructed.

Progressive reform could prove to be an undemocratic process. It was also intrusive, could often turn violent, and invariably demoralized a whole range of social, ethnic, and working-class groups to whom reform meant the criminalization of long-held personal, recreational, religious, or even sexual practices that provided welcome relief from the tedium and regimentation of work in industrial society.

We needn't look deeply to fathom the reactions of thousands of baseball fans on learning that the Sunday game had been enjoined by a handful of local clergy while Sunday golf was a weekly ritual for the upper classes. What were the feelings of a Jewish butcher, arrested for selling meat on Sunday, or those of Newark German-Americans whose beer gardens and concert halls were closed on that day while the factories operated? Crackdowns and police raids on brothels and gambling dens were to be expected, but we should not be surprised that agents of the Law and Order League, armed with legal warrants, received a chilly or even violent reception when they entered a neighborhood saloon on Sunday. Protestant hegemony weighed heavily upon large segments of American society, particularly upon the working classes, European immigrants, black people, and religious minorities such as Jews, Mormons, and Seventh Day Adventists.

The Social Purity crusade, the social hygiene movement, the Florence Crittendon Circle, the white slavery scare, and the career of Anthony Comstock provide evidence of a deep concern over sexual morality at the turn of the century, as did also the eugenics movement, the epidemic of lynching and race riots, and the prosecution of heavyweight champion Jack Johnson, in 1913, for violation of the Mann Act.[19] For Progressives, the intraracial American family represented the socio-sexual ideal. Deviations from that norm raised the twin specters of sexual anarchy and race suicide. But for a sizable portion of the working classes—again, particularly blacks—economic circumstances made that ideal all but unreachable, and intimate relationships between the sexes were formed in contexts that the larger society condemned as immoral and illegal.

The objects of Progressive reform were, by their own lights, neither corrupt nor contented. Yet certain of their behavior patterns had predictable and disastrous results for both themselves and for society. In 1908 the Reverend Ernest A. Boom, chairman of the Committee on Alcoholics and Narcotics of the New Jersey Dependency and Crimes Commission, reported that the net cost of dependency and crimes to taxpayers of New Jersey the previous year exceeded $8.5 million. The vital statistics for 1907 showed 265 deaths directly attributable to "alcoholism" and 298 to "cirrhosis of the liver," and that was only the tip of the iceberg. In the past six years 20,000 people in New Jersey had died of consumption. Autopsies on consumptives done in Germany showed that, in one instance, 44 percent, and in another, 78 percent, were alcoholics. Hundreds of studies confirmed the relationship between crime, disease, and dependency and the consumption of alcohol, and the same could be said of the relationship between sexual promiscuity and venereal disease. To secular Progressives and evangelicals alike, the evidence clearly indicated that the liquor traffic was a "menace to the mental, moral, and physical welfare of the state."[20] As historians now admonish, "However we may judge prohibition efforts historically, we cannot dismiss them as ridiculous attempts to change unalterable drinking habits."[21]

In city after city in New Jersey in 1908, state investigators confirmed the presence of eight-year-olds in poolrooms and intoxicated youths in saloons and dance halls. They discovered pornography on the Boardwalk, heard obscenities in the lyrics and jokes of vaudeville shows, were accosted by prostitutes, and found widespread evidence of gambling and fornication. My contention that Commodore Kuehnle's Atlantic City was no more wicked than Trenton or Paterson, and perhaps less so than Hoboken or Newark, or that racism, class conflict, partisan politics, and practical economics lay at the bottom of Progressive reform in the city, should in no way lead us to deprecate the seriousness of conditions in this city and in others that Progressives, including evangelicals, sought to correct.

I have said that Atlantic City was unique. But it was unique in that it catered to all segments of American society and became the prototype of the "popular" seaside resort.[22] On a given summer weekend, tiny Absecon Island seemed to groan under the weight of 300,000 tourists, principally from the Philadelphia and New York urban centers. "Atlantic City is one of the most amazing facts in America," said travel writer Harrison Rhodes in the *Saturday Evening Post* in 1915. "It is America in little; unless you prefer to say that America is really a little Atlantic City." The American Hardware Manufacturers convened in Atlantic City in 1915, and so did the New Jersey Baptists. At this relatively late date, the city still promoted itself as a health resort, and a retired university professor sat in his wheelchair on the Boardwalk contentedly watching the "procession of brokers, governesses and children, colored waiters, ladies of fashion, chorus girls, and gum chewers" who filed by. Especially since the 1890s, and even before, travel writers from both sides of the Atlantic had consistently expressed the theme with which the urbane Rhodes concluded his article: "Atlantic City lifts the lid from American life so that you may observe it freely."[23]

Long Branch, Asbury Park, and other coast resorts built boardwalks and made other efforts to replicate the development of Absecon Island, but they never attained the heights of Atlantic City. We are left as means of explaining the Atlantic City phenomenon with what its boosters always called "vision," a term more objectively translated as management and promotion. I have framed this study around the fifty-year evolution of the liberal policy, a management and promotional device that grew and changed incrementally in response to changing economic and social conditions. People, not historians, make history. The men and women, black and white, native and immigrant, and the wealthy, poor, and middle class, who built, applauded, deplored, enjoyed, or merely endured Atlantic City between 1854 and 1920, did so as the firm ground of traditional values trembled and, often, shook violently beneath their feet. I invite the reader to transcend the Kuehnle myth and to experience with them their agonies and uncertainties as well as their delights and aspirations, a journey that unfolds as a complex but intensely human tale of ordinary people who lived through an era every bit as baffling as our own.

Our odyssey begins on barren, windswept Absecon Island in the 1850s and continues as we survey the growth of Atlantic City to 1910 when it had emerged as the nation's foremost popular resort. Of critical importance to my thesis is the development of the black community, its relationship to the rest of the city, particularly the local Republican organization, and the voting behavior of black citizens.

Chapter 3 is an essay on Sabbatarianism. Its obvious importance to Atlantic City and to other commercial resorts lay in the six-day workweek and the Sunday excursion trade, but I soon discovered much larger implications. The Christian Sunday remained a powerful symbol of moral and social order during the Progressive era. To me, as to Solberg, the efforts of historians to understand the movement seemed trivial in the light of its apparent pervasiveness and influence. This chapter does not pose as a definitive work on the subject, even for New Jersey. It is meant for my purposes to suggest a larger place for the Sabbatarian movement in the total scheme of Progressive reform, to demonstrate its relationships to other facets of reform, both evangelical and secular, to penetrate the legal and social complexities and the depth of social and political conflict surrounding the state enforcement of Sunday laws, and finally, and more specifically, to place Atlantic City in the context of the widely differing perceptions Americans held of proper Sabbath observance.

Chapter 4 traces the nineteenth-century evolution of the liberal policy, and the fifth chapter recounts earlier reform efforts made locally in response to the growing influence of evangelical groups in the state, particularly Sabbatarians, and attempts to gauge the levels of vice and disorder in the city at the time the reform movement began. I know of no norms for vice and disorder, but the Crimes and Excise commissions' reports of 1908 provide a useful means for comparing conditions in Atlantic City with those of other cities in New Jersey and perhaps an answer to the question of just how wicked the resort really was. Chapter 6 is an account of the reform movement, and the final chapter describes its results and discusses its importance in terms of the national Progressive movement.

The liberal policy was essentially a compromise morality that satisfied no one completely. But, if not in its synthesis, certainly in its formulation, it took into account all of the social pressures that grew out of the Industrial Revolution. The hopes and fears of the residents for the city were seen in both their divisions and their unity and expressed in a variety of ways. At times the struggles that took place within Atlantic City amounted to no more than small-town politics. At others, particularly in times of crisis for the city's image, internal struggles produced decisions and evoked statements, from both within and without, that constituted remarkably frank and incisive commentary on the changing state of public morals. The appropriateness of Atlantic City as a laboratory for the study of this subject was perhaps best expressed by the cryptic statement often attributed to Enoch L. Johnson: "We always gave the people what they wanted."

CHAPTER TWO

From Pitney's Folly to World's Playground

Atlantic City presents a unique case study in urban development. Founded in 1854, it began as a speculative real estate venture, a creature of the railroad and of outside investors. By 1870 it stood as it had been envisioned, a quaint seaside colony of Philadelphia. Its coming of age in the waning decades of the nineteenth century paralleled the growth of the resort industry and the industrial and social maturation of the country. But to say simply that Atlantic City was called into existence by the inexorable forces of industrialization and urbanization is to neglect the efforts and expectations of the men and women who promoted and built the city during a period of rapid social and economic change.

At a dinner held in 1889, elderly residents described Absecon Island as they had known it early in the century: "In those days the greater portion of the island was sand hills, duck ponds, swamps, briar thickets, and nesting places for the wild fowl. Many of these wild fowl could be killed with clubs, and it is said that they were so numerous at times that in lighting upon trees the branches would break." In the summer, swarms of mosquitoes and greenhead flies buzzed incessantly over the low and swampy terrain. Foxes, rabbits, mink, muskrats, and huge blacksnakes infested the island. There was little indication that the intrusion of civilization would ever consist of much more than the six rude farming and fishing dwellings that existed there by 1850. "The whole island," said another old resident, "could have been bought very cheap then—much less than the price of a single cottage today."[1]

In retrospect we can see in these quaint descriptions of a seashore wilderness only sixty miles from Philadelphia just the thing from which fortunes were made. But in the 1850s railroads were in their infancy, and the prospect of building a resort city in this lonely place seemed as remote as the island itself.

The resort industry was also in its infancy. In 1833 the *New Jersey Gazetteer* compiled an index of the then known resorts along the New Jersey coast. By this time Cape May was well established as a "noted and much frequented watering place, the season at which commences in July and continues until September," and offered six boardinghouses, "three of which are very large."[2] It catered principally to the wealthy of Philadelphia, and until the Civil War was a summer ritual for many elite planter families from Virginia and Maryland.[3] Long Branch to the north offered "inducements to invalids, the idle, and hunters of pleasure to spend a portion of the hot season" in the several boardinghouses that existed for that purpose.[4] Along the rest of the coast resort facilities consisted of a scattering of "respectable farming families" in offshore villages such as Toms River, Tuckerton, or Somers Point, who advertised and took in guests for the season. Of the eight places listed, only Cape May and Long Branch had boardinghouses dedicated exclusively to the summer trade.[5]

Cape May and Long Branch, located on the mainland, were served by regular stage and steamboat lines from Philadelphia and New York. But Philadelphians reached Cape May only by a six-hour steamboat ride down the Delaware River or by a 104–mile stage route through the wilds of South Jersey. A trip to Long Branch, though somewhat shorter, required a similar ordeal over primitive roadways, a journey broken only by infrequent and incommodious taverns along the route.[6]

Most of the one-hundred-odd miles of coastline that separated the two resorts consisted of undeveloped barrier islands. The only thing that distinguished Absecon Island from the rest of this dreary expanse was that it stood in the path of the shortest distance from Philadelphia to the ocean. Yet speculation as to the resort possibilities of the area was discouraged by the belief that it would be impossible to build and maintain a roadbed across the meadows that separated the island from the mainland. A local skeptic expressed the consensus of area residents by calling the island "a sandpatch, a desolation, a swamp, a mosquito territory, where you could not build a city, or if you could, no one would go there."⁷

Atlantic City was the brainchild of Dr. Jonathan Pitney, a physician who had made his home in the mainland village of Absecon since 1820. Where others saw only waste and desolation, he saw a healthful and pristine wilderness, a delightful spot for summer cottages, and a perfect refuge from the debilitating atmosphere of the growing cities. Locals labeled the scheme "Pitney's Folly," and for twenty years treated the proposal with an amused tolerance. Although his vision was a modest one—a bathing village made accessible to the urban centers by a railroad across the meadows—Pitney set in motion the chain of events that created the great resort.⁸

In 1850 he began to promote the project by writing a series of letters to Philadelphia newspapers extolling the healthful atmosphere of Absecon Island and discussing the benefits of the proposed railroad to the hinterland. The letters attracted the attention of a group of glass and iron manufacturers whose operations dotted the pine barrens of Camden County and the western portions of Atlantic County, including Samuel Richards, who owned a glassworks and 50,000 acres at Jackson. Pitney argued that a passenger and freight line from Camden to the beach would benefit the glass and iron interests as well as create a lucrative resort trade. Moreover, the railroad would open up the entire region for development and enhance the value of their holdings. As the land developed into farms and other enterprises, new towns would be created, and the revenues to the railroad would increase. These men were easily convinced of the need for a railroad, but it was against their better judgment that they agreed to extend the line past Hammonton. In fact, two years later when Richards caught his first glimpse of Absecon Island, he exclaimed that it was "the most horrible place to make the termination of a railroad" that he had ever seen.⁹

In May they hired Richard Osborne, a civil engineer of national repute, who had worked on the building of Chicago. Osborne assured the group that within a generation the railroad would enable the new city to surpass Cape May as the nation's premier ocean resort and expressed a rare democratic view of the resort industry: "The work-worn artisan shut up in the close and debilitating shops of the city, whose limited means prevent a long absence from his calling, will find here the rest and recreation that he cannot now obtain."¹⁰ By 1852 Osborne had seen firsthand the transforming power of the railroads, and his prediction suggests that he had more than just an inkling of the broad recreational potential of cheap transportation. But at this time it is doubtful that the directors' plans for the island extended beyond the more modest vision of Jonathan Pitney.

On June 24, 1852, the Camden and Atlantic Railroad Company was organized in Philadelphia, and the company issued ten thousand shares of stock to the original thirty-eight stockholders at $50 per share. Construction on the railroad began that summer, as Pitney, now a director of the company, proceeded to buy up the island. The local owners banded together and demanded $25 per acre. After some haggling, they settled for $17.50. Some of these parcels sold for $300 per acre soon after the railroad's completion. Atlantic City's first land boom was underway.[11]

Fifty years later, speaking of the founding at the resort's Golden Jubilee, Atlantic City's congressman, John Gardner, said that in no sense was the city a speculative venture. "There was no object," he said, "to develop the island with an object of increasing land values." This was a strange protest from one who was called "Atlantic City's barefoot boy," and who had made sizable sums from resort real estate. The railroad had acquired land in such quantities that in March 1853 the state legislature, fearing a monopoly, prohibited further purchases. The directors formed the Camden and Atlantic Land Company and proceeded to buy up the rest of the island. For the locals it was a windfall. In 1884, one recalled, "The people who lived here made just as much money then as now, because there weren't so many of them after the pennies. With a capital of $1000 one could become a land speculator and clear a good round sum without waiting very long."[12] By this time the resort was well established. During the 1850s and 1860s, the railroad and the residents weathered severe storms, both natural and economic, as they proceeded to carve a resort city from the raw wilderness of Absecon Island.

The first train steamed into the city on July 1, 1854, in a puff of rosy optimism. On hand to launch the resort were over six hundred guests of the railroad, dignitaries, newsmen, and prospective investors. They met in the large saloon of the nearly completed United States Hotel and heard a round of laudatory speeches. Nearby, Bedloe's Hotel was ready to receive guests, and the Surf House and some twenty-five substantial cottages were under construction. Richard Osborne later recalled that the party, consisting of nine cars, left Camden at 9:30 in the morning, and by noon was steaming up Atlantic Avenue to the hotel. The two and a half hour journey had taken the old stage line a full day to complete.

During the first year, the Camden and Atlantic carried twenty thousand passengers to Atlantic City.[13]

The railroad began a vigorous publicity campaign, inviting Philadelphians to escape from the suffocation of the city to the stimulating breath of the ocean in less than three hours for a fare of only $1.50.[14] One South Jersey newspaper predicted: "Passengers will soon have the opportunity of running down in an hour and a half to one of the most agreeable bathing places on the Atlantic Coast. Absecom [sic] thus promises to become a formidable rival to Cape Island. The shortness of the trip will induce thousands to give it preference."[15]

Atlantic City in its first year was something less than the railroad's promotional brochures had led visitors to expect. Wrote an early resident: "At that time ranges of hills of sand spread out on every side; tangled underbrush and running vines impeded pedestrians; holly and cedar trees and bayberry bushes . . . made up the general landscape and furnished abiding places for foxes, rabbits, (and) rats."[16] Hotel accommodations were primitive. There was no running water, no indoor plumbing, and no bedsprings. An early guidebook advised visitors that when staying in an elevated story of a hotel, "a half inch rope as a fire escape may be a prudent provision." Streets, ungraveled and ungraded, existed mainly on paper, and numerous cattle, swine, and goats ran free on the island. The newly formed city government lacked the funds to effect improvements. Property owners, though anxious to see their holdings appreciate, were hostile to increased taxes, and the lack of fresh water and adequate sewerage facilities remained serious problems well into the 1880s. Visitors accustomed to the amenities of Cape May and Long Branch made plain their disappointment. One couple, having bought a lot sight unseen, found only a heap of sand on a deserted beach and wept when they saw it.[17]

By 1855 there were, by actual count, seventy-one structures on the island. Mostly boardinghouses, they stood among the remnants of the cedar and bayberry forest that had, until recently, thickly covered the area. Huge sand dunes, some fifty feet high, lined the beachward side of the village, shielding the houses from the ocean. Cattle scaled the dunes to feed on the beach grass. In the absence of refrigeration, provisions were scarce, and much of it had to be brought in live. A boardinghouse operator who braved the second season recalled: "Black snakes were almost as plentiful as huckleberries, and they were not as bashful. They came into our yard and even crawled into the cellar. We killed a monster on the porch one day . . . they were after the live chickens."[18] That year an August northeaster shortened the season and dampened the spirits of all but the hardiest of the resort's boosters.

During the winter, severe storm tides practically engulfed the island, leaving it isolated for days at a time. When the waters receded, ponds were left to stagnate and breed insects which, by summer, became a plague. In August 1858 the *Philadelphia North American* published a letter from an outraged visitor.

> Last week the place was crowded with visitors; now they are escaping the scourge as rapidly as possible. This house is now surrounded with bonfires, in the hope that the smoke therefrom will drive off the enemy. The horses attached to a carriage containing guests from the United States Hotel became so maddened from the attack of greenhead flies that they ran away near the Inlet, demolishing the carriage and broke the arm of one of the ladies.[19]

Horses, covered with blood, lay down in the streets, and cattle sought refuge from the torment by wading into the ocean. Men and women wore masks on their faces, children squalled, and people begged railroad conductors to take them away ahead of schedule. Although by 1860 the city had taken steps to eliminate the breeding places, insects remained a blight on the resort for some time.

The Panic of 1857 almost wiped out the railroad, and it offered one dollar round-trip excursion rates just to stay afloat. In 1860 the land company sold off portions of its holdings on the island to satisfy railroad bondholders.[20] Bad publicity threatened to strangle the resort in its infancy. Forced to live the entire year on the receipts from July and August, both the railroad and the city experienced the perennial difficulty of seaside resorts—a seasonal economy.

After September, the city practically shut down. In January 1856 a former Philadelphian complained of the bleakness and isolation of resort winters.

> Six months ago almost every Philadelphian thought and talked of this place; but who thinks of it now besides its inhabitants and real estate owners? Here are nearly two hundred persons on this sea-girt beach, storm bound prisoners. We have a telegraph, but the operator went to the mainland before the storm of Saturday night, and the wires are broken. We have a railroad, but when the cars will reappear is a question upon which opinions

are conflicting and unsatisfactory, and the floating ice forbids a small boat to navigate the bay and creek.[21]

The first mayor, Chalkley Leeds, "weary of the honors of office," resigned later that year, as did his successor after a month's tenure. The affairs of the city were in the hands of the railroad, which still owned much of the island.

Yet the city built slowly but steadily onward. The permanent population, estimated at 250 in 1854, grew to 687 by 1860. By 1858 the city boasted 130 buildings, not counting three churches, a market house, a lighthouse, and several large railroad structures. Two "first class hotels," the United States and the Surf House, could each accommodate 350 people, and several smaller ones, along with numerous taverns and boardinghouses, also took in guests. The railroad estimated that during July and August of that year an average of more than three thousand visitors were in the city each day.[22]

In 1866, D. M. Zimmerman, the secretary and treasurer of the railroad, began issuing free passes to prominent physicians of the Philadelphia area. He then solicited expert medical testimony on the unique health-giving properties of the climate of Absecon Island. Dr. William V. Keating of Locust Street in Philadelphia testified that the resort was not only free of mildew and malaria, but would afford "relief and cure to all cases of rheumatic fever and arthritis," even in the most acute stages. "I have ventured to send patients there in the height of an attack of rheumatic gout, in the months of May and June, who have had complete amelioration of all of their symptoms within forty-eight hours of their residence, provided they located themselves as near the ocean as possible, so as to avoid the land breezes."[23] Atlantic City also offered relief from "chronic bronchitis, laryngitis, incipient tuberculosis, and scrofula." The time was not distant, he predicted, when "the inhabitants of the great West, South, and Northwest, especially those suffering from the sequelae of malarial poisoning, with debilitated digestive organs, impoverished blood, and from what is termed a cachectic condition of the system" would all resort to the bracing atmosphere of Atlantic City. In 1878, when the city had begun to boom, a travel writer commented that the University of Pennsylvania seemed to have bred its doctors for the "express purpose of marshaling a dying world to the curative shelter of Atlantic City."[24]

An 1868 edition of *The Ladies Friend* described the resort as a retreat for

Philadelphia Quakers: "Atlantic City has the advantage for plain, quiet folks, that so many of its houses are kept by Friends, and resorted to by that class. It is another Quaker City. Now, wherever the sober-minded, clear-headed, pure hearted Friends most do congregate, there you are pretty sure to find more substance than show, more reality than sham, cleanliness amounting to nicety, wholesome fare, and home-like comfort."[25] During its second decade, Atlantic City established itself among well-to-do Philadelphians, but it did not exactly boom. By 1870 the population had risen to only 1,043. It was, in the words of an early resident, "but a struggling resort, with no winter business to speak of, and a summer season of but six weeks duration."[26] As the first era of its existence drew to a close, Atlantic City gave only faint indication of what it would become during the remaining decades of the century.

The 1870s in the United States was a decade of industrial strife, panic, and economic depression. Yet this was precisely the time that Atlantic City began to develop as a popular resort. The resident population of the city more than quadrupled from a little more than a thousand to 5,477 by 1880. Although these figures are small in terms of urban development, they reflect a corresponding increase in patronage. In 1871 the railroad carried over 367,000 passengers and showed a profit of over $131,000. In 1872 passengers numbered over 417,000 and profits exceeded $212,000. Based on the railroad's figures, we can estimate the resort's seasonal patronage for these years at well over 100,000 and the crowds in the city on a busy summer weekend at 25,000 people.[27] This dramatic prosperity in the face of general economic adversity illustrates the intensity of the demand for leisure which attended the growth of industrial society.

An 1873 promotion described Atlantic City as "The City of Homes by the Seaside" and proclaimed: "The solid character of its patrons, the better elements of society, the quiet home-like atmosphere of the place . . . all conspire to make Atlantic City the ideal of a summer resort."[28] "New passenger cars of elegant finish" beckoned the "overworked men" and "overanxious women" of Philadelphia to the genteel ambience of private villas, wayside inns, and comfortable hotels. By the 1870s travel time from the patron city had been cut to under two hours, and a substantial cottage could be had for $500 for the season.

The promotion also contained a gesture to the working classes. In addition to "counting house chiefs," the railroad invited "subordinates in their shirtsleeves" to sample pleasures of seashore life that were less genteel in character. Throughout the season, special trains for the accommodation of excursionists left each morning and returned in the afternoon. These were available at specially reduced rates and included the free use of an "excursion house with modern hotel conveniences and a large saloon for dancing and other amusements." The company frankly admitted that its objective was to "identify the interests of visitors and all of our patrons with its own to secure a mutual benefit."

During the summer of 1873, the railroad brought sixty-four excursions to the city. These included such diverse groups as the Sawmakers' Beneficial Association, the German Independent Congregation, the United Lodges of Mechanics Hall of Camden, St. George's and St. James churches of Philadelphia, the Anthracite Lodge, and St. Mary's Literary Institute. Atlantic City, proclaimed A. L. English, editor of the newly formed *Atlantic City Daily Review*, had become the excursion resort of the country, surpassing Cape May by a two to one margin. English admitted that the city was "crowded beyond reason" and that some of the excursionists were given to bouts of drunkenness and hilarity. But to the "certain classes" who found the excursionists a detriment to the city, he replied that on the whole they were orderly and quiet, and besides, they spent money. "Let them come," he proclaimed, "let them come by the thousands and in great multitudes. There is enough pure air for us all, and to the weary inhabitants of the dusty city we know it is a great and pleasant relief from the work-a-day life which many of them lead."[29]

Much later Mayor John Gardner, in a blush of candor, referred to the "hard business necessity" that had changed the nature of Atlantic City:

> In that early day, experiments had to be resorted to which nobody desired, because they were necessary to life. When the cheap excursion had to come, when questions about who came on them could not be raised, when the moonlight excursion had to come in September, after the guests generally were gone, when other desperate expedients to raise the cash to keep the engines and cars running over the rails, and the people in Atlantic City from default, were being tried, all deplored it, the railroad company not less than the others.[30]

The "moonlight excursion" referred to the practice of making the resort available to groups of black people in September after the regular guests had departed for the season.

Local tradition credits the building of the Boardwalk in 1870 with the beginning of the city's popularity. Atlantic Avenue had been the center of resort activity. Except for a few hours in the morning, the beach was

From Pitney's Folly to World's Playground • 23

deserted, dotted with the hulks of rotting shipwrecks. At night, it was a foreboding place, described later as "a scene of desolation, dark in the moon shadows of tufted hummocks, and sinister with the sounds of crawling crabs and the clank of their snapping claws."[31]

"Seabathing" was still more of a curiosity than a popular pastime, and a dip in the ocean required a trek through "tiresome areas of mosquito marsh" to the water's edge. Tiny wooden walks had been built across pools and swamps to bathhouses, and eventually became a popular convenience for onlookers. The first boardwalk was a temporary affair merely eight feet wide and a few blocks long. It proved so popular that it was enlarged each year until 1879, when it was replaced with a permanent structure. The Boardwalk gave the city a unique identity and made the beachfront both accessible and amenable to urban visitors.[32]

In 1874 the railroad's passenger total approached 500,000, and its revenues climbed steadily. In 1876 the Centennial Exposition was held in Philadelphia, and resort businessmen anticipated huge crowds from the overflow to the shore. But the expected bonanza never materialized, and the season was pronounced "a failure" despite the stay of President Grant at the United States Hotel that July. Yet during that year well over 160,000 people visited Atlantic City. Having tottered on the verge of bankruptcy for most of its twenty-two-year existence, the railroad reported earnings of almost $565,000.[33]

In 1875 a group of the railroad's directors, led by Samuel Richards, resigned in a dispute that reflected the divisions within Atlantic City. Richards, the driving force behind the railroad and the land company, had initially been slow to recognize the profit potential of the resort business. But as tourists and revenues increased, he wanted to expand the excursion trade. Rebuffed by the majority of the directors, Richards formed a rival company to accomplish that purpose. After a bitter fight, he organized and built the Philadelphia and Atlantic Railroad, a narrow-gauge line, in the astonishingly short time of ninety days.[34]

The completion of the Narrow Gauge in July 1877 touched off a rate war. Round-trip tickets which had cost $3.00 on the Camden and Atlantic were sold for $1.25 on the new rival line. As the fares dropped, the crowds swelled proportionately, and by the summer of 1879 were so great as to nearly exhaust the supplies of meat, milk, bread, and other provisions. So much building was taking place that year that a Camden newsman reported that "the sound of the bricklayer's trowel and the carpenter's hammer greeted one at every turn." Walt Whitman, who had visited the city on a bright January morning of that year, reported "a real sea beach city" of excellent roads lined with rows of "choice private cottages." The trip on the Camden and Atlantic inspired him to write:

> What a place (is it not indeed the main place?) the railroad plays in modern democratic civilization! How indirectly, but surely, and beyond all other influences to-day in America, it thaws, ploughs up, prepares, and even fructifies the fallows of unnumbered counties and towns!—the tough sward of morals and manners of the low average (nine-tenths) of our vulgar humanity! Silently and surely and on a scale as large and genuine as Nature's, it sets in motion every indirect and many direct means of making a really substantial community.[35]

In 1880 the West Jersey and Atlantic Railroad, a branch of the Pennsylvania, completed still another line to the city in an effort to attract the "middle and lower classes." The resulting competition proved too much for the Narrow Gauge, which was sold to the Philadelphia and Reading system in 1883. In the same year, the Pennsylvania absorbed the Camden and Atlantic, and the resort was now served by two interstate lines, including the mammoth facilities of the Pennsylvania Railroad. "Immediately," wrote one promoter, "the name of Atlantic City became familiar in every ticket office in the land in control of that great and powerful corporation. The reputation of the place became national, and people from all parts of the country began to appreciate its health imparting properties."[36]

During the 1880s, the city continued its rapid growth. By 1885 its population reached 7,962, and five years later, it increased to over 13,000.[37] Travel time from Philadelphia during the 1880s was an hour and a half, and within the decade would be reduced to less than an hour. What began as a trickle was now a deluge as thousands of middle- and lower-class excursionists swarmed onto the island during the summer months.

In 1882 George Howard constructed the first amusement pier which extended over six hundred feet into the ocean. It was quickly followed by Applegate's Pier in 1884 and the Iron Pier, more than a thousand feet long, built in 1887. Dances, shows, mechanical amusements, and exhibits of all sorts beckoned the visitors onto the piers and the Boardwalk. Wrote one impressed visitor: "We have here all kinds of catch-penny shows, the wonderful woman snake charmer, the man with the iron jaws, the learned pigs, the Johnny go rounds. . . . It is a real vanity fair."[38]

From Pitney's Folly to World's Playground • 25

Beer gardens, saloons, and popular opera houses appeared everywhere in the city to complete the menu of diversion. In Atlantic City there was something for everyone. Wealthy cottagers, and even city fathers, might sniff at the "shoobies," the shoe-box lunch crowd who prudently packed their meals in boxes and swelled the resort's summer population. But the railroads had no such compunctions. Scheduled commuter trains were regularly shunted aside to allow the excursion trains to pass through. In the summer of 1890, an official of the Pennsylvania Railroad estimated that the line carried thirty-eight thousand excursionists to the resort from Pittsburgh alone, and this did not count people who came on the regular trains.[39]

As Walt Whitman said, the railroads did indeed build Atlantic City, but this statement overlooks the fact that by 1880 the railroads were responding to a demand as well as creating one. Throughout most of the nineteenth century, vacations and tours were the prerogatives of the rich and well-to-do. After the Civil War, rising living standards, the gradual shortening of the work week, and the availability of cheap transportation brought vacations and excursions within the reach of the middle and even lower classes. These developments created a demand for mass resorts, one which Richard Osborne had anticipated perhaps a decade too soon.[40]

Large and fashionable hotels began to appear during the 1880s and became the symbols of wealth and refinement in Atlantic City. The Brighton, a rambling four-story structure of 150 rooms, stood near the ocean between Illinois and Indiana avenues. Opened in 1876 as Brighton Cottage by F. W. Hemsley, it grew in stages until it achieved the proportions of a hotel and was the first to stay open all year. The Hemsleys were one of a number of Quaker families who dominated the hotel business in Atlantic City. In 1856 Elisha and Elizabeth Roberts built the Chalfonte House, a "commodious first class boarding house" that featured mule-car rides over the dunes to the water. In 1869 they opened the Shelburne, a much larger cottage that became popular with New York luminaries including Diamond Jim Brady. In 1860 William Dennis, the headmaster of Burlington Friends School, built a family cottage on Michigan Avenue and gradually expanded it into a twenty-two-room hotel. The Dennis remained in Quaker hands until its sale in 1970. Chalfonte-Haddon Hall, later to become the city's first legalized casino, began as a family enterprise in 1876 when Henry West Leeds persuaded his mother and his life-long companion, J. Haines Lippincott, to enter the hotel business in Atlantic City. The Traymore, which hosted Vice President

Hendricks and his wife for an extended stay in 1886, began as a ten-room boardinghouse purchased by Daniel S. White in 1870. Nathan Leeds Jones, David Scattergood, Charles Evans, and Caspar Wister Haines also turned modest fortunes to the transformation of cottages and boardinghouses into hotels for the rich.[41]

The "Quaker houses," as they became known, set an aristocratic standard of accommodation that evoked an earlier, quieter, and more Victorian concept of seashore life. By the middle of the 1880s, armies of liveried black footmen met the wealthy at their trains and quickly whisked them away to their hotels. Once inside, auxiliaries of uniformed maids, waiters, and bellmen attended their every need. Sailboat rides, drives on the beach, and concerts and cuisine were amusements that the rich could share with their own kind. Broad verandas, glass-enclosed promenades, and elevated observatories provided the perspectives from which the wealthy looked down on a resort teeming with middle- and working-class humanity.

As the genteel insularity of hotel life was the exception in Atlantic City, the resort not only had to reconcile the interests of its diverse patronage, but also come to terms with its image. In an age of pronounced class distinctions, this was no easy task. The answer was to celebrate Atlantic City's diversity and to appeal to the democratic instincts of the people. An official guidebook for the 1885 season proclaimed that the success of the city was due "mainly to the unacknowledged distinction of class in society. The rich and the poor, the healthy and the invalid are equally well received."

> The center mile of the walk, which is opposite the city, well suits the mixed crowd that walks it from morning till night; such a conglomeration of all classes cannot be seen in any other seaside resort in the world. The rich banker does not look down upon the shop boy he meets, and the boy thinks himself equally as good as the banker for he feels the few dollars in his pocket that he has been so long scraping together to pay the expenses of his visit, and while he smokes his cigar he thinks he is indeed doing the grand, and hopes before his week is up to leave, that some millionaire's daughter will take a fancy to him.[42]

Democracy in America also meant social mobility. The opportunity to rub elbows with the rich or to act the part, if only for the day or the weekend, was a major attraction of the resort.

But the ideal of social harmony required a balance. Such a resort could have gaiety but not license or raucous hilarity. If it could not be exclusive, neither could it be vulgar. This left a broad middle ground. Yet, by 1885, the balance was beginning to tilt toward naughtiness as can be seen from the following.

> Atlantic City has no particular characteristics. It stands entirely by itself; as a seaside resort it combines all of the advantages of other places without any of their extreme views. People can enjoy themselves according to their own inclinations, as long as they remain within bounds. It is like one seaside resort without its beer and rowdyism-like another without its religion; another without its temperance and cheapness, and another without its dissipation and extravagances. Here the extremely good come to be moderately bad, and the extremely bad to be moderately good, if they can. Pleasure no doubt does here reign supreme, still religion has not been forgotten, for every denomination has its place of worship.[43]

If Mrs. Grundy disapproved, so much the better. The snobbish and tranquil world of Victorian America was giving way to a more democratic, less rigid concept of social order, one less burdened by the precepts of religion and moral uplift.

Beneath the intense boosterism lay the nagging suspicion that the popularity of the city wouldn't last. In 1889 a local editor warned that the city should establish a manufacturing base in case the resort business should fold.[44] Such advice was not often found in the pages of the local press, consumed, as it was, by the process of promoting the resort. Skeptics were also silenced by the city's continued prosperity. A railroad schedule for the summer of 1895 listed eighteen daily departures from Philadelphia to Atlantic City, and this did not count special excursion trains.[45] In July 1897 a travel writer for the *New York Times* marveled at the huge crowds and the democracy of the resort and characterized Atlantic City as "Coney Island grown a big, well-developed girl, with a little boarding-school culture and polish, and no one is quite sure whether either is more than skin deep."[46] Even sophisticates were at a loss to explain Atlantic City, and we should not be surprised to discover that the local entrepreneurs who led the city and shaped its policies were themselves wary and uncertain about its future.

To a correspondent from the *Philadelphia Press*, covering the Easter Parade in 1903, the rise of Atlantic City from a "miserable hamlet of fishermen's huts" to the world's greatest resort in just fifty years suggested "The Tale of Aladdin's Lamp." The huge hotels with their pennants flying from soaring roofs and cupolas resembled Arabian castles arisen from the sand. Bejeweled matrons promenaded in their Easter finery in an unending procession that included thousands of the not-so-elegant who were also dressed for the occasion. Tourists from France, Hungary, China, and Japan rubbed their eyes at the display of wealth and democracy on the Boardwalk, asking in a gaggle of languages, "Is this all true?" But the correspondent knew that this was no illusion. Atlantic City marched in step with the rest of the country in a continual journey of progress.[47]

In June 1904 the city marked its fiftieth anniversary with a lavish four-day fete, an extravagant display of boosterism that was more than just an act of faith. "There is something sonorous and virile about the name, Atlantic City," proclaimed the souvenir program, "and there is no danger of its being confounded with any other place or institution on earth." What New York was to finance, Atlantic City had become to entertainment, distinctly New World and democratic. "It has taught the American people the science of rest and recreation, and the lesson was needed to the strenuous American worker." Boosterism notwithstanding, the city began its second half-century on a note of strident self-confidence that seemed to dispel the doubts of the previous decades.[48]

The resort celebrated its Golden Jubilee with parades, solemn ceremonies, and a huge triumphal arch spanning Atlantic Avenue capped by a statue of King Neptune drawn in a seashell chariot by six seahorses. At the foot of Maryland Avenue rose a huge granite column inscribed at the base with the names of Jonathan Pitney and the other founders, symbolizing the foresight and the efforts of the pioneering residents. Mayor Stoy had conceived the celebration some months before, enlisting one hundred "representative citizens" to plan the event. "The Jubilee is for everyone," declared the mayor, and the planners and the paraders included hotel people, the yacht club, policemen, firemen, social and political clubs, unions, liquor dealers, the churches, the Women's Christian Temperance Union (WCTU), and Northside groups. But in the end, the whiteness of the celebration matched the gleaming whiteness of the founders' column as, at the last moment, the black groups withdrew from the parade to settle a storm of protest from white lodges who refused to march with them. "Atlantic City is equipped to entertain the world," proclaimed the program, and its mission had just begun.[49] The truth is, Atlantic City was not one resort; it was many.

"If a student of our national characteristics should wish to understand the American people," wrote Katherine Busby in 1910, he should look to Atlantic City. "For this great middle-class playground is the eighth wonder of the world" and "bears witness to the whole panorama of American life."

> Nothing is omitted from the repertoire to make the American dollar feel at home. And still not all the visitors at Atlantic City are as opulent as they look when on the Boardwalk parade grounds. Many have saved the year through for a two weeks' holiday there, and are staying not at one of the magnificent hostelries clustering around the waterfront, but in a side street in one of the packing box-type flimsy honeycombs of pine which look as if they might be pulled to pieces by your fingers-or at a boarding house in the city proper.[50]

By 1910 Atlantic City had made good its boast of being "The World's Playground," annually hosting over three million people.[51] A summer population of 250,000 was not unusual. "There is no one," wrote a Philadelphia journalist, "that can visit Atlantic City, from the King of England to the $10 a week clerk, who will not find accommodations to suit his taste and pocketbook."[52]

Between 1890 and 1915 the resident population grew from 13,037 to 51,667. Fifteen percent of the adult population owned business establishments that were dependent either directly or indirectly on the resort trade, which flourished mainly during the summer months.[53] These ranged from large hotels to small boardinghouses, restaurants, saloons, and amusements, as well as the supporting businesses necessary to any small city. Of course the bulk of the resident population consisted of the thousands of skilled and unskilled workers who built the city and who staffed the resort facilities that were the mainstay of the city's seasonal economy. Despite the city's efforts to cultivate the convention trade and to promote itself as a year-round resort, its lifeblood remained the huge crowds of excursionists and vacationers that swelled the city during the summer months.

Observers were often critical of the get-rich-quick mentality that seemed to fuel the city's rapid growth. A Philadelphia journalist characterized the resort as a "carpetbag city." People came for many reasons but stayed only to make money. Even Pittsburgh, "in its balmiest days of boom," had not created as many fortunes. The "so-called native" acquired "a taste for champagne early in his seashore career."[54] These comments reflect the prevalent attitude that resort building was an ephemeral enterprise, fit only for the amusement operator who, building nothing of permanence, lacked civic responsibility. To be sure, the resort business was nothing if not risky. By this time, Cape May, Long Branch, and even prestigious Saratoga Springs had experienced periods of difficulty from which they were only beginning to recover.[55] But this was the age of Horatio Alger, and if Atlantic City did not boom in steel, it did boom in tourism, a field which created opportunities for the small investor.

In 1900 local historian John Hall wrote: "Perhaps in no other town on the Western continent do the hotel interests so dominate as here. Atlantic City is preeminently a hotel town. . . . The story of this stupendous extension and expansion is the story of the last fifty years of this town."[56] With the exception of a commercial fishing industry located in the Inlet section, almost the entirety of Absecon Island was devoted to the accommodation and entertainment of tourists.

In 1915 the municipal assessor estimated that 80 percent of the city's real property consisted of hotels. Of the 587 buildings listed as hotels for tax purposes, 187 were classified as boardinghouses—cottages of ten rooms or less that advertised and took in guests. Beyond these, there were "a good many hundreds, perhaps thousands" of cottages similarly engaged which had escaped the assessor's notice. Next in line were 300 large boardinghouses or "small hotels" of between ten to one hundred rooms. Frequently operated by women, they were of such a size that proprietors could take a personal interest in the management and the guests. Dependent on personal reputation, those that survived the "second season" provided steady and lucrative rents.[57]

Kuehnle's, a rambling frame structure on Atlantic Avenue opposite the Camden and Atlantic depot, was one of the most popular small hotels. The Commodore himself would often tend bar and wait tables, and on Sundays stood at the door collecting half-dollars for the hotel's famed "fifty-cent family dinner." Catering to the working and middle classes, the boardinghouse and the small hotel formed the staple of the resort economy.

In Atlantic City, the larger the hotel, the more exclusive and expensive it tended to be. A third class of hotels consisted of seventy-five houses of between one hundred to two hundred rooms. Catering to the family trade, they were "with few exceptions managed and conducted in a quiet and a dignified way." Their coaches met the trains, and they featured uniformed bellmen, printed menu cards, and private baths.[58] Aspiring to an upper-class status, these hotels occupied a higher ground among the three groups of hotels that accommodated the working and middle classes.

Economic and class divisions among the resident population became more pronounced as the city grew. The building of the Boardwalk between 1870 and 1896 determined its social and political configuration. Before the beachfront developed, trains ran down the middle of Atlantic Avenue, dropping off visitors at the various hotels at which was then the center of resort activity. Later this became known as the "old system," and Atlantic Avenue as the "Old Town" section. As the Boardwalk developed, hotels which sat modestly near Pacific Avenue were moved beachward to front on the ocean and enlarged to opulent proportions. The largest of these, such as the Dennis, the Traymore, the Marlboro-Blenheim, the St. Charles, and Chalfonte-Haddon Hall formed the nucleus of the "beachfront," which during the 1890s developed into the city's most valuable section.

Rising cathedral-like above the glitter of the Boardwalk amusements, the beachfront hotels testified to the progress and permanence of Atlantic City and to its continued popularity among the rich. The Marlboro-Blenheim, completed in 1906 at a cost of over $2 million, was the first of a new generation of large hotels. Built in stages, its evolution reflected the nature of development along the Boardwalk. In 1887 Josiah White purchased the Luray, a forty-room wooden hostelry at the foot of Kentucky Avenue. Its owner was willing to sell, White later said, because "Atlantic City had reached its peak.... From here it could go only backward." But White and his sons added 210 rooms to the hotel and prospered.[59]

In 1900 the Luray burned down, and the Whites quickly replaced it with the Marlboro, an immense fireproof structure that was the last word in luxury and refinement. Later, when a roller coaster appeared practically under the windows of the hotel, they surreptitiously bought out the nuisance and in its place constructed the Blenheim, a magnificent addition of reinforced concrete designed by Thomas Edison.

The Whites' success touched off a boom in luxury hotel building that did not abate until the Crash of 1929. The Marlboro-Blenheim was followed by the Dennis, Chalfonte-Haddon Hall, and finally by the Traymore, completed in 1915 by second cousin Daniel S. White at a cost of $4 million. A huge three-domed monolith of concrete and steel, the Traymore could accommodate more than three thousand persons. Built in the Renaissance style, the hotel provided the genteel magnificence that prosperous vacationers had come to expect in Atlantic City. While the city would wait until the next decade for another hotel of the proportions of the Traymore, by 1916 several "skyscraper" hotels dominated the beachfront, among them the Breakers, the Strand, and the St. Charles, all of which rivaled the Traymore, if not in size, then in luxury, service, and appointments.

The Boardwalk hotelmen constituted the economic and social elite of the city. Though largely self-made, they were anything but nouveaux riches. Alan K. White, Charles D. White, Daniel S. White, Ezra Bell, Henry Leeds, Walter J. Buzby, Newlin Haines, and J. Haines Lippincott were descended from old and venerable Quaker families. They began life in comfortable but unpretentious circumstances. They built their fortunes on the great hotels that dominated the city's skyline—solid, sedate, yet elegant houses that welcomed the rich and reflected the social outlook of their proprietors.

The hotels of Atlantic City provided economic opportunity of a different sort for large numbers of black people who, beginning in the 1870s, flocked to the resort in droves seeking employment in the hotel-recreation industry that was rapidly developing. Blacks first came as workers, later as visitors, and finally, by the mid-1880s, had settled in Atlantic City in numbers sufficient to constitute a significant and stable part of its population. In their roles as workers, visitors, and residents, black people in Atlantic City presented a vivid and comprehensive reflection of the black experience in the North following the Civil War.

In an era when the great industrial centers of the North were not ready to employ blacks, the island became a mecca for legions of black men and women who became waiters, porters, bellmen, maids, servants, cooks, and domestics. By 1905 blacks made up 95 percent of the hotel work force in Atlantic City. This was not unusual, as the majority of blacks working in the North during this period were employed in "domestic and personal service," a census category that included hotel work.[60] As the industrial economies of Trenton, Newark, Paterson, and Jersey City were built on the backs of immigrant labor, the resort economy of Atlantic City rested on the service of black workers.[61]

When Atlantic City began to boom in the 1870s, the onus of slavery still lay heavily upon the United States. Blacks who trickled north to form the vanguard of the great migration that would begin to materialize a generation later soon saw that the peculiar pattern of race relations in the South was merely transposed northward.

In 1876 Charles West Cope, the president of the Royal Academy of England, dined as the guest of a Quaker hotel owner. His impressions provide a rare glimpse of black hotel workers during the formative years of the resort.

> The meals were excellent, and the service conducted by a staff of black waiters under the command of a chef, a very handsome, compactly-built man, in the finest linen and the smartest satin ties of primrose or pale blue, which set off his dark skin to advantage. I was interested in these black people. They were very zealous in their duties, and when dinner was over they all adjourned to some rough ground near the sea and played at rounders. They seemed a happy, contented, merry set, constantly singing and laughing. Their peculiar laugh, a sort of "ugh, ugh," seemed to come from deep chest recesses; and one of them, while running after a ball, fell into a depression of the ground hidden by a bush of weeds, and his heels appeared above it in the air. The general laugh was contagious, in which the negro who had disappeared heartily joined when he rose, as his white teeth glittering in the sun showed us.[62]

In this portrait, which appeared as a delightful vignette, we can perceive the role that blacks were expected to play in the resort. Their efficiency and contentment must surely have been the subject of the dinner's conversation between this curious upper-class Englishman, unfamiliar with American racial mores, and his kindly Quaker hosts who no doubt basked in self-satisfaction at the happy condition of their help. We cannot know the feelings of these particular black workers, but seasonal employment in Atlantic City must have seemed a bright alternative to life on a tenant farm in Virginia, Maryland, or North Carolina.[63]

In June 1893 a waiter, dissatisfied with the employees' food, committed the bold and symbolic act of ordering a regular meal for himself from the head steward. When the steward refused, the entire staff walked out in the first of only three strikes known to have been conducted by black waiters before the advent of unions in the 1920s. The hotel summarily dismissed the strikers and that evening replaced them with the hotel's chambermaids. On the next morning the dining room was staffed by "a new force of colored waiters."[64] In August 1899, at the height of the season, the entire force of waiters at the Albion Hotel walked out and attempted with no success to get the other hotel employees to join the strike. The manager discharged the strikers, sending immediately for the police and a new force of waiters. The *Union* reported that "the managers greatly deplored the occurrence and received the sympathy of the guests who realized the dilemma they were in."[65]

A third, more disastrous, strike occurred in the Marlboro-Blenheim Hotel in the summer of 1906. The hotel made temporary wage adjustments which lasted until the end of the season, but then introduced the "European Plan" at the Blenheim, replacing all of the black waiters with whites at the same rate of pay. The incident had citywide ramifications. Later, black waiters referred to the period before 1907 as the "golden era." After the strike, increasing numbers of white workers, particularly women, appeared in the hotel dining rooms of Atlantic City.[66]

Waiters' wages could vary from $8 per month in the smaller establishments to $25 in the exclusive hotels. Often the pay was supplemented by room and board, but the regular compensation was a pittance compared to the gratuities. Recalled one "old hotelman": "I have been tipped more money for waiting on a party than that particular party paid for his board at the hotel."[67] Although many black males did relatively well in Atlantic City, as a rule wages were low, conditions poor, and competition for the few year-round jobs was intense.

William M. Ashby was one of a number of Lincoln University students who worked as a waiter in Atlantic City during the early 1900s. During the day he worked at a small hotel and at night he waited tables at the Ilesworth, a hotel that featured a huge block-long cabaret. A favorite haunt of Lillian Russell, the cabaret was one of the busiest and most popular places in the resort.

Ashby was on duty at the Ilesworth on the night of July 4, 1910, when Jack Johnson knocked out Jim Jeffries for the heavyweight championship of the world. "The patrons," he recalled, "were in an ugly mood. Jeffries had let the whole white race down . . . by letting that nigger beat him up." The crowd vented their anger on the waiters, calling them "ugly, profane, and degrading names." According to Ashby, the humiliation of black waiters was a common sport. "We suffered from rude or half drunk guests who called us degrading names because of our color." Such treatment had to be borne in silence, but there was retribution of sorts: "We could in a way always get back at them. We could spit in their soup or in their beer. This was sometimes done. But this was a vicarious triumph. They would never know of our repulsive act. . . . Rebellion caused us to think of ways to get even the very minute we stepped on the floor."[68]

To get on the floor at the Ilesworth, one purchased a towel for 25 cents from Johnny Johnson, the black headwaiter. This was a common practice in resort hotels, one that "no waiter would dare challenge." Said Ashby, working in the Ilesworth was like "being in a jungle." Ownership, management, and the workers were out to cheat the patrons and each other. On a busy night, glasses, plates, and silver were in short supply and waiters habitually stole from one another, which often resulted in "fierce fights." Even if a waiter were caught stealing from a customer, he ran "no great risk of retaliation."

Black males constituted the most vulnerable segment of the resort's population, a situation worsened by the constant threat of their replacement by white women. Critical to the resort economy, they were nonetheless expendable. Yet black workers in the resort probably fared no worse than those in similar occupations in other Northern cities, and the opportunity for employment continued to draw them to the city in large numbers.

As early as the 1890s, the black presence created serious problems for the resort's image. In 1893 the *Philadelphia Inquirer* asked:

> What are we going to do with our colored people? That is the question. Atlantic City has never before seemed so overrun with the dark skinned race as this season, probably because the smaller proportion of visitors makes their number more prominent. At any rate, both the boardwalk and Atlantic Avenue fairly swarm with them during bathing hours, like the fruit in a huckleberry pudding. This has gone so far that it is offending the sensitive feelings of many visitors, especially those from the South. . . . Of the hundreds of hotels and boarding houses which stud the island from one end to the other, it is probable that not a dozen could be found in which white help is employed. And when to the thousands of waiters and cooks and porters are added the nurse girls, the chambermaids, the barbers, and bootblacks and hack drivers and other colored gentry in every walk and occupation of life, it is easy to see what an evil it is that hangs over Atlantic City.[69]

The article appeared after a financial panic and during a severe depression. Hard economic times tend to heighten racial tensions, and the *Inquirer*'s observation sent an ominous message to area blacks.

One week later the *Philadelphia Tribune*, a black publication, sent a reporter to Atlantic City to investigate, and his findings were recorded by the *Daily Union*.

He found no serious "problem" agitating the public. His people were here in great numbers because they were needed and had been sent for as servants. As a rule, they kept in their places becomingly, and did not intrude to offend those who were over-sensitive as to race prejudice. The colored people are natural born servants, taking bossing more meekly and gracefully, than white help, and are for these and other good reasons, generally preferred.[70]

At worst, we may view the *Tribune*'s compromise as acceptance of the caste system that was already entrenched in Northern cities, and, at best, as a strategic retreat of the sort that Booker T. Washington would make in Atlanta two years later. If not the hoped-for millennium, Atlantic City was one of the few precarious footholds for blacks in the urban North, one in which significant numbers had lived and worked in relative peace for twenty years.

Seen from still another perspective, the item indicated that the city had taken no steps to exclude blacks from the beach or the Boardwalk. However, the nature of the Boardwalk and the other public areas of the city made rigid controls difficult to impose, and before the turn of the century, blacks managed to enjoy at least some of their attractions. Moreover, when blacks were relatively few in number, they did not overly excite white racial anxiety. As their numbers increased, tensions rose proportionately.

In 1884 one Charles Edwards, having been refused admission to two concert gardens on the Boardwalk, brought suit under a state civil rights law passed that year. Editor Heston of the *Review* expressed surprise at the incident, noting: "While the colored people have never attempted to secure accommodations at a hotel, however they have in perhaps all cases been supplied with refreshments at the bar; at least if ever refused, there was never any noise made about it and up to the present time they have except in one or two instances gone into all places of amusements upon perfect equality with the whites."[71] We may well question Heston's succinct history of the city's racial policy. Racial segregation was practiced by blacks themselves who would invariably know the limits.

As the black presence increased, the color line stiffened. In August 1896 amusement operators forcibly ejected George Clinton from a toboggan slide. Clinton, a delegate to the Republican National Convention, put up a struggle but was thrown into a rubbish heap, handcuffed by the police, and taken away. Clinton also threatened to bring suit, but nothing came of either case.[72]

Between 1899 and 1924, George Walls operated the only black-owned business on the Boardwalk, a bathhouse at the foot of Texas Avenue in the excursion district. The establishment served both races, but blacks bathed at the designated beach at Missouri Avenue, two blocks away. In 1899 Walls addressed a prospectus to black investors, and gave clear indication that his venture had the blessing of the city's white leadership, and that it was, from their point of view, a solution to the city's racial problem.

Atlantic City, said Walls, "employs more Colored men and women than any other city in the country," and they "enjoy more privileges than in any other city of its kind in the United States." The eight thousand blacks in the city owned more than $500,000 worth of property. But none had yet bought south of Atlantic Avenue. For blacks with means, it was a golden opportunity; the directors of the corporation had been "invited" and "encouraged" by "White friends," who stood ready to help. Most of Walls's prospectus read as though it were taken from the pages of *Heston's Handbook*. "Our wives and our children are subject to sickness and nervous breakdown, just like other people, and need a place that will most quickly and most thoroughly restore our health, strength, and beauty." Walls had high expectations of his bathhouse. He envisioned the city as a Northern base for American blacks, a place where people of substance could congregate and discuss the problems confronting the race.[73]

In 1980 an elderly black resident described the reality of the beachfront as it existed early in the century:

> [The colored beach] was at Missouri Avenue. It's where everybody went to meet. . . . The other beaches . . . were concessions of the hotels. . . . Now there wasn't any law that you couldn't go on those beaches, but the reason was that the people gathered more or less at the Missouri Avenue beach, and that's where the majority of the people were. . . . If you said, "Well, I'm going to be in Atlantic City over the weekend, you knew that if we went to Missouri Avenue, that's where we'd find them; there was a million of them there.[74]

In 1906 Walls actually petitioned city council for an ordinance prohibiting blacks from bathing outside of Missouri Avenue. Other black residents who saw mixed bathing as a danger to their employment situation supported the effort.[75] But by this time, the city had no need for such an ordinance.

The beach was public domain, and nothing prevented venturesome blacks from traversing its entire length. Discrimination on the Boardwalk consisted of innumerable private acts. Soda fountains and mineral water booths used separate sets of glasses for blacks and whites. The "Jim Crow" glasses were larger, thicker, and held more, but this minor bargain did not assuage the feelings of indignant blacks who vigorously, but vainly, protested the practice.[76]

Beginning in the summer of 1904, police ordered blacks off carousels and other amusements on the Boardwalk. In 1906 a notice posted in the employees' sections of hotels and restaurants called attention to the resort's increasing Southern patronage and read: "We therefore request that you, our colored employees, and your families and friends, not to bathe or lounge in front of our respective properties, . . . feeling sure that you will appreciate the appeal in the spirit in which it is made and that its observance will benefit both yourselves and ourselves."[77]

The hotelmen made that spirit plain by concluding that "there would be fewer colored employees" if the practice continued. In urging compliance, the *Sunday Gazette* was even more explicit:

> The colored man is dependent on the white man for his living, and when the white man says it is necessary for the colored man to join him in improving business by a little self-denial, he should promptly agree to the request. For years the colored bather has been an issue on the oceanfront. Hints that he was not wanted were of little consequence. Until the Southern man arrived, the hotel men were disinclined to force the issue, which to them would look like discrimination. When it reached the issue of dollars, the hotel men acted.[78]

In 1906 the policy of racial segregation crystallized in Atlantic City, but it does not appear that it resulted from an increase in Southern patronage. Racial tensions predated any large influx of Southern visitors, an indication that Northerners were no more tolerant than Southerners. Later that summer, precisely the same thing occurred in Cape May, a resort which had had a proportionally much larger Southern clientele since before the Civil War.[79]

Commercial resorts carried a high potential for racial violence, particularly outside of the Deep South where codes governing the association of the races were not officially drawn and the recognized rules of segregation were often murky. This was most tragically illustrated by the swimming incident in Lake Michigan during the summer of 1919 which touched off the Chicago Race Riot, resulting in the deaths of thirty-eight people. The events that led to the riot began when *The Whip*, a black newspaper, urged black Chicagoans to make the Twenty-fifth Street beach "our Atlantic City."[80] In Keyport, in June 1888, a number of white youths "thought it would be funny to spoil the fun of a negro, who astride a wooden horse, was enjoying himself to the utmost." The youths purchased ten pounds of flour in separate bags and took turns dousing the black man as he whirled around the carousel. Either in panic or anger, he drew a pistol and began firing at his tormenters, severely wounding a bystander.[81] Seaford, Delaware, also experienced a serious racial conflict during the summer of 1906.[82] No such incident occurred in Atlantic City. After 1904, the color line, though unofficial, carried all of the weight of municipal ordinances.

In September 1896 the *Philadelphia Inquirer* noted: "One of the harbingers of fall is the annual excursions of colored citizens from Pennsylvania, Delaware, and New Jersey to the seashore."[83] By the 1890s the annual September excursions of black people to the resort had become an institution, allowing the city to extend the season for another weekend. With the enactment of Labor Day as a national holiday in 1904, the black excursions came during the second week in September. During these holidays, blacks may have enjoyed a respite from the usual restrictions, but not from humiliation.

In 1892 the *Union* remarked: "There's more than one new coon in town today; fully 8,000 of 'em."[84] In 1898 the *Union* observed:

> They are patronizing the street cars and the busmen are doing a good trade. The lunch counters and the buffets are gathering in plenty of nickels and dimes, for the colored folk are generous and, like Pittsburghers, spend every dime they bring with them and have only the return coupons of their tickets left when the day is done. . . . Tomorrow they will be gone, and it is estimated that they will leave behind no less than $20,000 in hard-earned cash.[85]

The same tone was struck by Walter Evans Edge's Republican *Press* in September 1900:

> Yesterday was a great day for the colored population. Over eleven thousand were brought in by the two roads on the excursion train. . . . A great long line of sambos and Liza Janes was seen like a huge cineograph moving picture along the ocean front. . . . The loud laugh of the happy negro and

the "yaller girl" made the Boardwalk ring. . . . Considering the event and the low price of razors, it is wonderful that so few disturbances occurred during the day.[86]

Negative coverage for blacks was by no means unusual in the Northern press in either Democratic or Republican papers. But for local newsmen, ridiculing the September excursionists was an annual sporting ritual and served as another reminder for blacks of their place in resort society.

The black presence in Atlantic City dates from the city's inception in 1854. Black laborers worked on the construction of the railroads and, to some degree, in hotel and road construction in the 1850s and 1860s. As most of the workers were transients, they had little effect on the city's resident population. Massive black immigration coincided with hotel development, which began in earnest in the 1870s and 1880s. Most were seasonal employees, but a large number of black people chose to settle in the resort and made up a significant portion of its resident population. By 1910, when blacks accounted for 6.4 percent of the population of Camden, 3 percent of Newark, 2.7 percent of Trenton, 2.2 percent of Jersey City, and only 3.5 percent of the urban population of New Jersey, Atlantic City's 9,834 black people made up over 21 percent of its total, which by this time exceeded 46,000. By 1915 the population of Atlantic City rose to 51,667, and the black population, at 11,069, kept pace at 21 percent.[87]

During the early years, blacks lived in clusters throughout the city, either in servants' quarters or in makeshift housing near their employment. As the southern or beachward section began to develop with summer cottages, hotels, and permanent residents, blacks were increasingly forced into the northern portion of the city beyond Atlantic Avenue. By 1905 the "Northside," Atlantic City's black community, had taken shape. Its boundaries were clearly defined and included the area north of Atlantic Avenue to the meadows, extending to Arkansas Avenue on the west, and to Connecticut Avenue on the east. In 1905 only 3.3 percent of the city's blacks lived outside of this area, and by 1915 blacks with white neighbors would constitute less than one percent of the black population. Practically all the blacks who resided in white areas of the city either lived in the hotels in which they worked or were live-in help at private residences.[88]

If the business cycle made life precarious for white industrial workers, the seasonal economy of Atlantic City created conditions for native blacks that were almost nightmarish. By 1881 city council was setting aside funds in October for "taking care of the poor in winter."[89] In 1888 Alfred Heston, the city's chief publicist, wrote: "Colored people come here for the purpose of doing laundry and waiting, and their children are bottle fed and neglected."[90] The winter of 1905 was particularly harsh, and the Overseer of the Poor was overwhelmed with requests for aid. He reported: "As usual, those applying for relief are mostly colored, but a number of white families have been among the recent applicants." Republican clubs in all four of the city's wards, along with Mayor Stoy, Louis Kuehnle, and other prominent citizens, were active in charity work, in one day distributing forty-five gallons of soup and 369 loaves of bread.[91]

Margaret Brett, a social worker investigating the conditions of blacks in Atlantic City in 1912 for the *Survey*, reported: "Irregularity of employment, the most serious problem of modern life, reaches its apex in Atlantic City."

> "In season" relatives and acquaintances are urged to come to this El Dorado, and come they do in battalions, happy with the vision of picking up like shells from the beach gold that the visitors waste. And then they wake up. "Out of season" a city of 300,000 all of a sudden in the moisture of a cold wave has dissolved to 100,000, and in two weeks the recently arrived are paying room rent with promises and subsisting on sea breezes.[92]

Then as now, Atlantic City was a study in contrasts. On the avenues, "an army of blithesome Negroes" served the visitors and at day's end retreated to a "labyrinth of alleys, lanes, and streets" of two-room shacks and worn-out homesteads, "all cellerless and few sanitary," and whose rents were high in winter and even higher in summer.

The seasonal economy created special problems for the entire city, but winters fell with a particular harshness on the black community. Social services fell under the aegis of the Overseer of the Poor, whose meager handouts meant only bare sustenance for the unemployed during the difficult cold months. Churches and private charities were also active in aiding the poor, but such efforts could not begin to address the problem of seasonal unemployment, which was a fixture of the resort economy.

In 1909 the city's social services were combined under a branch of Organized Charities, a national organization which maintained agencies in over two hundred municipalities. Its motto, "Not Alms, But a Friend," reflected its "scientific" outlook on poverty.

Their research in Atlantic City confirmed the popular suspicion about the underclass that, as a rule, "the cry for bread was simply a demand for booze; that the whine of poverty was simply the trained cadence of laziness."[93] Margaret Brett observed paternalistically but not unsympathetically that "the Negroes dwell in a state of intermittent prosperity. Always living from hand to mouth and with rents in arrears, they take refuge in the morrow. In winter they reason with cheerful philosophy that it is the city's duty to take care of them." At this time, the city committed but $5,000 per year to Organized Charities.[94]

To the vast majority of black residents, Atlantic City offered little beyond seasonal and menial employment. Outside of the world of work, there were few institutional relationships between blacks and whites. After an unsuccessful experiment with school integration in the 1890s, the Board of Education adopted an official policy of segregation in 1901. The municipal hospital treated blacks in separate wards, and black children could not play in public parks outside of the Northside. As a result, the Northside turned inward and developed parallel institutions, agencies, and leadership, most of which centered about the church. Black fraternal organizations such as the Prince Hall Masons, organized in 1881, and the Lighthouse Lodge of the Elks, founded in 1900, were active in community work and charitable activities and provided social life for the black upper classes. Saloons, restaurants, and dance halls operated by local blacks catered to both natives and black tourists and provided social amenities that could not be obtained south of Atlantic Avenue. The Northside developed not merely as a physical ghetto, but also as an institutional one, in the city, but not of it, an enclave distinct and separate from the mainstream of resort life.[95]

The beachfront and the Northside represented the extremes of Atlantic City's class structure. Atlantic Avenue, the main thoroughfare that ran west from the Inlet, bisected the entire city and developed as the business center. Once-grand cottages, remnants of the avenue's more exclusive days, were being renovated into storefronts and boardinghouses and small hotels. In 1912 a boomlet in the building of apartment houses added to the commercial atmosphere that the "Old Town" section was beginning to take on. Except for the profusion of taverns, restaurants, and saloons that were jammed during the summer months, Atlantic Avenue resembled the business district of any small American city. Between Arkansas and Connecticut avenues it formed the southern boundary of the Northside, a dividing line between two distinct and separate worlds.

The Inlet section at the northwestern point of the island had become a district of working- and middle-class whites. Once an exclusive cottage section and the site of the Royal Palace Hotel, it too had fallen out of fashion with the rich with the development of the beachfront. Before the turn of the century, Mary Riddle had led a group of enterprising women in creating Chelsea, a fashionable area of imposing homes and summer cottages in the southwestern portion of the city.[96]

West of the Northside, in the vicinity of Arctic Avenue, stood the nucleus of an Italian community known as Ducktown. Although the foreign-born population reached 6,485 in 1910 and represented 14 percent of the total, its diverse mixture precluded the formation of substantial ethnic communities within the city. The largest groups were the Italians at 1,383, the Russians at 1,148, and the Germans at 835.[97] Assuming that national immigration patterns held true for Atlantic City, the majority of the Russians were Jewish. But like the rest of the foreign born, they were represented at all levels of the social spectrum. With the exception of the black Northside, ethnicity was not a large social or political factor in the city.

With the completion of the Philadelphia and Atlantic Railroad in 1877, the area surrounding its terminus at Arkansas Avenue quickly grew into a small amusement center for the working classes. The Narrow Gauge Excursion House and the Seaview Excursion House afforded inexpensive accommodations near the beach and became the nuclei of a variety of booths, rides, and pavilions catering chiefly to the excursion trade. Saloons such as the Poodle Dog, the Hole-in-the-Wall, and O'Neil's Tavern could become rough. In 1891 a correspondent to the *Union* complained: "In one avenue down town there are thirteen saloons in a block. Here is where the excursionists go. Some of these have been a little better than dives and every little while we would get a case of a man who had been drugged and robbed or beaten and robbed while drunk."[98] By the 1890s the section had become known as "the Bowery," and policemen patrolled it in twos for their mutual protection. (See map on p. 44.)

At the bottom of the social pyramid rested its foundation, the fifth of the population who had nothing to sell but their labor. The vast majority of Northside residents defined economic goals in terms of survival. Yet, on election day, Republican leaders counted on the Northside to vote

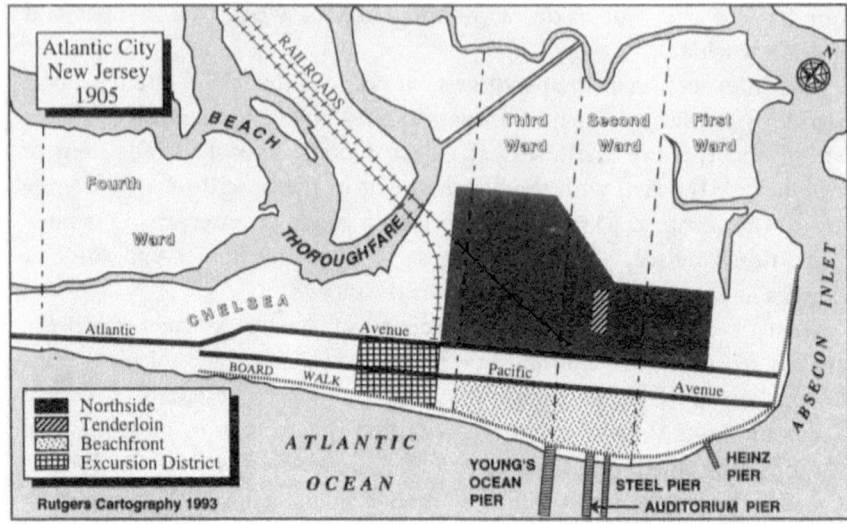

Atlantic City in 1905.

solidly for the organization line. Observers summerized local politics with the axiom, "The beachfront pays the taxes, but the Northside does the voting." At this time the Democrats were the party of white supremacy, lynching was a national scandal, and the Republicans were, after all, the party of Lincoln.

Between 1854 and the advent of commission government in 1912 when citywide mayoralty elections were no longer held, Republicans elected fourteen of the sixteen mayors, and had, with rare exception, controlled city council. We might assume that during the nineteenth century local residents took their party allegiances seriously and that Atlantic City was a solid Republican town. Neither was the case. Willard Wright, a Democrat and a popular local physician, won one-year terms as mayor in 1877, 1878, 1880, and 1882, and a two-year term in 1892. The voters elected local attorney and municipal judge Joseph Thompson to the mayoralty in 1898.

In 1890 Smith E. Johnson, the perennial Republican sheriff of Atlantic County, won an assembly seat by 195 votes but carried the city by only 105 of its total of 2,017 votes. In 1891 Republican mayor Hoffman captured the same seat by a majority of 281 over the Democratic tax assessor, William Riddle, but lost the city by seven votes.[99] Riddle, a follower of Henry George, created a local sensation by assessing beachfront properties at significantly higher rates. He won reelection to that office in March 1892 by the more substantial majority of 591 votes.[100] The picture that emerges from the political hodgepodge of the 1890s amounts to nothing more than small-town politics driven by personal affinities and local interests in which Democrats were able to mount a viable opposition.

Not untypically, the leadership of both political parties during the nineteenth and early twentieth centuries was drawn from the rising class of small businessmen and professionals whose interests were primarily local in scope.[101] The transition from the "old system" to the "new system" meant that political and civic leadership fell to the Atlantic Avenue or Old Town interests. The expanding resort economy created a number of local business elites who built modest fortunes in enterprises tied both directly and indirectly to tourism and entertainment.

Here we find Louis Kuehnle, Jr., the most successful among the Old Town businessmen, by 1905 a reputed millionaire and a highly respected citizen of Atlantic City. Louis, Sr., a German chef, had immigrated to the United States in 1849. In 1858 he brought his wife and three sons to Egg Harbor, the newly created German settlement located twelve miles north of Atlantic City on the Camden and Atlantic Railroad. He opened the New York Hotel, served several terms as the Democratic mayor of Egg Harbor, and won a seat on the county Board of Freeholders. In 1875 he opened Kuehnle's Hotel at the southwest corner of Atlantic and South Carolina avenues and placed it under the management of his eighteen year old son, Louis, Jr.[102]

A Democrat, young Kuehnle had little time for politics. He never married, spending his young manhood building his hotel business, where he worked feverishly cooking, tending bar, and waiting tables. When the Pennsylvania Railroad absorbed the Camden and Atlantic, it built its main depot just opposite the hotel, and Kuehnle's prospered enormously. Its sixty-foot bar was constantly filled with travelers waiting to entrain, and conductors announced departures by running into the building to yell, "All aboard." Working behind the bar or in the hotel dining room, the huge, jovial Kuehnle met people coming and going, including County Clerk Lewis Scott, Sheriff Smith E. Johnson, and Gardner, for whom the hotel was a convenient meeting place.

In 1890 Kuehnle waged a legal fight with the Pennsylvania Railroad over a property encroachment and became a local hero when, backed by one hundred citizens, he faced down a railroad work crew who attempted to remove curb stones from his hotel sidewalk.[103] In 1896 Mayor Stoy appointed him water commissioner, and Kuehnle emerged from his first term a Republican. Although by 1900 he achieved a measure of local influence, there is no evidence of direct political activity, much less of his being a political boss. In expanding Atlantic City, Kuehnle found a fertile field for the investment of his hotel profits, and he absorbed himself in business.

In 1900, Kuehnle bought a brewery, and the *Press* reported the transaction as follows:

> Louis Kuehnle, emperor of business and the king projector of enterprises, has again launched out. This time his venture is in the line of hops and malt on a gigantic scale. . . . There is probably no man in Atlantic City better qualified to do this. His liberal means and perhaps still more liberal business views will be vested in the hands of men of unquestionable ability and sound judgement, and while he still will be at the head of his great Telephone Company, and the several other important branches of business that he is pushing, he will keep his best eye upon the new enterprise in question.[104]

Allowing for the booster mentality of the local press, in this instance that of Walter Evans Edge, the tribute was not unwarranted. Kuehnle helped create the Atlantic Coast Telephone Company because of the high rates of the Bell system. Any project for the betterment of the city, especially ones that freed residents from the dominance of Philadelphia-owned utilities, found a willing backer in Louis Kuehnle. He was a founder and the first president of the Atlantic City Electric Company. Acting with other local capitalists, he formed a water company, which they eventually sold to the city, a traction company, the Consumers Gas Company, and he was the principal investor in an ill-fated scheme to bring top-rated vaudeville acts to a plush theater constructed on Atlantic Avenue. While most of these ventures were profitable, in some he lost heavily, including a steam heating plant to provide heat and hot water to city hotels.[105]

In 1900 he joined a group of prominent citizens in a plan to make the Inlet a port of call for East Coast pleasure yachts, and they formed the Atlantic City Yacht Club. Kuehnle's sixty-four-foot craft became the club's flagship, and Kuehnle became "The Commodore," a title that remained with him long after the club disbanded.[106] By 1910 he directed several banks and had financial and personal connections with every segment of the business community. He served as treasurer of the United

States Fire Company for ten years, and his charitable endeavors, particularly in the Northside, were legendary.

Although a recognized civic and financial leader, the Commodore wore his mantle lightly. Despite his wealth, he retained a common touch and a self-deprecating sense of humor. With his little dog Jerry, his constant companion of fifteen years, he cut a familiar and avuncular figure throughout the city. Seated in a barber chair in 1901, the 230-pound Kuehnle responded to good-natured taunts about his weight from an equally large Philadelphia whiskey dealer by challenging him to a footrace. Each man put up $100, and onlookers staged the race with great ceremony. Kuehnle led until a Saint Bernard dog jumped in his path, but the Philadelphia man spent the better part of his purse treating spectators at the bar of Kuehnle's Hotel.[107] The portrait that emerges from numerous turn of the century newspaper accounts shows a man without guile or pretension, more adventuresome than shrewd in business, a big fish in a small pond, and one held in awe by local townsfolk for his generosity and his alleged "Midas touch."

Accounts of Kuehnle's career written near and at the time of his death place him at the helm of the city as early as 1900. In 1931 Victor Jagmetty, who, by his own account, had Kuehnle's confidence and as a reporter had followed city politics closely since 1885, wrote: "There was no discussion over appointments or perquisites. Either The Commodore did, or he didn't, and that was all there was to it. There was one, and but one, political boss of Atlantic City, and Louis Kuehnle, seated firmly in his chair at The Corner [South Carolina and Atlantic avenues], was IT.[108] According to Jagmetty, Kuehnle was known as the "easy boss" because of his generosity toward defeated adversaries, yet he maintained an "iron discipline."

> The delegates were hand-picked by district leaders who assured the "big boss" of individual willingness to "take orders." Boss Kuehnle consulted political leaders behind closed doors and they agreed upon a "slate," that is the framing of city and county tickets, which were certified to district leaders, who in turn were required to keep their followers in line in supporting organization selections in the conventions and then in the polls.[109]

There can be no doubt that Kuehnle was a man to be reckoned with in the small resort city whose politics were dominated by business interests. In New Jersey, prior to the passage of the Geran Act in 1911 and the advent of primary elections, the winnowing process of factional battles waged before or within nominating conventions whereby the winners made peace at the top presents a likely scenario. In a world grown large and impersonal by the 1930s, the picture of Kuehnle determining the destiny of a city and dispensing patronage from his hotel porch had a nostalgic appeal. But it is not supported by the evidence.

The Republicans gained political control over the city by default. The popular Democratic mayor, Joseph Thompson, declined to run in 1900, presumably weary of Sunday closing conflicts and anxious to attend to his own expanding business interests. Democratic leadership then fell to attorney Clarence L. Cole, who was tainted locally because he had represented a reform group in a recent crusade against commercial vice. William Riddle, a political maverick, had broken with the national organization in 1896 over Bryan's free silver platform. In the absence of effective leadership, the organization crumbled, and local Democrats defected to the Republicans in wholesale fashion.[110] The absence of a strong labor movement or powerful ethnic groups within the city who might have coalesced into an effective Democratic opposition meant that the business-dominated Republicans had a clear field, and it was within this group that Kuehnle exercised leadership. But Kuehnle as czar is a role that was much overrated. In fact, the course of political developments during this period points in the opposite direction, to a faction-ridden city controlled by a faction-ridden Republican party that was unable to mobilize the populace behind movements supported by its leadership, which was itself divided and fragmented.

A few examples will suffice to illustrate this point. In 1900 the city still operated under its original charter an antiquated document that vested most of the appointive power in the hands of the common council and limited the city's capacity for bonded indebtedness. A new charter, ratified by the voters in 1902, raised the debt ceiling by 25 percent and paved the way for much-needed city improvements. A modern sewer system, a municipally owned water company, a paid fire department, improvements to the Boardwalk, as well as street paving all flowed from the new charter between 1904 and 1910. Each measure was delayed or opposed by majorities in city council who were more influenced by tax-paying constituents than by the business wing of the local Republican organization.

The charter was written and sent to the state legislature for approval only after a protracted struggle within the council. According to a local source, Governor Franklin Murphy signed it in a moment of rare drama.

With pen poised, Murphy was set to veto the charter because the debt ceiling was too high when an aide ran into his office and announced, "Atlantic City is burning down." The great Boardwalk fire of April 3, 1902 destroyed thirteen hotels, twenty-five stores, and several homes along a two-block section of the Boardwalk. Inadequate water pressure hampered the efforts of volunteer companies, and the fire threatened to consume the entire city. The fire was contained and the disaster averted. But Murphy relented, and the voters ratified the charter the following month.[111]

Opposition to the regular Republican organization centered about the person of William Riddle, who, by 1902, had jumped on the Republican bandwagon and was firmly entrenched as a councilman from the Fourth Ward. The Riddle obstructions consisted of amendments to city-let contracts providing for minimum wages and union workmen and of objections to council not accepting lowest bids on such projects as street paving, curbing, and the laying of gas and water mains. Walter Evans Edge constantly fumed against the "turncoat Democrat" who controlled ten votes in council. In one day in 1902, by a vote of eleven to five, council voided a host of city contracts, discontinued a city lawsuit, and delayed the referendum on the city charter. To Edge, Riddle was a demagogue who threatened to take over the city.[112]

Riddle's version of these events is contained in a document he prepared, probably in 1916, in which he summarized his tenure in council between 1902 and 1910 as a time when he "fought every franchise grab and every contract grab attempted by this powerful combination."[113] Senator Edward S. Lee, a brick contractor, built City Hall, and party stalwart and later mayor Edward S. Bader, a cement contractor, bid successfully on many city contracts. Although Riddle owned valuable properties in the resort, he sought to build a constituency of the working classes, particularly among blacks, the unions, and city employees. As a council member, he busied himself with repeated resolutions in support of striking Pennsylvania coal miners. His term as tax assessor found him constantly embroiled in controversies arising out of low assessments for favored supporters and high ones for his political enemies.[114] Some levels of graft, demagoguery, and favoritism undoubtedly attached to both sides, but that is not at issue here. To accept either or both versions, or something in between, is to admit to a political situation sharply at odds with that of Atlantic City dominated by an all-powerful machine.

Although it is clear that in the business of mobilizing votes and keeping recalcitrant lieutenants in line the local Republican organization operated with less than machinelike efficiency, the question remains as to Kuehnle's position within the party hierarchy and the extent of his personal influence in the city. It is not resolved by a front-page article that appeared in the *Sunday Gazette* in September 1906 under the headline, "Kuehnle Says Council Must Pave Atlantic Avenue." Kuehnle and the Atlantic Avenue League of Businessmen had organized a huge protest parade of five hundred citizens to resolve the paving issue. Said Kuehnle, "We will show City Council that they must yield to public sentiment in regard to paving Atlantic Avenue." The writer was frankly at a loss to explain this development.

> Commodore Kuehnle, the recognized boss of the majority in City Council, rather astonished the reporter. He is given credit, whether he possesses the power or not, of being able to command a majority on the floor of council whenever he wants it by simply issuing requests. . . . That he has determined to compel Council at the head of a formidable array of citizens to do the bidding of the public is a political move which will not injure his reputation as a politician. Commodore Kuehnle says he is going to do it, and that practically means that it will be done.[115]

The poor condition of Atlantic Avenue had been a sore point among all segments of the business community for at least a decade. Kuehnle had led the paving forces at least since 1901, when he was elected chairman of a joint committee of city council and the Board of Trade to investigate the matter. When work finally began that winter, paving was an idea whose time had come.

The charter and street paving owed less to a powerful political combination than to the Boardwalk fire and the advent of the automobile. In an unguarded moment in 1903, an exasperated Walter Evans Edge, impatient with political infighting and the slow progress of municipal improvements, declared that "boss rule" would be the salvation of Atlantic City.[116] Four years later, local leaders were still clearing political appointments with John Gardner, not Louis Kuehnle.[117] The years between 1900 and 1910 were the most critical period in the development of Atlantic City into a modern municipal entity. In later life, Kuehnle may have basked in the reveries of local newsmen that he guided the city to greatness; or he may have bristled at the allegations of reformers that he bossed a regime as corrupt as that of Enoch L. Johnson. The events of this period provide evidence of neither and, in fact, suggest the opposite—a

From Pitney's Folly to World's Playground • 51

city rent by factions and slow to effect municipal improvements pushed by the Republican organization.

Finally, there is the issue of the black vote. Beginning in the 1890s, seasonal unemployment, the nemesis of the black work force, created a unique opportunity for Republican leaders, especially in an atmosphere of closely contested elections. Numerous transients from Camden and Philadelphia, who swelled the population during the summer months only to return to those cities after the season, could be registered, and for a modest fee, be easily imported back to the city to vote, and this with at least a modicum of eligibility. But Republicans in Atlantic City were slow to exploit this potential bloc of faithful voters, and, before 1908, blacks were a dubious asset to party fortunes.

The municipal elections, held in March 1892, and the general election that November illustrate the relationship of blacks to the local political establishment prior to its dominance by the Republicans in 1900. After the March election, Editor Hall noted that the city was doing well to poll 2,754 votes on a rainy day. In November, Harrison carried the city by 361 votes over Cleveland in a total vote of 3,119.[118] Neither election carried much importance except that each provided a very early instance where black voters carried a critical balance of power in a Northern city.

In nominating Willard Wright for mayor, the Democrats fell back on a popular and proven candidate. The Republicans nominated Robert Stroud, city councilman and a political ally of Mayor Hoffman. For the council seat in the Third Ward, the Democrats nominated Somers Doughty, who operated a saloon at Indiana and Atlantic avenues and was conspicuous only for his racial hostility. Opposing Doughty was Samuel B. Rose, a three-term incumbent who, as the *Bulletin* noted, had "shouldered a musket in the Great Rebellion" and had been a consistent friend to his black constituents.[119]

Editor Hall of the Democratic *Union* set the tone of the race in his comment on the Republican caucuses: "The number of colored men that attended the Republican precinct caucuses last evening surprised the whites. They were in the majority ten to one. A colored chairman [Northside saloon keeper William H. Furney, who it should be noted, enjoyed wide respect as a businessman in both the white and black communities] presided at City Hall, and two colored men were elected to the city Executive Committee from that precinct.[120] Precinct lines ran from the ocean to the bay, cutting the Northside into several divisions. Blacks at this time could not have mustered a majority, let alone 90 percent, in any precinct. But to him the event stood in stark contrast to the Democratic caucuses where "the large attendance of white men was the special feature."

The *Philadelphia Bulletin* noted: "The colored people are taking more than usual interest in this election because of the well-known antipathy to their race on the part of several of the Democratic candidates." Thomas W. Swann, a Democrat and "the well-known colored journalist and politician," arose from a sickbed to campaign for Stroud because, as he was quoted: "Mr. Stroud has always been alive to the best interests of the city, and at the same time has never forgotten that they too were a part of the municipality. They are well aware of the prejudices that exist here against them, and have nothing to hope from his opponents."[121] Swann may have worked for the *Tribune*, which understandably took a judicious interest in the election, particularly in the candidacy of Somers Doughty, whom it described as "a man of mean and contemptible spirit": "Last summer a party of colored gentlemen, representing the best culture, standing, and education of Philadelphia, entered Mr. Doughty's place on their way to the beach and were charged a double price for everything they ordered. Upon one of the gentlemen remonstrating, he was told, 'The boss of this place does not care for nigger trade no way, so I hope you will all keep out of here.' "[122] Doughty won by a slim majority of twenty-four votes. Wright won by twelve votes, and another Democrat managed to win another of the four council seats by the same margin. In two other council races, the Republicans won by majorities of twenty-three and thirty-nine.[123]

Given the racial climate in Atlantic City, the black impact on the election was almost certainly negative. Black participation carried the penalty of alienating substantial numbers of white voters, especially in a small community where they had high visibility. Even the Republican *Bulletin* accused the Democratic henchmen of Governor Abbett of buying up black votes in preparation for the upcoming statewide elections in November.[124] Editor Hall celebrated Wright's slim victory with the well-worn comment that "the coons and the gamblers no longer control Atlantic City," and frankly attributed the result to the presence of blacks in the Republican caucuses.[125] Among the few certainties that emerged from an investigation in 1890 was that blacks accounted for only a small portion of the city's vice problem. Yet the persistent association of blacks with gamblers and prostitutes further confounded their efforts at a meaningful participation in the political process.

The November election found William Riddle running against Samuel Hoffman for the state senate. Riddle lost the election by 55 votes and the city by 184. Riddle contested the result to the Democratic-controlled senate, charging that Hoffman had "colonized the colored Republicans" of the city. The Riddle probe, conducted in January 1893, was strictly a partisan affair, but its findings shed considerable light on the political role of blacks in Atlantic City at this time.

Riddle's protest centered about the illegal registration of blacks in Atlantic City, which he described as follows:

> Such fraudulent registration being in many cases from empty houses and from vacant lots; and in some instances of as many as eight negroes from one small two-story house which had been occupied for several years continuously by but one family, containing only one man. . . . And in another instance as many as nineteen negroes being registered by a negro Republican from his own home, a small two-story building, with the lower floor being used for a cigar store, kitchen and dining room, and the upper floor for sleeping apartments; said negroes being said to belong to a Republican club having its meeting place there . . . and did register and vote from somewhere else during the election . . . yet, so registered, were in many cases voted on from said house by negroes.[126]

The indictment respectively described a hotel belonging to William H. Furney and Joshua Foreman's cigar store, allegedly the instruments in a Republican scheme to vote the names of nonresident blacks who worked in the city during the summer.

Both Furney and Foreman had come to the city in 1888, lived in their establishments on Baltic Avenue, and let rooms to transient workers. But the similarity ends here. By 1892 Furney was a pillar of the black community, a member of the Republican City Executive Committee, and his hotel had become a gathering place for "respectable" Northside residents. Foreman's cigar store was a reputed gaming establishment and the frequent target of police raids. Both places served as political headquarters of sorts, but the evidence spoke more to the living and working conditions of black males in Atlantic City than it did to the existence of vote fraud.

The Furney household included his son and father-in-law, but eight men had registered to vote at that address. On the day of the election, four of the remaining five were lodging at the house, and the fifth, Robert Mickens, actually owned a large boardinghouse three doors away. Three of the four in residence worked intermittently for Furney during periods when the house was busy, and would either work at other places in the city or travel to Philadelphia to work when Furney's was slow.

For example, James Brown had worked for Furney for three years, but twice during the previous year had gone to Philadelphia for a month or more to find work. Living and working conditions were similar for two of the others, and the remaining individual, John Peterson, had been constantly employed by Furney as a cleaning and maintenance person for three years and lived there permanently. Aside from the Furney family, only Brown and Peterson voted in that election.[127]

Joshua Foreman produced the records of the Young Men's Union Republican Club containing the roll of twenty-five members, seventeen of whom supposedly registered and voted from Foreman's address. The club was formed in 1890, but the minutes were blank until October 1892. Foreman had given canvassers the names of twelve people residing at his house and those of others living in various parts of the precinct. In error, they listed all of the names at Foreman's, a mistake that Foreman actually clarified at a meeting prior to the election, having struck from his residence all but the twelve. Of twelve people registered from 901 Baltic Avenue, only four voted.[128]

One voter, William Wood, a waiter from Philadelphia, had "lodged" there between jobs at various hotels for three years. During the summer of 1892, he had stayed with Foreman briefly in June and then worked and lived at two different places. Laid off in September, he returned to Foreman's and worked there until some time after the election. Wood was one of a number of transient workers who "kept his trunk" of permanent possessions in one of the sleeping rooms, and it was evidently the nearest thing to a permanent address that he could claim. He had been registered there for three years, and his right to vote from that address had never been questioned.

Fourteen black men had registered to vote at Haddon Hall, a large beachfront hotel. Working as seasonal employees, most returned to Philadelphia for the winter. If they lived in Atlantic City for only four months of the year, it is not difficult to believe that the hotel was their most steady source of employment and their most permanent of residences. The investigation failed to show that any of the individuals in question had registered to vote elsewhere.[129]

The Democratic majority on the investigating committee summarized the situation accurately: "During the summer months many colored men are employed in the hotels which are open for the season in Atlantic City. They leave in September and October, but their names are registered from the places where they slept in the summer. These names are voted upon by somebody. It may be that the colored men who are registered return from Philadelphia, Washington, and more distant points to vote on election day."[130] But, they concluded, this would be unlikely as most of the men were not listed in the city directory.

In all, Riddle challenged the votes of eighty-nine people, all blacks who worked in Atlantic City. For the Democrats, eligibility turned on whether the voters in question actually slept at the designated residences on the night before the election. At Foreman's this would have been difficult, and impossible at Haddon Hall, which was closed for the winter. From the Republican point of view, they had conclusively established the right to vote in all but one instance. One's view of the matter depended upon a legal definition of residency. But this was not a court of law, and the majority decided in favor of Riddle.

The Democrats needed only to establish the illegality of fifty-five votes in order to reverse the election. But to have accepted all of their charges at face value would not have established much of a Republican conspiracy to colonize the Northside. If anything conclusive emerged from the investigation, it was that in 1892 the Republican organization of the Northside was at best very loose. Even the *Union*, which constantly made vague charges of Republican vote buying, condemned the proceeding as improper and partisan and conceded that Hoffman had won the election.[131]

Interestingly, Riddle's only charges of vote buying were against whites in other municipalities in the county, and William Furney testified that the Democrats had purchased a few votes in the Northside for a fee of seven dollars each.[132] Blacks were indeed dependable Republicans, but the party held them at arm's length. Irregularity of employment and residence patterns made organization difficult. Unlike white immigrant groups in the industrial cities who saw in the Democrats a party of tolerance and a means of employment and socialization, for blacks the Republicans were merely the lesser of two evils. In 1881 a "non partisan" group of forty-four citizens suggested to city council that in view of the growing black population, "it was only a matter of justice" that a black be appointed to the police force. Council appointed a black in 1886, but eleven years later a Northside preacher complained that after two decades of devotion to the Republican party, blacks in Atlantic City had "separate schools with mixed teachers" and but three policemen and three janitors to show for it.[133]

With the collapse of the Democratic organization in 1900, the black vote became expendable and the "organization" even less attentive to the interests and aspirations of Northside Republicans. Ironically, among white politicians only William Riddle, the former Democrat who as a councilman from the Fourth Ward had the smallest black constituency, made a serious effort to court the black vote before 1908. A resolution he introduced in 1902 providing for the appointment of a "colored boy" as page failed by a vote of fourteen to two. When, in 1906, blacks in the Third Ward organized a "Colored Republican Club" in an attempt to elect one of their members to city council, the organization quickly squelched the effort.[134]

By 1908 Atlantic City was indeed a Republican stronghold in New Jersey. In matters of state and national politics, the resort seemed to speak with one voice. In its promotional literature, it posed as an outgrowth of American democracy a resort where rich and poor, though not black and white, could find equal welcome in a haven of social harmony. Local promoters had published four histories of the resort, and official guidebooks were full of quaint anecdotes recounting the tribulations of the pioneering residents.[135] All extolled the wisdom of Jonathan Pitney and attempted to convince a wary public, and perhaps themselves, that, despite appearances, Atlantic City was not built on the sand, that it was a city of brick, not wood, and that it had substance, permanence, and respectability.

American democracy made up the core of the liberal policy, and local historians painted all classes of people in Alger-like proportions as they struggled to build a great resort on the wastes of a barrier island. All of the white citizens could share in this epic, as history served the internal function of creating a synthesis of the city and of knitting the community together. Harmony required compromise by all of the contending elites, including the evangelical community, a process that produced the liberal policy. This compact long predated Republican ascendancy in Atlantic City. Transcending the local realm of law and politics, the liberal policy only barely covered a cauldron of conflict simmering just beneath the surface of the small resort community.

CHAPTER THREE

The Robbery of the Sabbath

Social and political historians have continually seen World War I and the 1920s as critical turning points in American society, "the crisis of the Protestant establishment," the time when Protestant churches became "sharply aware that their ancient sway over the nation's moral life was threatened."

> The debacle of Prohibition functioned both as evidence and cause of the churches' loss of authority in a culture where urban values became primary. The decline of the Puritan Sabbath despite strenuous campaigns in its behalf, the emergence of new attitudes towards recreation despite old Puritanic suspicions of play, and the expansion of the amusement industry served meanwhile to weaken the disciplinary aspects of church membership. Modern thought and social change were slowly bringing down the curtains on the "great century" of American evangelicalism.[1]

The evidence suggests that by the turn of the century, at least in the Northern industrial states, Protestant hegemony was more of a social veneer than a consensus or, if there was indeed a crisis, it occurred well before the war and Prohibition.

To be sure, most evangelicals, and many secular reformers, veiwed the decline of the Christian Sabbath and the rise of commercial recreation as symptoms of spiritual and moral deterioration. But the social anxieties that fueled the Sabbatarian movement, and the Progressive movement as well, went far deeper. To examine the relationship between Sabbatarianism and Progressive reform in Atlantic City is to plumb the depths of an ongoing social crisis within American society, one whose principal ingredients were race, class, and ethnic conflict and profound anxiety over social, economic, and sexual change.

In 1908 Charles J. Fisk, chairman of the governor's commission to investigate the enforcement of the state's liquor laws, made the following assessment of conditions in Atlantic City:

> We find here a state of affairs that probably does not exist in any other part of the state. We find a city that is one of the largest watering places in the State of New Jersey, where some of the laws relating . . . to liquor and moral matters are not only not enforced, but are absolutely ignored. We find a condition of affairs here where the saloons and liquor places are wide open, where in connection with a number of saloons we find that there are music halls and dance halls, rendeveux for disorderly people, for prostitutes and demimondes, where young girls are taken in and led astray, . . . and they hold licenses granted by the city.
>
> We find places that are in the hands of gamblers, regular hell holes, . . . and then we go further and find the officials, from the Judge of the Court of Common Pleas down to the police officer who acts under the order of the municipal government, saying that it is impossible to . . . enforce the law as far as the liquor question is concerned, because the people do not want it and won't stand for it.[2]

Many found this judgment harsh, but it could not be said that Fisk was uninformed. A "churchman" and a Wall Street banker, he was the "reform" mayor of Plainfield, a delegate to the Republican National Convention, and at the time had presided over exhaustive hearings on the liquor traffic throughout the state, documenting the connivance of local politicians with saloon keepers, gamblers, and prostitutes in Paterson, Newark, Jersey City, Hoboken, Camden, and Trenton, and also in rural parts of the state. As the foreman of a grand jury in his native Union County, he had discovered that the liquor interests dominated both municipal and county governments. In all of these places, saloons were open on Sunday.[3]

What then was uniquely evil about Atlantic City? Sifting the lengthy indictment, we come to the end before we identify the difference. Municipal officials were unable to prevent Sunday liquor sales because "the citizens wouldn't stand for it." For middle- and upper-class professors of the Protestant ethic (it would be difficult to find a better example than Fisk), the violation of the Fourth Commandment, if not trivial among the catalog of offenses, was certainly less grave than prostitution, gambling, and political corruption. Yet it was principally on this point that the city had stumbled, and by 1908 Atlantic City had become a national symbol of an ethos already in crisis.

But before we can begin to speak of the problems of Atlantic City, we must first deal with the Protestant ethic, and "Protestant hegemony," the term historians have used to explain its dominance of American culture. More precisely, we need to identify the place of Sabbatarianism in that continuum of values that for generations of middle- and upper-class Americans has defined "respectability" within American culture.

Defining respectability in this context is a task similar to that confronting the Supreme Court justice who could not define obscenity but simply said that he knew it when he saw it. If respectability, decency, and such milder terms as rectitude and propriety were defined in the culture within the parameters of Protestantism, a problem immediately arises. By 1900, forty-one Protestant denominations were active in the United States; their very existence speaks to doctrinal differences and varying levels of piety among the sects.[4] Moreover, the practices and beliefs of such groups such as the Mormons, Seventh Day Adventists, and Unitarians differed radically from the dominant Methodists and Presbyterians. Even within sects, the extrapolation of social policy from religious doctrine could differ substantially. For example, in 1914 the New Jersey Methodist Conference commended Walter Rauschenbusch for his "social passion," but found that his writings had "no foundation in Scripture" and were "destructive in their character." His book, *Christianity and the Social Crisis*, was proscribed for church use. On the same list appeared the Reverend D. H. Meyers's *The Graded Sunday School in Principle and Practice* because: "the book fails to appreciate the Christian conception of sin, apparently teaching that to protect a person from vice and crime and rudeness of manner is to keep him from sin, so that his salvation will be one of prevention rather than rescue."[5] The conflict between "faith and works" had begun the Reformation, and the question of how the faithful should confront a sinful world is as old as Christianity itself. But the problem here is to identify the significant elements of Christian doctrine common to American Protestants that admitted to public policy, and hence became the synthesis on which Protestant hegemony was built.

We might begin with the International Reform Bureau which professed a "full orbed Christianity," and in 1908 was waging a campaign against the opium traffic in China and the sale of liquor to East Africans and other "uncivilized races." Its letterhead proclaimed its platform: "The International Reform Bureau promotes those Christian reforms on which the churches sociologically unite while theologically differing. It proffers cooperation to all associations that stand for the defense of the Sabbath and purity; for arbitration in the place of industrial and international war; for the suppression of intemperance, gambling, and political corruption."[6] Much in the platform suggests a unity of social outlook. Most Protestants of the day would have agreed that vice, crime, and even "rudeness of behavior" were proper objects of public policy. Few would dissent from the proposition that the savage of all races needed to be protected from themselves. We would also find that arbitration, both foreign and domestic, could only take place among "civilized" disputants; the record of imperialism and the suppression of the IWW, to cite but one domestic example, are sufficient to validate that consensus. But on the first principle, "the defense of the Sabbath," the consensus breaks down.

Strict Sabbatarianism found favor only among the literal minded. Refusal to "take the cars" on Sunday or to read a Sunday newspaper were practices that most American Protestants found anachronistic. The achievement of a "Puritan Sunday" was the most radical, and in one sense, the most reactionary goal of evangelical reformers; Sabbatarian stridence often proved an embarrassment to Progressives such as Theodore Roosevelt and the "New Idea" contingent in New Jersey, the forerunner of the Progressive movement in that state. The rural mentality and the religious sensibilities which led to Sunday restrictions have drawn the sarcastic wit and comic indignation of social commentators and historians for decades; H. L. Mencken and Richard Hofstadter immediately come to mind.[7] But during the period in question, Sabbath observance was no laughing matter. Blue laws, which came first to colonial Virginia, not Puritan New England, were widely passed in the nineteenth century and just as widely defied. They lay at the bottom of much social and political conflict, particularly in the cities.

If, on the one hand, blue laws were legal absurdities in a modern industrial society, on the other, by 1890 they constituted the most pervasive and practical manifestation of Protestant hegemony in America. After the Civil War, church-based reform groups sprouted profusely. The International Reform Bureau, the National Reform League, the American Union League Society, the Women's Christian Temperance Union (WCTU) and its men's counterpart, the Knights Templar, and later, the Anti-Saloon League and the Lord's Day Alliance, all founded between 1863 and 1909, were national in scope. An almost endless number of local and state societies, such as the Philadelphia Sabbath Association founded in 1888, and churches themselves supported their efforts. Dominated by Protestant elites and dedicated, either primarily or prominently, to the preservation of the Christian Sunday, they were "ecumenical" only in the fact that they embraced dominant Protestant sects. In 1899 the American Union League Society found the chief peril to "Anglo-Saxon" institutions of state, school, and church in "Politico-Ecclesiastical Romanism," and declared that "offenses against God and his laws (including Sunday laws) cannot be punished . . . unless they are also offenses against society."[8] By 1920 every state, save California and Oregon, forbade the sale of liquor on Sunday.

Yet to view Sabbatarianism principally in terms of a fundamentalist adherence to the Fourth Commandment is not only to misconstrue the modern movement but also to obscure its origins. The movement to legislate Sunday observance began in Elizabethan England, during another period of social and economic upheaval. Not solely the product of Calvinist theology, it sprang from the new urban commercial classes who saw ritual festivals as dangerous relics of Catholicism and Sunday sports as the Medieval orgies of the savage peasantry. Bull baiting, cockfights, and equally bloody football games were ritual Sunday pastimes, and even Shakespeare's theater could degenerate into a pageant of drinking and obscenities. The Sunday proscription and eventual abolition of these pastimes were clearly seen by Puritan reformers of that day, and later by historians, as progressive, not reactionary measures. In the words of Winton Solberg:

> The Puritans constituted a pressure group to advance a radical message which a large segment of the population found increasingly attractive. Since Puritanism made its greatest headway in urban and settled communities, while traditional sports retained their strongest hold in rural and backward areas, the attack on Sunday pastimes may be interpreted as an attempt to impose the ethos of an urban civilization upon the "dark corners of the land."[9]

Clearly, Protestant Sabbatarianism, as it first emerged in sixteenth-century England, was much less a matter of theology than social control.

Historians of the Prohibition movement have seen Sunday restrictions, like Prohibition itself, primarily in terms of the agrarian/urban dichotomy in American culture which became more pronounced after the Civil War with the advance of industrialization, urbanization, and immigration.[10]

62 • *The Robbery of the Sabbath*

Illinois passed a statewide closing law in 1841, but in Chicago it was almost entirely ignored. Sporadic efforts at enforcement by reform mayors led to riots and brought swift political retaliation. Between 1870 and 1910, Newark experienced a protracted conflict over Sunday observance between native Protestants and the swelling numbers of German immigrants who were at a loss to understand the native antipathy to the concerts and beer gardens that were a traditional part of their Sunday leisure. During the summer of 1895, the energetic new police commissioner of New York, Theodore Roosevelt, created a national stir by enforcing a succession of "dry Sundays" in that city. His zeal in enforcing the Sunday laws did much to enhance his national reputation, but made him the "most hated man in New York" and caused much embarrassment to the reform administration of Mayor Strong.[11] In Chicago, Newark, New York, and elsewhere, the conflict took the form of antagonism between native and immigrant groups. But this outward appearance touches only one aspect of an issue that went deep into the social consciousness of the nation.

In 1890 William Addison Blakely, a legal scholar and noted civil libertarian, published *American State Papers Bearing on Sunday Legislation*, a lengthy collection of legal briefs and other polemics against Sunday laws which he saw as a "revival of the religio-political ideas of the Middle Ages." At this time only Arizona, California, and Idaho among the states and territories had no Sunday restrictions, and in each of the other jurisdictions the sale of liquor on that day was prohibited. In every instance, except for Delaware, New Hampshire, and New Jersey, the laws in force were either passed or revised into their current forms within the previous decade. The oldest law, passed by Congress in 1868, imposed Sunday restrictions on the District of Columbia.[12]

For Blakely, the particular genius of American institutions lay in the deistic and Enlightenment theories of government held by Jefferson, Madison, and others who had banished from the statute books "Sunday laws, compulsory attendance at church, and laws against Unitarians, witches, infidels, and Quakers." In that same spirit, Congress, beginning in 1810, had resisted persistent appeals by Sabbatarians to stop the passage of mails on Sunday. The middle decades passed with no agitation for religious laws in Congress and relatively mild enforcement of Sunday laws by the states.[13] But now an alarming reaction was setting in. "In certain localities we see some of these same laws being revived, and new and more stringent ones being demanded. From thirty to fifty cases of the prosecution of Sabbatarians (Seventh Day Adventists) for Sunday work have come to the editor's notice within the past few years, among them being an ordained minister."[14] A new generation of zealots had arisen to impose Christian morality on the nation, and the centerpiece of the movement was Sabbath observance. The National Sunday Rest Bill, proposed in 1888, was the first of 117 religious measures introduced into Congress between that time and World War II. Of these bills, ninety-six demanded Sunday legislation.[15] Sabbatarianism may have been a reactionary movement, but it was also a powerful modern phenomenon.

Blakely devoted a long career to the study and monitoring of the "religious right" in the United States and took a grim view of the proliferation of religious laws. How accurate were his perceptions? To begin with, we must take the reformers at their word. Modern Sabbatarians, like their Puritan forebears, continually and unabashedly proclaimed their intention to establish a Protestant theocracy in America. Moreover, the negative and nativist aspect of that impulse is abundantly manifest throughout the movement. The National Reform League was founded in 1863 expressly for the purpose of placing "all Christian laws, institutions, and usages of our government on an undeniably legal basis as the fundamental law of the land."[16] Their official publication, the *Christian Statesman*, proclaimed that the government "must enforce upon all that come among us the laws of Christian morality. . . . If the opponents of the Bible do not like our government and its Christian features, let them go to some wild desolate land; and, in the name of the devil, and for the sake of the devil, subdue it, and set up a government of their own on infidel and atheistic ideas, and then, if they can stand it, stay there till they die."[17] "A true theocracy is yet to come," declared Frances Willard, who saw the ballot for women as a means of the "enthronement of Christ in law." Nor was Willard, who was among the more ecumenical of evangelical reformers, above nativist appeals. In 1876, early in her career as a temperance lecturer, she committed herself to the suffrage issue by declaring that the woman's voice was essential at the polls, "where the Sabbath and the Bible are attacked by the infidel and foreign population of our country."[18]

To the Seventh Day Adventists, Sabbatarians stood convicted by their own declamations of a scheme to impose inquisitorial Catholicism under the guise of Puritan reform. In 1884 the *Christian Statesman* "cordially and gladly" conceded the fact that in Catholic Europe and in the South American republics, Roman Catholics were the "recognized advocates of national Christianity and stand opposed to the proposals of secularism," and stood ready to join hands in the effort. As for the Church, she crouched like a Cheshire cat, "marvelous and shrewd in her cunning. She can read what is to be. She bides her time, seeing that the Protestant churches are paying her homage in their acceptance of the false Sabbath, and that they are preparing to enforce it by the very means which she herself employed in bygone days. . . . Who understands better than the papal leaders how to deal with those who are disobedient?"[19] If Sabbatarians were neither the dupes of Rome nor engaged in setting up a latter-day inquisition, it surely must have seemed so to the Seventh Day Adventists, and for that matter, to growing numbers of American Jews who also felt the weight of Sunday restrictions.[20]

If we look to the courts for the preservation of minority rights, then much of the conflict that attended the Sabbatarian movement must be laid at the door of the judiciary. Federal and state courts upheld Sunday laws on the basis of principles and practices, that is, by the recognition of Christianity as the basis for common law and the police power of the states. In 1892, Justice David J. Brewer expressed the state of judicial thinking on the Establishment Clause in the nineteenth century when, speaking for a unanimous court, he declared: "This is a Christian Nation." Actually, the case in point, *The Church of the Holy Trinity v. U.S.*, was not at all involved with the Establishment Clause. It arose from an oblique attack on the Contract Labor Law of 1887 in which the church was cited and convicted in the lower courts of New York for violating that law by contracting for the services of an English clergyman. An indignant Justice Brewer, a member of the National Reform League and a frequent lecturer on their behalf, seized upon the opportunity to expound on church/state relations, devoting more than half of the decision to a discourse that firmly planted Christian doctrine within the common law.[21] At this time, Christian communicants barely made up one-third of the nation's population.[22]

Brewer's Christian nation theory actually broke sharply with Supreme Court precedent on Sunday laws. Beginning in 1885 and continuing for most of the twentieth century, the Court treated Sunday laws as civil regulations.[23] The issue has therefore devolved upon the states, and we are left with fifty-one separate Sunday jurisdictions, many containing a myriad of differing county and local regulations.

In 1798, the New Jersey Legislature passed "An Act for the Prevention of Vice and Immorality," which provided that no travelling, worldly employment, or business, ordinary or servile labor or work, . . . nor shooting, sporting, fishing, hunting, gunning, racing, or frequenting of tippling houses, or any interludes of plays, dancing, singing, fiddling, or other music for the sake of merriment, nor any playing at football, fives, ninepins, bowls, long-bullets, or quoits, not any other kind of playing, sports, pastimes, or diversions, shall be done . . . by any person . . . on the Christian Sabbath.

"An Act Regulating Inns and Taverns," passed in 1847 and revised in 1872, forbade the sale of intoxicating beverages on Sunday.

In New Jersey, the news dealer who sold the Sunday edition and the person who bought it were no less guilty of a Sunday violation than the keeper of an open saloon. Nor was the youth who played baseball on Sunday, or for that matter, the Pennsylvania Railroad the moment its second train steamed in or out of a city.[24] Although a few municipalities within the state, most notably, the Methodist settlement of Ocean Grove, attempted to enforce the law to the letter, enforcement generally followed the customs and usages of dominant groups. In the absence of a provision of enforcement by the state, the law made censors of local officials.

Local censorship of Sunday activities therefore fell to mayors, municipal councils, police officials, and local magistrates, who, in passing and enforcing local ordinances, reflected the mores of their constituencies. County prosecutors seeking to punish violators under the state law confronted sheriff-picked grand juries who would or would not indict according to the political whim. Moreover, the maximum penalty under the 1874 law was a one-dollar fine that rendered such prosecution useless to begin with. Thus few Sunday cases progressed to the state bar, and the conflicts generally remained local in scope.[25] Where the population was not homogeneous there was conflict. We may well sympathize with the German-Americans of Newark, who, when denied their Sunday concerts, questioned the "business necessity" of running the factories on Sunday.

In 1923 the borough of Linden indicted a Jewish congregation for conducting a religious parade through the town on Sunday, a Jewish butcher for delivering meats, and a woman, "past sixty years of age," for carrying seven apples from her neighbor's house to her own on Sunday morning. A 1937 revision of the state criminal code left the 1798 law virtually intact, a fact which led one civil libertarian to comment that the most urbanized state had "the most drastic blue laws in the union." New Jersey's Sunday law was not repealed until 1978.[26]

For William Addison Blakely and the Religious Liberty Association, the Washington-based group that carried on his work, the operation of Sunday laws "before the bar of reason" amounted to nothing less than "backward drift" that struck at "the very roots of human advancement and progressive civilization."[27] Blakely, like most secular intellectuals, saw the Sabbatarian movement simply in terms of religious enthusiasm. But the growth of the movement itself reveals growing social pressures far in excess of the kind exercised by Puritan minorities.

The transformation of Sabbatarianism from a matter of religious doctrine to one of public policy began seriously after the Civil War. This was illustrated by the proceedings of the Evangelical United Brethren Church, founded in rural Pennsylvania in 1800 by a group of pietistic German-Americans. Among the Brethren, Sabbath observance had been an article of faith from the beginning. In 1866 their national conference, representing a greatly expanded church, entered a "solemn protest" against efforts to rescind the Sabbath laws and "respectfully prayed the honored Senators and representatives to reject all proposals tending to lessen the observation of the Lord's Day." By 1880 the issue had assumed much wider implications. "Should the sanctity of the Sabbath be displaced by the simple holiday of the European pattern, our surest stronghold against the assaults of socialistic and communistic influences will fall into the hands of those who are the enemies of the Christian family and Christian marriage."[28] As a friend of the working classes, the Church also appealed that workers "counteract the despotism of consolidated capital" by refusing to work on Sunday.

By 1893 the Brethren had become the National Evangelical Association. No longer supplicants, they now saw themselves as arbiters of social conduct. Meeting in Chicago, they pronounced "Sabbath Reform" as one of the four great moral questions of the era, the others being slavery, now abolished, social purity, and temperance reform. Reaffirming their allegiance to the rules of Sabbath observance contained in the first *Discipline of the Church*, published in 1809, the Congress declared its opposition to all forms of Sunday business, including newspapers, and specifically to "all pleasure rides and excursions." Interestingly, as if to corroborate Blakely's assertion that the Protestant churches had been less than consistent on these matters for most of the nineteenth century, the Association congratulated itself in the following manner: "The Evangelical Association has from the beginning . . . taken a very prominent part in the temperance reform. . . . At that early day (1809) the sentiment of the

Christian Churches on the temperance question was by no means what it is today, and with the possible exception of one or two denominations, the Evangelical Association stood alone in her attitude toward the temperance cause."[29] A similar claim was not made for their consistency on the Sabbath question, but the report closed by calling for a "closer union of the Church with the cause of temperance," and declared that now the influence of the Evangelical Association on Sabbath observance was "felt and feared all over this land."

The minutes of the New Jersey Methodist Conference date from 1798. Like the Brethren, with whom they would later merge, Methodists had always had a strict Sabbatarian doctrine. But the Conference did not formally address the issue until 1871 when a committee on "Sabbath Desecration" noted a "growing tendency throughout the country to disregard the sacredness of the holy Sabbath by making it a day of pleasure seeking in steamboat excursions and the running of Sunday trains." But more addressed to their own communicants than to the public at large, the report lamented: "Our own people to some extent participate in these Sabbath desecrations, especially in Sunday visiting," and called for a stricter enforcement of Sabbath doctrine within the Church to the point of disapproving Sunday camp meetings "unless the most careful arrangements are made to prevent Sunday travel to and from the ground." In 1880, Sabbath Desecration became a standing committee of the Conference and continued to recommend "closed gates" at Sunday camp meetings so as to remove the temptation to railroad managers to "make gain out of Godliness" by transporting people to the sites.[30]

By 1893 the Church had become clearly more public and political in its pronouncements. The Committee on the State of the Church reported:

> It is with rejoicing that we note the increase of the power and of the efficiency of the church in its opposition to all forms of evils. To its uncompromising attitude toward the rum traffic. To its determined purpose to have the iniquitous race-track bills repealed, and to present a bold and united front against all corrupt politicians and political machinery. To its untiring appeals for a more strict observance of the Sabbath.[31]

The Temperance Committee, while not presuming to dictate the political conduct of the members, urged that they use "their solemn trust in the elective franchise" to rescue the country from social evils and alternately praised and condemned Congress and the state legislature for actions on various excise and gambling bills. The Committee on Sabbath Desecration had become the committee for "Better Observance of the Sabbath" and had reason to rejoice that year as Congress had "closed the gates" of the Columbian Exposition in St. Louis.

Sabbatarians not only forged ties with temperance and social purity reformers, but by the beginning of the twentieth century had emerged as a powerful movement in their own right. In 1884 the Philadelphia Sabbath Association was formed (John Wanamaker later became its president) to "save the Sabbath from desecration and secure a day of rest for all." In 1888 a group in New York City formed the American Sabbath Union. In 1909 they incorporated as the Lord's Day Alliance and became the parent group of Sabbatarian societies that had been founded in every state. Their increased militance and political sophistication were illustrated by the following excerpt from their annual report in 1911: "In nearly all the states, bills looking toward commercializing the Lord's Day are introduced as regularly as the legislature convenes. In all instances, excepting in Ohio, where a local option sports bill was permitted to become law without the governor's signature, the Christian forces have been able to prevent these bills from becoming laws."[32]

The Alliance was especially concerned with sporting events and theatricals, and an Illinois group had targeted a Sunday Chautauqua. On Long Island, an Alliance member succeeded in having a Sunday air show canceled, and on neighboring Staten Island the Sunday Observance Association of Kings County successfully prosecuted a real estate agent for selling shore lots on Sunday. Quoting the *New York Daily Mail*, the report concluded: "As matters now stand they cannot show property on the first day of the week without running the risk of being fined or landed in jail or both. Perhaps this will pave the way for the annihilation of the Sunday paper, which would undoubtedly be the greatest accomplishment in reform movements yet achieved."

In New Jersey, Sabbatarians not only saw the Continental Sunday as evidence of social and moral deteriorioration, but Sunday laws as an important tactical wedge in the effort to cleanse society of drink and commercial vice. Attacks on the Sunday sale of liquor had the dual advantage of depriving saloon keepers of profits by merely insisting on enforcement of the law. In 1891, the Reverend A. Nelson Hollifield, pastor of the Third Presbyterian Church in Newark, delivered a sermon that became New Jersey's "Sabbatarian Manifesto" and drew the lines for the thirty-year conflict within the state that would profoundly affect the fortunes of

Atlantic City. Entitled "Shall We Legalize Sabbath Desecration and Races and Gambling on Race Courses?", the sermon articulated the deep evangelical anxiety over urbanization, immigration, and the secularization of American society.[33]

Hollifield saw the Continental Sunday as an alien menace that threatened the very fabric of American society. Of the 1,173 saloon keepers in his native Newark, 850 were foreign born. The clamor for an open Sunday did not reflect a change of sentiment "on the part of Americans," but an insidious foreign influence. Saloon keepers who defied the Fourth Commandment were "destroying the character, health, fortunes, and souls of individuals; breaking the charmed circle and wrecking the joy and contentment of peaceful homes; and filling the community with paupers and criminals." The working classes were especially vulnerable on Sundays because their wages received the night before went "into the pockets of saloon keepers" instead of providing "food and raiment for dependent families."

Hollifield concluded with a clarion call for the church to step beyond the spiritual realm and deal with the problems that affect public morals. Declared another Newark clergyman:

> The ministers of this state are not politicians, not enough so. But now we serve deliberate notice on the liquor dealers that the war to bring to the church into politics is to bring politics into the church. If that Sunday law be repealed, let it be distinctly understood that the clergy will start an agitation which will put it back on the statute books with additions that will make the present status of saloons seem as life compared to death.[34]

The sermon was so well received that it was published in an effort to "mold public opinion and to influence legislation on these important matters."

If the broad-based opposition to Sunday laws belied Hollifield's assertion that Sabbath drinking was an alien and a working-class problem, appeals to race and class prejudice were powerful elements of the Sabbatarian position. And there was the majesty of the law. In describing the lawlessness of the Sunday liquor traffic, Hollifield drew heavily upon Edmund Burke's lurid portrayal of the anarchy of the French Revolution. But if his imagery was extreme, his logic was unassailable. Municipal officials who winked at Sunday sellers and grand jurors who refused to indict offenders violated solemn oaths of office. Selling liquor on the Sabbath was, no less than burglary, a crime against the laws of the state.

Within a decade, Sabbatarians and temperance reformers, unified in such groups as the Knights Templar and local law-and-order societies formed solely for the purpose of obtaining evidence against lawbreaking saloons, had set the pattern for the antisaloon crusade in New Jersey. In 1901 William Black, a local attorney carrying the Knights' banner, waged a strong but unsuccessful struggle against the Sunday sale of liquor in Newark. Black hired detectives to secure evidence, affidavits were sworn and notarized, and charges were filed with local prosecutors. But grand juries, bowing to public and political pressure, refused to indict, and the courts were helpless to enforce the law.[35] In Long Branch, the problems with saloons involved gambling and prostitution, and the local law-and-order league was more successful. A presiding elder of the Methodist Conference praised the effort: "It gives me great pleasure to report that at some places our brethren have been making aggressive warfare against this curse of all curses. Notably this has been true of Long Branch where public sentiment has been aroused, licenses have been refused, and violators of the law have been punished."[36] Inevitably, raids against saloons resulted in sensational newspaper exposés that embarrassed local police and public officials.

In Camden, the Reverend Samuel H. Hann formed the Camden County Law and Order League. Hiring detectives and marshalling sympathetic lawyers and judges, Hann harassed Camden saloon keepers and branched out to neighboring Gloucester and Cape May counties. The New Jersey Methodist Conference blessed the efforts of the "tried and trusted Hann" by relieving him of his pastoral duties to become the state temperance agent of the Methodist Church, a position he held until his death in 1919. In 1901, the Law and Order League incorporated as a statewide organization in order to give it standing in other counties, and Hann became secretary.[37]

The year 1901 brought particular ferment over the liquor question and commercial vice, both nationally and in New Jersey. February found Carrie Nation en route from Kansas City to Chicago, where police were stationed in readiness to contain her saloon-smashing crusade. In Long Branch, Joseph A. Poole, the editor of a small paper, was serving a thirty-day jail sentence for libel, a conviction rendered by a local jury as a result of his crusade against vice and Sunday selling in which he accused the mayor of extortion. In Newark and Jersey City, the bars were open on Sunday, and whole sections of working-class districts contained gambling operations including slot machines, policy games, and betting on bicycle races. Reformers in Essex, Hudson, and Monmouth counties were consistently stymied by local police and grand juries who refused to indict lawbreakers despite notarized affidavits and other indisputable evidence. To reformers and law enforcement officials, the jailing of Editor Poole was the most outrageous example of a pattern of judicial abuse which tied the hands of county prosecutors and judges in their efforts to prevent gambling and the Sunday sale of liquor.[38]

In March, Governor Foster M. Vorhees sent the legislature a bill providing that whenever the governor, attorney general, a county prosecutor, or judge of the state court system notified a mayor or local official of illegal activity, failure to act on that information within ten days would constitute a misdemeanor punishable by a fine or a jail sentence. Aimed specifically at saloon gambling operations in Newark, Jersey City, and Long Branch, the Vorhees Act was quickly and unanimously passed. Although the ultimate power remained in the hands of county grand juries, the law curtailed the obstructive power of police and local officials.[39]

In June, Supreme Court Justice Thomas Hendrickson, hearing cases in South Jersey, applied the Vorhees Act to the Sunday sale of liquor and ordered Mayor Stoy to close the bars in Atlantic City. But Sunday closing in Atlantic City was short lived, and little came of that move to enlist the state in the effort to close the bars on Sunday. In Essex and Monmouth counties, Justices Skinner and Fort failed to follow the Hendrickson lead, and Governor Vorhees declined comment as to whether the law that bore his name applied to the Sunday sale of liquor.[40]

In an extensive comment on the Atlantic City situation, the *Newark Evening News* quoted a "prominent Democrat" as saying that Hendrickson had gubernatorial ambitions. Hendrickson believed that "there were enough good Democrats and independent Republicans to sustain a candidate who had the moral courage to make the attempt to stop liquor selling on Sundays and to crush an evil that has by sufferance been allowed for many years." But the Democrats stood ready to make "personal liberty pledges in return for organized support." The Hendrickson order had also galvanized a powerful array of Republican forces, including the Pennsylvania and West Jersey railroads, Senator Sewell of Camden, and the wealthy Boardwalk hotelmen of Atlantic City who were heavy contributors to Republican coffers. They were determined to force a revision of the law in the state legislature.[41] As it turned out, neither party took a stand on Sunday closing, and efforts at revision, like Hendrickson's candidacy, were unsuccessful.

Throughout the state, local reformers continued their crusades against the Sunday sale of liquor. In February 1902, newly elected governor Franklin Murphy received a letter from the Philadelphia Sabbath Association reminding him that the liquor laws in New Jersey remained unchanged, and that their lack of enforcement was doing "great harm" to the people of Pennsylvania. Others called attention to open saloons in Keyport and Belleville. An affidavit, notarized in Camden, attested that saloons in Atlantic City, including Kuehnle's Hotel, were habitually doing business on Sundays. Only four complaints survive, but contemporary newspaper accounts of vice wars throughout the state suggest that Murphy's files are incomplete on the subject. The lone surviving reply—to the protester in Keyport—has the suspicious ring of a form letter: "The proper method to pursue in order to break up this evil is to make a complaint to the Prosecutor of the Pleas of the county in which the violation is alleged to take place, or to file a remonstrance against the renewal of the license of the person who has violated the law. There is no authority vested by law in the Governor to interfere in the matter."[42] Murphy's successor, Casper Stokes, proved no more inclined than Murphy to close the saloons on the Sabbath, and the Sunday war in New Jersey entered a period of stalemate.

Yet, by now the churches had grown comfortable in their militance and remained very much alive to the possibilities of Sunday closing laws as a legal weapon against the liquor interests. This was clearly expressed by the resolutions of the Temperance Committee in its report to the Methodist Conference in 1902. To consent to the "robbery of the Sabbath" would give tacit consent to "all the licentiousness that follows in its train," including drunkenness, "especially among women," and the demoralization of the home and of society itself. They pledged united support to Hann's work, but added: "We . . . ever feel that we must go on to the perfection of Prohibition."[43] If to the Methodists in New Jersey, Sabbatarianism had become subordinate to the greater goal of Prohibition, it remained, nonetheless, both a means and an end.

By 1906 the saloon was under siege in New Jersey, and Sunday raids had become a weekly ritual throughout the state. A branch of the Anti-Saloon League organized in Newark, along with local law and order societies, good citizenship leagues, and other groups such as the Civic

Righteousness Federation of Jersey City, formed a network of local reform groups that blanketed the state. Saloons adopted the policy of locking front doors on Sundays and screening the front windows. But if the side-door business muted Sabbath desecration, it produced a situation where reformers gained entrance to saloons through side and back doors and uncovered a multitude of back-room evils. Whether they burst into a neighborhood poker game or upon a group of women drinking beer, to reformers gambling was gambling, and the mere presence of women in a saloon could only mean one thing. They dubbed children dispatched by their parents to the saloon to buy a bucket of beer the "growler brigade," youth whose innocence was compromised by exposure to the saloon. Of course there was a good deal about the saloon that was less than innocent. In city after city, saloons were controlled by breweries, and licensing procedures were often irregular or corrupt. There were gamblers and prostitutes, and the influence of the saloon in the politics of, for example, Jersey City, was by 1906 an article of faith among observers of New Jersey politics. But Sunday raids had the effect of documenting these evils, and in the hands of reformers even normal activities took on the lurid aspect of the saloon. Obstructive police tactics and grand juries who refused to indict Sunday sellers only reinforced the sinister notion that the state was "controlled by the rum power."

A Sunday campaign in Trenton closed the bars for a time, but in Newark, Jersey City, Hoboken, and Elizabeth, cities with larger immigrant populations, police harassed reformers, and citizens' leagues witnessed spectacle after spectacle of wholesale defiance of the law. Even in Bridgeton, a dry factory town in rural Cumberland County, reformers discovered that a hotel speakeasy was also a brothel, a family business that had quietly thrived for twenty-five years.[44] In this atmosphere of exposure, the time was ripe for reformers to strike a blow at the saloon by enlisting the state authorities in the campaign for Sunday closing.

In February 1906, a statewide interdenominational group of clergymen met in Trenton and framed a bill, and Governor Stokes signed it that summer. Known as the Bishops' Law, it provided for license revocation and stiff fines for Sunday selling. It also banned back rooms connected with saloons and provided that saloon interiors be open to public view on Sunday to make evasion of the law more difficult. Although the liquor interests managed to draw some of the teeth from the measure with an amendment providing for local rather than state enforcement, the law promised to wreak havoc upon the Sunday liquor trade if properly enforced.[45]

The wrangling over the provisions of the Bishops' bill revealed the potential for political embarrassment that lay in the state enforcement of Sunday closing, and apparently Stokes signed it with no little trepidation. A "loyal Republican" warned state chairman Frank O. Briggs of the "serious effect" state enforcement would have on the party. Not only would it drive the liquor interests into the arms of the state Democracy, but he was in possession of a petition containing some 200,000 names in opposition to state enforcement including "leading business men, churchgoing men, honest laboring men, voters all," whose voices deserved "very careful consideration."[46] Another correspondent whose travels took him throughout the state reported: "Wherever I went, I heard more opposition to the Liquor Law than I did of any reform movement, and I am inclined to believe that it is losing ground every day."[47] But the Methodist Conference warned the governor that it represented 462 ministers and 104,143 lay members who insisted on strong protection from Sabbath desecration and the other evils of the liquor traffic.[48]

The Bishops' Law burst upon New Jersey as a "political powder barrel." The New Idea movement was well under way, and the prospect of neutralizing the saloon as a political instrument had drawn the unanimous support of these early Progressives. In Essex County, New Idea sheriff Frank Sommer alienated urban voters by conducting a vigorous Sunday enforcement crusade, and regular politicians from both parties were quick to saddle the Progressive forces with responsibility for this "obnoxious act."[49] The law sparked a wave of Sunday closing campaigns throughout the state, and the gubernatorial election of 1907 took place amid a flurry of excitement over the liquor issue and Sunday closing. Yet the election proved a classic study in the avoidance of that controversial subject.

Both candidates, the Republican John Franklin Fort and the Democrat Frank S. Katzenbach, Jr. ran on nearly identical Progressive platforms. Neither was disposed to make the Bishops' act an issue in the campaign, but Fort did, on one occasion, pledge that he would enforce it. Fort won the election by a scant eight thousand votes, and later attributed his narrow victory to that pledge, lukewarm though it was. An active Methodist churchman, he would later lead the New Jersey contingent of the Lord's Day Alliance. With Fort in the governor's chair, by 1908 evangelicals looked toward a period of vigorous enforcement of the Sunday liquor laws and stepped up raids throughout the state.[50]

Upon taking office, Fort was deluged with complaints that the Bishops' Law was not being enforced. Actually it would appear that the law had resulted in considerable tightening of the reins on saloons by local authorities, but in many localities the law had little effect. In an open letter to Mayor Otto Wittpenn of Jersey City, Samuel Wilson of the Civic Righteousness Association complained that saloons still shrouded their windows and were open on Sundays despite Wittpenn's public assurances that the law was being enforced. Saloon keepers employed police and other sentries to warn of the presence of Association detectives, and grand juries still refused to indict Sunday sellers.[51] Reformers in Newark, Hoboken, Elizabeth, and Paterson met with the same resistance, and city after city declined to pass the ordinances required by the law banning screens and back rooms in saloons.

The Bishops' Law had given the state no more power than it previously had to close the saloons on Sunday. Yet Fort's repeated reminders that he had no authority under the law to compel compliance with the excise regulations did little to assuage reformers. Vice, crime, and the liquor traffic were serious issues in New Jersey in 1908, and Fort was under considerable pressure to act. In May he appointed two commissions, one to investigate crime and dependency and another to investigate the liquor traffic. Simultaneously holding hearings throughout the state during the summer of 1908, the Crimes Commission and the Excise Commission together gathered almost six thousand pages of sworn testimony on conditions in the state. Yet their findings, both presented to the governor on December 15, only documented what informed people had long known about vice, crime, and the liquor traffic in New Jersey and further stirred up passions on both sides of the Sunday controversy.

Arriving in Atlantic City Sunday, August 1, Fisk and the other commissioners were no sooner settled in their hotels than they personally witnessed over two hundred saloons and hotels doing a rushing Sunday business. Fisk immediately summoned Mayor Stoy and Police Chief Woodruff, who informed him that the bars had always been open on Sunday and would remain so because the "visitors demanded it."[52] The astounded Fisk abruptly dismissed his callers, setting the stage for a hostile confrontation between the city and state authorities.

At the outset of the hearings, County Prosecutor Clarence Goldenberg freely admitted that while the Bishops' Law was being observed in the county at large, "as far as Atlantic City is concerned, it has never been nor is it now being enforced." To William Winter, president of the Good Citizens' League, the conflict was between "religion and morals" on the one hand, and "the love of money" on the other. One James Steelman, chairman of the evidence committee, testified that they would enter a saloon on Sunday, "buy the stuff, . . . label it with the name of the place and the very hour and very minute we bought it, swear out the warrants, have the man arrested, bound for the grand jury, and take this same evidence to the grand jury." During the previous eighteen months, citizens' raids had produced some sixty arrests, but five separate grand juries had failed to return a single indictment, despite conclusive evidence.[53]

Sheriff Smith E. Johnson, who had been in office since 1884, testified that he had never seen a drop of liquor sold in Atlantic City on Sunday in his life, not that he didn't believe it, he just hadn't seen it. "I don't have to go hunt up business as I understand the law. I know of no law that will make me do so." As for the grand juries, Johnson swore that he didn't stack them, and Judge Higbee of the Court of Common Pleas washed his hands of the matter by saying that he did not believe that a grand jury of twenty-four men could be found in Atlantic County that would indict for Sunday violations. In the police department, attitudes ranged from defiance to exasperation. Officer number seventy-three, speaking to a commission detective posing as a visitor, referred to commission members as "a lot of bum hoboes" who should mind their own business. "I will tell you that we have got a sheriff in Atlantic County that can't be beat. He has the making of the grand jury and it is hard to get by that combination." Police Chief Malcomb Woodruff complained that there was no use arresting anybody for Sunday selling because grand juries simply would not indict.[54]

City license holders had formed a branch of the Royal Arch, a national organization pledged to the "responsible conduct of the liquor business." But the commissioners were not relieved to hear from the mayor and the wealthiest hotel owners in the resort that the code governing Atlantic City's liquor traffic represented a compromise among the Royal Arch, city officials, and even members of the clergy. Entitled "Regulations to Take Effect June 1, 1907," they required saloons to lock front doors and screen windows on Sunday, forbade music in barrooms and cafes so as not to entice the young, and placed restrictions on gambling. The eighth section declared: "We pledge good faith in the above, and will see them carried out honestly and faithfully by the Mayor and City Officials who shall do their duty in exacting from all obeyance. Any neglect of the above shall be the signal for the enforcement of the present and more rigid conditions that exist now."⁵⁵ In other words, irresponsible saloon conduct of any sort would result in Sunday closing. To Charles Spiedel, president of the Royal Arch, and to the resort business community he represented, this was a reasonable compromise. To the commissioners, it was an open conspiracy to evade the laws of the state. Actually, the code represented the final revision to the liberal policy and a solution to the thorny conflict over Sabbath observance that had raged within the resort for more than two decades.

John J. White, the owner of the resort's most exclusive hotel, reminded the commissioners that Atlantic City brought more than $2 million per year into the state and urged that this alone warranted special legislation for the city. But the crux of the city's case was contained in the following:

> Some people may think that it would make not make much difference to a man whether or not he could have liquor served with his meals on Sunday, the same as other days and the same that he does at home. I tell you, gentlemen, we who have made a careful study, who have chanced not only what we have on it, but what we have been able to get through the confidence of others in us, know that it is a very small thing which decides people where they will go on their vacations.⁵⁶

In White's view, the enforcement of Sunday closing would mean "ruin" and "disaster" for the nation's largest seaside resort. The accuracy of this observation matters less than the fact it expressed the view of practically the entire community.

The commissioners left Atlantic City unimpressed by the argument that Sunday liquor sales were critical to the survival of the city and much outraged by what amounted to blatant defiance of the laws of the state. Throughout the month of August the city remained wide open. On August 15, a defiant Mayor Stoy as much as announced that the Sunday law would not be enforced and called for its repeal. Although there were token indictments for gambling, another grand jury failed to indict a number of hotel men clearly guilty of Sunday selling. Supreme Court Justice Trenchard dismissed the panel in "dishonor," declaring that they had violated their oaths of office. But the jury foreman, Joseph Salus, who was president of the Businessmen's League, made a heroic stand, declaring that the panel was as representative of men as could be found in Atlantic City. "We are willing to stand before God and man and accept the consequences. It is manifestly unfair to reprimand us. We represent the will of the people in Atlantic City; we represent five million dollars of property; we do not intend that our action shall be made political capital of by any man."[57] Actually, the grand jury included Harry Graf, the proprietor of the Hole-in-the-Wall Cafe who was one of twenty-six people under indictment. But in the persons of White and Salus, Atlantic City had put its best foot forward. White was the spokesman for the "beachfront," a contingent of Quaker hotel owners who operated the largest and most prestigious establishments in the resort. Salus owned several Boardwalk cafes catering to the most refined element of the resort's patronage. Both men were prominent in state Republican circles and enjoyed a personal acquaintance with the governor. But, if Fort was not merely dealing with an unruly saloon element, he was faced with a nullification policy that challenged the very basis of executive authority.

On August 27 Governor Fort, calling the city a "Saturnalia of Vice," reacted with a withering proclamation and threatened to call out the militia and place the city under martial law to enforce the Bishops' Law. The proclamation, along with accompanying open letters to the mayor, the sheriff, and Judge Higbee contained a combination of truths and falsehoods and was a blistering indictment of the moral status of the city based entirely on the evidence of the Excise Commission, which, in the governor's words, "astonished all good citizens of the state. . . . No one in office or before that commission questioned the fact that street walking, gambling, houses of ill-fame, people of ill-repute, and obscene pictures, and open violations of the excise law existed in Atlantic City. . . . The citizens [of Atlantic City] are alarmed. . . . Never in the history of the city has it been worse."[58] There was indeed a tenderloin in Atlantic City, and there were also gamblers—facts freely admitted by the resort's best citizens who had for the past few years been engaged in an earnest effort to eliminate those blights from the "family resort." Moreover, commissioners had revealed to the *New York Times* that conditions in Asbury Park, a temperance resort, were no better than in Atlantic City, and even the Methodist enclave at Ocean Grove contained twenty places where liquor could be had.[59]

At a town meeting, Joseph Salus denounced the governor's proclamation as "the damndest lies ever put out." While most of the state press had nothing but harsh words for the city, the *Philadelphia Bulletin* praised its orderliness, and the *New York Times* castigated Fort for "harsh and extreme measures."[60] Although Fort had been a compromise candidate for governor, once in office, he had cast his lot with the New Idea faction of his party. The blatant defiance of the state by the city authorities had placed the executive authority squarely on the line, and in view of his campaign pledge, he had little choice but to act forcefully.[61] But why the severe condemnation of the moral status of the city?

The use of the state militia would never have stood on the issue of Sunday closing alone. From the beginning, agitation for the Bishops' Law, although aimed at Sunday closing, was couched in deeper evils. The original petition to Governor Stokes from the clergy made absolutely no mention of Sabbath desecration and read in part as follows:

> The proprietors of many places wherein intoxicating drinks are sold and consumed . . . in back rooms, not only offer opportunity to the abandoned and the profligate to gratify their bestial appetites by debauching the innocent of the poor man's home, but actually encourage and solicit the patronage of the vilest of men and women, who with the appetite of the brute and the arts of the demon recruit from the children of honest laborers . . . the wretched victims of promiscuous prostitution.[62]

Efforts to enforce Sunday closing on its own merits had never been successful in New Jersey except in rural areas, and even in those areas evasion had been, if surreptitious, widespread.

To be sure, there was a large constituency for the Puritan Sunday in New Jersey. But for most, even evangelicals, the conflict in Atlantic City transcended Sabbatarianism and became an issue of social control. Fort's proclamation made him a national figure. In the weeks that followed he was deluged with petitions and letters of commendation. A campaign among New Jersey churches produced 146 petitions containing 67,496 names in support of Fort's heroic defense of the Sabbath. But typical of the many letters and telegrams Fort received was a communication from the Methodist Sunday school in Gothenberg, Nebraska, commending his "Christian resolution" and "firm and manly determination" to enforce the laws of state. Josiah Strong declared that "lawlessness" had become "one of the greatest perils of our institutions." Oswald Garrison Villard believed that matters in Atlantic City had approached a "critical state. . . . What is being done there is at all fours with the lynchings in Springfield and other forms of lawlessness. . . . You are confronted with but one phase of what is the all-important question of the day in this country, the enforcement of the law and the creating of respect for it."[63]

Nor was the issue confined to temperance. The Burlington County Local Option League telegraphed: "Congratulations on your honorable stand. We are with you 3,000 strong against *lawlessness*" (italics theirs), and Edward Black, the Newark Sabbatarian of the Knights Templar, saw the conflict in terms of "public righteousness."[64] Later, Fort confided to Chancellor Mahlon Pitney: "The Atlantic City situation was a troublesome one. It was not a question of temperance or Sunday selling, but it reached a point where it became simply a question whether the laws of the state should or should not be obeyed, or whether certain sections could nullify the state law at will."[65] Aside from the church petitions, among the 242 encomiums contained in Fort's files one looks in vain for a commendation specifically for his defense of the Sabbath.

Almost lost in the stack of correspondence was a letter from Christian Fisher, a Bergen saloon keeper, one of only three individuals who wrote in protest of the governor's action.

> I am now ruined. I made an honest living. But when I can sell no lager on Sunday my friends stay away. They must work hard in the week and cannot get any fresh air until Sunday comes. They will not drink ice water that makes them sick at the stomach. But what is it that we cannot do in Bergen as they do in Guttenberg and in Unionhill and all over when one that knows it can get all the beer that is good for him and more too when he goes to the right door and knows the watch, his friend. You are not a just man. We are all as good as the other.[66]

The Bergen barkeep was not alone in his belief that the Bishops' Law was class legislation that could not be enforced. At a later commission hearing, a prominent Hoboken citizen stated that the conditions found in Paterson, Hoboken, Elizabeth, and Atlantic City were not exceptional.

> They are purely typical. They will prevail everywhere you have a sumptuary law which cannot be enforced. The people are not worse than others. They have their own ideas as to the proper method of observing Sunday and are not willing to be dictated to by temperance societies as to what they shall drink and when they shall drink it. . . . If we send the militia to Atlantic City to see that the saloons are closed on Sunday, who is going to look after the militia. I would like to see a company of soldiers from Hoboken called out and stationed at a side door in Atlantic City on a Sunday afternoon.[67]

Even Samuel Wilson, while praising Fort's firm stand, complained that the law was still was not being enforced in Jersey City, despite the governor's assurances to the contrary. "Nullification is just as positive, less bold, but more hypocritical and in every way as despicable."[68] Of the few protests that Fort received, Wilson's was the most disturbing. If he sent troops to Atlantic City, would he also send them to Jersey City, or for that matter, to the state capitol in Trenton?

For the moment, Fort was spared this dilemma. The specter of troops patrolling the Boardwalk and the streets of Atlantic City was enough to make the mayor and the Royal Arch back down. Stoy announced that Sunday selling would cease as of August 30, and the Royal Arch whipped the license holders into line. Resort saloons were draped in black and one displayed a sign declaring: "No liquor sold on Sunday and damned little on Monday." Nonetheless, Fort's attorney general reported that the city was "as dry as last year's bird's nest," and it appeared that his victory was complete.[69]

But within two months Atlantic City had returned to her old ways. Reformers gathered more evidence against Sunday sellers, but again there were no indictments. In October, William Winter reported to the governor that many saloon keepers were now more defiant than when the order was issued. League detectives were threatened, and one was assaulted in a saloon while securing evidence and "barely escaped severe injury at the hands of a half-drunken crowd. . . . The feeling is so bitter against our men, that it is hardly safe for them to enter some of the places any more, but we are certain that should we cease our vigil, every place in the city would be wide open."[70] Winter pleaded for the governor to send aid. In January the local chapter of the WCTU sent the governor a notarized petition certifying that Sunday selling was again wide open and ended with another plea for the governor to use the power of his office to enforce the law. Fort replied that his hands were tied because the legislature had refused to grant his request for power to remove local officials who were derelict in their duty.[71]

In March the Methodist Conference roundly denounced Fort's inaction, and Easter Sunday saw the Boardwalk thronged with visitors, many standing three deep at every drinking place along the beachfront. That summer, raids by the Lord's Day Alliance and blaring headlines proclaimed the city's defiance. The *Trenton True American* declared Atlantic City "A City in Rebellion" and castigated the governor for his inaction. Fort directed his attorney general to order Mayor Stoy to enforce the excise laws. Stoy defiantly refused and was arrested on a warrant issued by a special magistrate, all of which generated much publicity and made the mayor a heroic figure in the city.[72]

If Fort had expected the commissions to deflect the Sunday issue or to provide some sort of mandate for legislative action, he was sadly disappointed. The commissioners, Protestants all, were as ambivalent on the issue as the public at large. Both the Excise Commission and the Crimes Commission presented their reports to the governor on December 15. Not unexpectedly, Fisk and the majority of the excise commissioners harshly condemned the conduct of the liquor traffic in the state and singled out Atlantic City for special opprobrium for its blatant defiance of the law. The most frequent and flagrant violation of the excise laws was Sunday selling, particularly "at shore resorts and in large cities," a fact they attributed to the "apparent disinclination of officials to enforce the law" and the "persistent determination of the drinking public to procure drink during prohibited hours . . . simply because they know it is contrary to the law." Yet the ninety-page report devoted but one paragraph to the defense of the Sabbath, recommending no change in the current regulations.[73]

The minority, consisting of Assemblyman John Howe of Newark and Caleb Van Husen Whitbeck, editor of the *Hackensack Record*, concurred "in large part" with the findings of the majority, but interpreted the evidence differently. They declared that excise conditions were not the result of political corruption but rather an expression of the will of the people.

> The case of Atlantic City, to which probably reference was had by our fellow members in charging mal-administration, is in point. The rules of the Royal Arch are cited as a conspiracy to defeat the law, yet these rules were drafted and approved by a committee composed, in equal number, of delegates from the Businessmen's League, the Hotelmen's Association, and the Good Citizens' League, as well as the Royal Arch. To maintain that the Atlantic City Law violations are due to political domination of liquor dealers, rather than to the opinion and wishes of a vast majority of all its citizens, is to shut one's eyes willfully to perfectly patent facts.[74]

They concluded with the observation that legislators should make laws in accordance with the wishes of those they represent, not in accordance with "the legislators' ideas of what is good for them," and recommended that "certain hotels and restaurants" should be allowed to sell liquor to their guests on Sundays.

The Crimes Commission was even more ambivalent on the Sunday question. Defiance of Sunday restrictions had bred a contempt for the law that was unprecedented in the annals of the state, particularly in Atlantic City. They were unanimous in recommending criminal indictments against Charles Spiedel, the members of the Royal Arch, city officials, and other "interested parties" who, as the commission sat, were engaged in a conspiracy to defy the laws of the state. But almost in the same breath they concluded that "harmful dead letter laws" were not only "unpunished" but "unpunishable" and should be repealed. The majority recommendation on Sunday closing was identical to the minority recommendation of the Excise Commission, to allow the sale of liquor to restaurant and hotel guests on Sunday. This was precisely the legislation that restaurant and hotel interests in Atlantic City had been pursuing for years.[75]

If laws for the prevention of vice and immorality were civil regulations intended to promote social welfare and public order, many, particularly social reformers and law enforcement officials, found them counterproductive. The Crimes Commission concluded that the state had pursued a narrow policy with respect to wholesome sports for the young.

> Young people, thousands of whom are forced to work six days in every week, have only Sunday for relaxation; harsh laws, made to fit other times, other peoples and other conditions, prevent the youth of today from finding harmless and healthful occupation on this day of idleness by witnessing ball games and other outdoor sports, and thus encourages them to spend their time gambling and drinking and in places where they ought not to be.[76]

The commission, with but one dissenting vote, recommended that the legislature expunge "the blue law relics" and make sports and amusements legal at least on Sunday afternoons.

Of the fifteen commissioners, only the Reverend Ernest A. Boom of Merchantville, a Methodist and a member of Hann's Law and Order League, saw fit to defend the Sabbath. Boom wrote a lengthy scientific treatise on the Sunday liquor traffic. Studies done in Switzerland and Germany, where there were no Sabbath restrictions, had shown that a disproportionate number of violent crimes occurred on Sunday. In Zurich the figure was 42.55 percent, in Heidelburg, 45 percent, and in Luther's Worms, it was 35.13 percent. Given the onerous financial burden of crime and dependency, the state simply could not afford to legalize liquor on Sunday.[77]

In January 1909, the New Jersey Sabbath Association merged with the National Lord's Day Alliance as Protestant groups throughout the state mobilized to prevent the repeal of the Sunday laws. Legislative delegations from Jersey City, Newark, Atlantic City, and other coast resorts introduced a number of bills to liberalize Sunday restrictions by permitting liquor, sports, and other entertainments through local referenda. The most conservative bill was introduced by Senator Wilson of Atlantic City. Similar to the Raines Law in force in New York, it allowed hotels to serve drinks to bona fide guests with their meals.[78]

During February and March, delegations representing the churches, the liquor dealers, and the cities descended upon Trenton, and the hearings often became heated. An Atlantic City hotelman declared that the resort was at the mercy of a "handful of fanatics." Joseph Salus, a Jewish restaurateur, struck a more conciliatory tone, pleading that Atlantic City license holders had no intention of violating the law. They just wanted personal freedom and a "fair deal." A Trenton clergyman responded that "Jews should go back to Russia where they could learn what personal freedom they enjoyed under the American government." Salus could only reply that he hoped that such uncharitable attitudes would not survive the century.[79]

Sunday baseball failed in the assembly by one vote, but a *Trenton Times* canvass indicated that there were, at most, only nine votes in favor in the senate. None of the bills on Sunday liquor sales reached the floor. "As for an open Sunday," said the *Times*, "the political party that endorses it will hardly know that it had a candidate in the election which follows the passage of such a law."[80]

Protagonists on both sides of the Sabbatarian conflict agreed that Sunday restrictions presented the most serious problem of law enforcement in the state, but the exhaustive hearings and the detailed reports resulted in no change in the law with respect to Sunday closing. In New Jersey, and particularly in Atlantic City, the Sunday conflict simply raged on, and the voluminous proceedings from the Excise Commission and the Crimes Commission were filed and forgotten.

Although pockets of enthusiasm remained, by 1912 the Sabbatarian movement in New Jersey began to show signs of serious decline. References to the issue in the Methodist Conference reports become briefer, more scattered, and more perfunctory, and by 1914 Sabbath Desecration had ceased to be a standing committee of the conference. Sabbatarianism had, at least since the turn of the century, stood in the shadow of the Prohibition movement, and in New Jersey that movement was now under the leadership of the Anti-Saloon League, which was pursuing the tactic of local option as a means of eliminating the saloon.

A Methodist clergyman, who compiled an exhaustive history of the southern New Jersey conference in 1986, referred to the "flickering flames of revivalism" that occurred just before and during World War I, and suggested that "often a fire may burn bright and seemingly intense as it begins to near its end." In retrospect, he wrote that the struggle to preserve the Christian Sunday in New Jersey had been a long one, and, in this secular age, few could understand the intensity with which his forebears waged the fight. "As a matter of fact, no concern received more attention in the New Jersey Conference in the opening years of the twentieth century, apart from temperance, than proper Sunday observance. Today, we may take pride in our liberty, but church after church laments the competition which draws children, youth, and adults away from the church."[81] It is interesting that a Methodist historian, immersed in the evangelical sources, saw the Sabbatarian issue in terms of competition as opposed to piety. In 1919, Justice James Mintern, testifying before a legislative committee, said that as a churchman he cherished the "beautiful ideal of the Christian Sunday" but, in the words of Edmund Burke, added: "You cannot indict a whole people." Conditions had changed, and the urban population now sought "air, rest and recreation from the putrid and confining environment of shop and factory."[82]

Atlantic City offered air, rest, and recreation, and a good deal more. The period between its founding in 1854 and 1920, the time by which it had come into its full fruition as a commercial resort city, Atlantic City stood consistently, though unwittingly, as both a symbolic and a practical counterpoise to evangelical reform. Sabbath desecration symbolized a broad range of social anxieties felt by middle-class Americans as they viewed the process of urbanization. Their approach to reform was conditioned by alarm over the increasing levels of commercial vice and municipal corruption, evils they perceived as stemming from the values and predilections of the working classes, particularly ethnic and racial minorities. These threats to society, both real and perceived, provided the external pressures on Atlantic City and constituted the broad social context in which the reform movement took place.

But the politics of urban reform in Atlantic City was also a local phenomenon, generated by the interests and perceptions of a resident population as diverse as the people who patronized the resort. By 1908 there existed within the city a "moral economy," similar, in historical concept, to the long-held practices and expectations of the English working classes at the dawn of the industrial era described by historian E. P. Thompson.[83] Those practices and expectations were essentially embodied in the liberal policy and obtained, in one form or another, throughout the community, even among blacks and others who had no part in its formulation. Mores and practices governing the relations between the classes, the races, and the sexes, recreational habits, as well as the structure of the family, had changed significantly since 1854. Responding, on the one hand, to social change, and, on the other, to evangelical and middle-class anxiety over social change, the liberal policy was, like the larger society, a compact at war with itself. Hence, the very forces that created the liberal policy would eventually destroy it in the wake of Progressive reform.

CHAPTER FOUR

Low Resorts

The development of Absecon Island brought to the wilderness the amenities of urban life. It also brought its maladies. Gambling, prostitution, and the liquor traffic marked every stage of the development of Atlantic City. It was one thing to build a resort city on the wastes of a barrier island, and another to manage its attractions within accepted standards of social and civic morality. City leaders confronted this problem from the very beginning, but it became increasingly difficult as the city grew. The evolution of the liberal policy during the nineteenth century reflected changing life styles and recreational habits and also changing attitudes toward race, class, sex, and commercial vice. But more importantly, from its inception in 1854 to century's end, it signaled, if not the opening, at least the significant widening of a cultural chasm between the Protestant churches of America and the masses of the people.

Beginning in 1848, the Reverend Allen H. Brown, a Presbyterian missionary, devoted more than thirty years of a long career to the spiritual needs of rural South Jersey. Traveling by horseback over primitive roadways, he preached to the isolated inhabitants and organized and built sixteen churches in the area. Brown's work continually depended on the financial support and hospitality of local capitalists who saw church building as an agent of progress and development. The frequent guest of Jonathan Pitney, Brown was well acquainted with Samuel Richards and the other directors of the Camden and Atlantic Railroad.[1]

Even to one accustomed to the rigors and privation of a rural ministry, Atlantic City in its infancy did not present an inviting prospect. Brown first visited the island with Pitney on a pleasant June morning in 1854, one month before the arrival of the first train. After "a tedious passage on a sailboat," Brown found the place "not very comfortable" and dismissed the new city with the terse comment: "The time indeed does not seem to have come to build a church on the Beach."[2] Evidently, Pitney was able to convince Brown that the city had a future, for within the year Brown accepted a choice parcel near the ocean from the land company for a church site. Two of the church's five trustees were railroad directors Richards and Bell. But the company revealed its priorities shortly thereafter, when in the flush of rising land values the directors tried to substitute a less valuable lot for the church. Brown, however, found the original site "just fine" and plunged into the project with characteristic zeal.[3]

Yet the city was barely a year old and the church not yet built when one of Brown's followers lamented in 1855 that "more places than we can now count are open for the sale of intoxicating drinks and hold out their allurements even on the Sabbath contrary to all law."[4] Twenty years later, when the city was served by nine churches representing "practically every [Christian] denomination," another Presbyterian complained of the "moral frigidness" of the place and of "the tide of dissipation that creeps, oft unseen, over our own, our neighbors', and our children's souls." He wrote:

> We look upon the dissipating influence of the summer vacation with fear. . . . Has it not occurred to you that it is a fearful ordeal to which young souls and receptive natures are exposed in hotels, where they see drinking as a pastime, and hear the popping of corks from champagne bottles oftener than they hear prayers; where they see card playing, and often gambling, . . . and hear the profanity that breaks forth from the lips of the profane.[5]

After 1855, Brown's diary was strangely silent on Atlantic City. Yet it must have been clear to him, as it was to many others—drinking and gambling notwithstanding—that the very nature of the modern resort was an affront to the evangelical preoccupation with salvation.

Most who visited the city in 1876 would have agreed with the writer who saw "a happy village devoted to nothing but recreation," a city with "no gloomy warehouses . . . no soiled pavements vexed with thundering drays, . . . and no hot factories giddy with steam and belted wheels . . . in short, none of the curse laid on fallen Adam." In this "jaunty little town," one, after a good meal in a hotel, could "stretch himself out on a good beach and go to sleep, without evil thinking or evil speaking."

"Seabathing," by this time, was no longer a novelty, and the sight of hundreds of young men and women frolicking in the surf was no cause for alarm, the sea receiving the bathers "with decorum and gentleness, lifting its waves high around them in a privacy of foam." Nor was the fact that by the bathing hour many of the gentlemen (at sunrise) had "already tested the billows . . . without the inconvenience of flannel."[6]

These disparate views of Atlantic City in its formative years underscore one of the basic conflicts of Victorian culture. Evangelicals deeply and genuinely feared secular amusements. Fraught with temptation and the danger of sexual intimacy, these libidinous pursuits were bad enough in and of themselves. Worse, they led to the ultimate degradation of drunkenness and prostitution. But what evangelicals saw as beginning the progress of the rake and the harlot, others saw merely as an innocent and healthful release from the bleak routine of industrial life. This conflict was by no means confined to commercial resorts, but here we see it in its sharpest focus.

In 1866 Mayor D. W. Belisle devoted more than half of his inaugural address to the "social, moral, and religious interests of society," which, according to his own observations, were not entirely being served by the city. "Small and rudely constructed shanties" had appeared, dealing out "many of the vices that the flesh is heir to." But worse: "Such places are found during the bathing season on all the principle streets and in goodly numbers along the shore in close proximity to the bathing grounds. Intemperate and dissolute persons frequent them, become . . . beastly intoxicated, and are then in a fit condition to shock the ears of respectable . . . visitors with their course and vulgar language."[7] The threat to the city was clear. "Individuals of standing and character . . . are unwilling to bring themselves and their families in proximity to the society that usually inhabit such vicinities." Yet to ban the tavern altogether would, according to the mayor, be neither "safe" nor "wholesome." The mayor did not explain what was unsafe or unwholesome about a temperance resort, but such was not the future of Atlantic City.

The mayor's address contained the seeds of the liberal policy. By the 1860s the saloon was already a fixture of the resort experience, and a decade later games, shows, and mechanical amusements would occupy a similar position. But the city had staked its fortune on the great middle class, and the working-class diversions would have to be managed so as not to offend middle-class morality. In practice, the liberal policy meant that the city would function all of the seven days, but that Sundays would be appropriately toned down. Establishments that crossed the bounds of decency and propriety would be eliminated. In the hands of city officials, themselves middle class, this form of censorship recognized the special status of Atlantic City as a resort yet enabled them to bring order and at least a semblance of decorum to a potentially riotous situation.

While many evangelicals would eventually come to terms with the "innocent" pleasures of seashore life, few would become reconciled to the spectacle of resort Sundays. In 1873 Editor English of the *Review*, himself a stern and frequent critic of resort improprieties, admitted without much indignation that "the Sabbath at a watering place is not observed with the sacred reverence which marks the day at other places."

> A stranger would be apt to judge from the general hilarity which marks our streets on the Sabbath that religion is the last thing thought of. While our churches are liberally attended, their patrons would compare feebly with those of our groggeries and hotel verandas. . . . Sunday is little different from any other day of the week. The saloons are thrown open for the entertainment of guests and revelry indulged to a greater extent than at any other time.[8]

In defense of the city, he offered that for workingmen and business people alike, Sunday was the only day of recreation and that for this transient population, "provision must be made."

During the 1850s and 1860s, when Atlantic City was basically a cottage resort, conflict over the Sunday issue was muted. As the city began to develop into an amusement center and a working-class resort, the conflict increased. In 1884 Alfred M. Heston, city historian and now the editor of the *Atlantic City Review*, proclaimed the merry-go-round a "positive nuisance." Its "discordant organ and large crowds" disrupted the serenity of the Boardwalk. He also reported that the increasing infraction of the Sunday laws was leading to a "speedy deterioration" of the resort, warning: "If it becomes thoroughly and generally understood that there is not much Sunday here, . . . it will not be long before it will be also thoroughly understood by the best class of people that it is an exceedingly good place to keep away from."[9] An alarmed Mayor Maxwell agreed, declaring, "Sunday has stopped at the bridge." In August 1884, the city council passed "An Ordinance Prohibiting the Exhibition of Shows, Plays and Amusements on Sunday." The law forbade "bowling alleys, shuffle board, ten pins, nine pins, billiard tables, pool tables,

revolving swings, or any other implements or contrivances for public use
. . . on the first day of the week."[10]

The city's approach to the Sunday issue reflected the nature of class conflict during the Gilded Age. The admixture of working-class visitors brought much to Atlantic City that was alien to middle-class culture. On a summer Sunday in 1885, a little boy wandered into the "excursion district" where he witnessed a "shocking" display. Beer gardens, gambling schemes, shell stands, cane fakirs, "the obscene baboon," and the "endless variety of claptraps" were in full operation, along with "the barkers and buttonholers doing their South Street act."[11] South Street was a notoriously ill-behaved working-class district along the Philadelphia waterfront, and the obscene baboon caused much comment during the summer of 1885. For a nickel a patron purchased three balls to knock a dodging monkey from its perch. The monkey's reputed cleverness in dodging the balls did not assuage the indignity of many who witnessed the spectacle.

The mayor responded with a strict enforcement of the Sunday ordinance in the excursion district, but Sabbath desecration was not the main issue. "Booths and peanut stands" had also appeared in the hotel district. Heston reported:

> For several years the whole front was free from this contemptible nuisance except in the immediate vicinity of the excursion houses. This did not matter so much, as the better class of patronage did not trouble that neighborhood very much, and the fakes, peanut vendors, and daily excursionist held full control. But last year the same element began to crop out about Applegate's Pier, and this year Applegate himself built a number of booths outside the Boardwalk above Kentucky Avenue, where the swarthy Italian and the head fez of the Turk claim public attention and obstruct the public view.[12]

In September 1889, a severe hurricane devastated the city, carrying away the Boardwalk, peanut stands and all. Five years later, the city obtained eminent domain over the beach and prohibited further construction outside the Boardwalk. But neither succeeded in eliminating "Turks and swarthy Italians" from the fashionable areas of the beachfront.

Thirsty patrons created a high demand for liquor licenses in the booming resort. But under the city charter a license petition needed to be signed by twelve freeholders who would vouch for the moral character of the applicant. By 1884 the population of the city had not yet reached eight thousand, and property owners willing to sign such petitions were scarce. To satisfy this requirement, a group of license holders purchased the Ram's Head, a worthless tract of meadow in the extreme Northside, so named for an ancient gnarled stump that resembled the head of a horned sheep. They divided the five-acre piece into postage-stamp lots and distributed them among 1,460 citizens who were willing to sign license applications. The Ram's Head became "Whiskey Tract," and licenses proliferated throughout the city.[13]

An anecdote published in English's *History of Atlantic City* in 1884 illustrated both the economic importance of the liquor traffic and its place within the liberal policy. Alois Schaufler, an impoverished German immigrant, came to Atlantic City in 1857. Having worked at blacking stoves in Philadelphia, he eked out a meager existence renting a shanty in the Inlet to Philadelphia sportsmen. When one of the men suggested he keep beer, he bought a keg but thought little of it. His fortune began when the word got out.

> Sheriff Magee and six or seven other Philadelphians, . . . hearing of my purchase, came to my place and . . . said, "Dutchy, have you got some lager beer?" I replied in German that I had, but that my place was without glasses. The sheriff said that the beer must be communicated to their stomachs in some way, and I went into the kitchen and got a small pitcher with a broken handle. Then I discovered that I had no spigot. I ran to Thomas Bedloe's hotel, . . . and borrowed a tin molasses spigot, but when I inspected the bung-hole, I saw that it was very large and the spigot very small. . . . I tore off a part of my jacket, wrapped it about the spigot. . . . Then the beer flowed, and all hands drank eagerly from my broken pitcher, the sheriff paying me twenty-five cents for each pitcher-full.[14]

Said Schaufler, "This was my first business encouragement." By 1884, Alois Schaufler was a leading citizen, and Schaufler's Concert Garden, a respected resort landmark featured Strauss waltzes and Wagnerian concerts played by "Professor Boehm's Military Band." To add to the joviality of the place, bartenders struck a gong every time a keg was tapped. But English carefully pointed out that concert gardens in Atlantic City "should not be judged by the standards at which they are held elsewhere."

> They are conducted with order and decorum. Many people who never venture into them at home visit them in the cool of the evening here, and enjoy the excellent music which is provided. Solid businessmen of

irreproachable reputation, distinguished people from all parts of the country, and church-going people are frequently seen in these places.[15]

German concert gardens became a popular upscale feature of Atlantic City nightlife during the 1880s. The largest, Fred Schwamb's Columbia Garden at Missouri Avenue and the Boardwalk, seated fifteen hundred people among potted palms imported from South Africa. Schwamb made a yearly pilgrimage to Berlin to pick out the best plants. Customers drank beer and sang to the strains of "Professor Kalitz's well-known military band" of eighteen pieces and a $12,000 electric pipe organ, "one of the largest made." But the measured din of the Sunday evening concerts did not trouble the city, for as Henry Adams wryly observed in another context, things German were "in the full tide of fashion." Later, Walter Evans Edge, protégé and successor to both English and Heston as the city's principal spokesman, observed: "It has always been said that the summer is never inaugurated until this amusement resort [Schaufler's] is opened." Schaufler had come a long way since the hard winter of 1857 when his wife died of sickness in childbirth for want of a warm place to convalesce because, as one hard-bitten resident put it, "We show no favors to foreigners."[16]

In July 1885, Heston defined one of the limits to the city's tolerance of the liquor traffic as he reported: "We saw several young girls in short dresses drinking beer in one of the gardens along the Boardwalk. These same girls staggered when they left the table. Four or five beers is a small item, but twenty-five cents worth of beer may kill your resort. Chase out the girls in short dresses and save your place."[17] Had the women been underage, Heston would surely have made that an issue. Unescorted, and obviously working class, the women represented deeper and unspoken dangers to the wholesomeness of the Boardwalk. Later, the city banned unescorted women from the Boardwalk cafes altogether.

"Girls in short dresses" would shortly pose a severe problem for the city's image, but evidence of commercial vice in Atlantic City before 1890 is sketchy. In 1884, Heston warned:

> If half the reports about gamblers and gambling houses are true, then it is clearly the duty of the authorities . . . to suppress them. There have been quite a number of Philadelphia and New York gamblers here all season, and it is currently reported and generally believed that they have been running games of chance in several parts of the city . . . without making any great effort to conceal their business. We have been informed that in

one or two places the "poker rooms" are immediately in the rear of the bar and that anyone who chooses to do so enters and that gambling is carried on night and day.[18]

In July 1886, Heston again warned that there were "gamblers among us," as police arrested a group of Baltimoreans for operating a den on South New York Avenue. Later that summer, police apprehended a group of blacks on Baltic Avenue for the same offense. One Edward Scott told a story "unfit for publication." "The place for a long time has been a house of ill-fame and is frequented by colored and white of both sexes."[19]

During the 1870s and 1880s, English and Heston provided a fragmented but consistent commentary on the moral status of the city. As the resort's chief spokesmen, their efforts at history, journalism, and promotion defined the terms of the liberal policy and reflected an acute sensitivity to the morals and anxieties of middle-class America. Atlantic City was a democratic resort, but the working classes were welcome only on the condition that they looked and behaved like the middle classes.

On Sundays, Young's Pier held only "sacred concerts," and local churches drew huge crowds to open-air services on the Boardwalk. But such concessions to the Sabbath could not hide the fact that the fundamental purpose of Atlantic City was to dispense pleasure, not religion. On Sunday, the merry-go-round was silent while the gong at Schaufler's rang more often than at any other time.

In August of 1890, the city council strengthened its hold over Sabbath amusements with a stiffer and more specific "Ordinance for the Suppression of Vice and Immorality." More in line with the diversions then in vogue, the ordinance offered good comment on the state of the amusement art in Atlantic City: "Be it ordained . . . that no merry-go-rounds, carousel, hobby or jumping horses, toboggans, figure 8 scenic railway, switchback, card writers, glass engravers, phonograph performances, museums, dancing, ball playing, sand throwing, bowling alleys, shooting galleries, or other kindred games or diversions . . . shall be performed on the Christian Sabbath."[20] In the same breath, council also forbade drunkenness, disorderly behavior, and the disturbance of religious meetings on Sunday, which did more to categorize amusements than preserve the sanctity of the Sabbath as these offenses were presumably illegal on all of the seven days.

To the *Philadelphia Bulletin*, council had "very queer notions about vice and immorality": "The City Council last night stamped the toboggan as 'vicious,' the merry-go-round as 'immoral.' Even the phonograph was declared a disturber of the peace, while card writers and glass engravers were described as coming within the bounds of 'vice and immorality.' "[21] The editors of the *Bulletin* saw that the city was particularly vulnerable on this point; and there was more: "Innocent children are denied the pleasure of riding on the merry-go-round but excursion loafers can revel in free flowing beer and whiskey. The industrious glass blower and the harmless card writer are denied the possible profits of the heaviest day of the week, but the crimson woman can flaunt her purchasable charms in the open mart." By this time, Atlantic City hotelmen advertised heavily in the Philadelphia papers, and their resort sections regularly contained complimentary features on the city. What explains the sudden discovery that the resort was riddled with vice?

The summer of 1890 was a time of crisis for Atlantic City, yet the season began promisingly enough. The Boardwalk, destroyed the previous September, was enlarged and almost completely replaced, and a "reform" city council seemed to have the city well in hand. On June 1, the *Philadelphia Inquirer* reported that the "fair sex" were to be more carefully protected than ever from the insults of "mashies" and "rowdies," or as Mayor Hoffman called them, "corner loungers who travel in their shape." Of course the season had not yet begun, but there were only two or three instances of ladies being subjected to vulgar glances and speech, and one unseemly encounter resulted in summary punishment. Authorities quickly jailed the two culprits, fined them heavily, and ran one out of town.[22]

The agent of this swift justice was probably Officer Harry Marks, locally noted for both his devotion to duty and his skill with the blackjack. But on one occasion his diligence went unappreciated. On the morning of July 23, at 2 A.M., he arrested and roughly handled three young men who came out of a bar and were singing loudly while walking along Atlantic Avenue. One of them happened to be Herbert Ker, the son of Robert Ker, the assistant district attorney of Philadelphia. Two days later, Ker personally undertook his son's defense in Recorder Gouldey's court and mercilessly grilled Marks, a former Philadelphian with an unseemly past. The court cleared the young man of all charges, except for "temporarily falling into bad company." Despite Ker's efforts to discredit Marks, Mayor Hoffman stood by his man, and Marks too was exonerated. Thus the affair appeared to have been a standoff, except for the two companions who, found by the court have been more drunk and more roisterous, were fined and released.[23]

This seemingly minor incident says much about the prerogatives of American justice in 1890 and about Atlantic City's dependent relationship with Philadelphia. It also explains the *Bulletin*'s crusade. On August 5, following an outraged column on the Ker affair, the *Bulletin* flatly stated its intentions. "On Thursday next, and on several days after that, this paper will present for your attention . . . detailed and minute reports concerning the degraded dives, the gambling halls, the houses of ill fame and other low resorts that openly and flagrantly violate the city ordinances and state laws."[24] "There is no purpose to harm the town," said the *Bulletin*, "nor to throw mud upon the good name of Atlantic City." It would war only upon "those vicious members of society who have made this place their field of profitable action." But few were taken in by this pious qualifier; revenge was imminent, and the city was squirming.

Beginning in August, at the height of a record season, the *Bulletin* launched the first of many probes of commercial vice that the city was to experience. In the name of public decency, city officials had closed the amusements on Sunday, yet tolerated gambling dens and houses of prostitution that flourished in their midst. The same people who censored amusements licensed saloons that ran on Sunday and sold alcohol to minors. Beginning with generalities on this theme, the *Bulletin* soon got down to specifics.

William "Dutchy" Muhlrad, who served time in Philadelphia in 1888 for operating a gambling den on Eleventh Street, now operated the Lochiel Hotel in the Inlet. "He controls and directs what may be called the leading gambling den of the city. . . . 'Dutchy's,' on Delaware Avenue, where some of the best known politicians and down-grade businessmen of Philadelphia stake their five and ten dollars on the deal of the little cards that have sent many a man to destruction and death."[25] The Lochiel, "named after the celebrated (political) headquarters in Harrisburg," catered not only to politicians, but to players "from Pittsburgh all the way to the Everglades of Florida."

Dutchy Muhlrad was the most notorious of a "vile fraternity" who ran gambling operations "from way down below Mississippi Avenue (the excursion district) where they play a five-cent limit" to "Levy's aristocratic gambling den on Maryland Avenue, just opposite the United States Hotel," just a stone's throw from the residence of Mayor Hoffman.

The stakes at Levy's were no higher than at Dutchy's, but Levy was more discreet.

> The first look at the Levy hell as one gazes at it from Maryland Avenue, gives one the idea that it is just the spot for a murder. It is a mysterious looking affair. The interior is still more mysterious, as the building is constructed on a novel plan and has a curious covered porch in the center. . . . Those gamblers who do not care to come in the front door can secure a more private entrance through an alleyway, access to which may be had on Virginia Avenue.[26]

The sinister aspect of the place was matched by Levy himself, who, under the gaze of a watchful *Bulletin* reporter, stole silently through his garden one night, seemingly oblivious to the gaming going on in the shrouded second story of the house.

At the western boundary of the Northside, on Arkansas Avenue, "mulatto" Charles Coleman ran a "low negro gambling den" which actually had an interracial clientele. "It is largely patronized by hotel waiters who regularly lose their wages in this hole. Poker is not unknown here, but 'crap' is the mainstay of the house, and the clicking dice rattle there every night."[27] Like Dutchy, Coleman had apparently been run out of his native Baltimore where he had been "in a good deal of trouble." Black men also played crap at Alexander Coot's on New York Avenue, at a "dive on Baltic Avenue," and at a good many more informal operations throughout the Northside.

Establishments of a more middle-class character included the Cigar Store on Atlantic Avenue and the "well-known upper room of the Extra Dry Cafe." In a modest cottage district, two women with two men, "said to be their husbands," ran an indiscreet gambling operation at 9 South Pennsylvania Avenue.[28] It would appear that gambling in Atlantic City respected neither race nor class.

But the *Bulletin* found its old nemesis, Dutchy Muhlrad, the worst among resort miscreants: "Your business is horrible—its history floats upon an ocean of criminals, defaulters, robbers, suicides, broken homes, sad hearts, and untimely graves. . . . You have no friends except those you have to buy; mothers and wives hate you, Dutchy Muhlrad; even children despise you."[29] In painting Dutchy as a defiler of the family, the *Bulletin* touched a raw nerve. By 1890 the social purity movement had gathered considerable momentum in the United States. Feeding principally on widespread anxiety about the effect of industrial society on the sanctity of the family and on sexual mores, the social purity crusade focused on the very real threat of prostitution and the more lurid and imagined dangers of white slavery. By 1890 journalists on both sides of the Atlantic had discovered the insidious underworld described by purity crusaders to the shock, or perhaps titillation, of the reading public.[30] In this atmosphere of heightened moral awareness, Atlantic City was particularly vulnerable. The term "low resorts" was a sinister euphimism that could apply to the whole range of conduct unsanctioned by the larger society, from saloons serving minors and women to those that harbored gamblers and prostitutes.

On August 9, the *Bulletin* published the names and addresses of twenty-four "disorderly houses." Twenty-one stood within a block or two north of Atlantic Avenue, and three were located on the ocean side, but within the excursion district.[31] By 1890 the city had begun the transition from the "old system" to the "new system," and Atlantic Avenue had taken on more of a commercial aspect as the better hotels and cottages were moved toward the beach. This presupposes some attempt, probably informal, at segregating prostitution within linear districts away from the Boardwalk.

The failure to contain prostitution caused problems for local residents and severe embarrassment to the city. Next door to the cottage of the pastor of the First Methodist Church stood the disreputable house of Bella Thomas. "Every action of the inmates is plainly to be seen by those occupying cottages across the way." The "despicable Mrs. Jeannette Barrett . . . was allowed to carry on a den at 136 North Tennessee Avenue," next to the house of James Latimer, "a well-known citizen." Latimer complained: "Bus loads of drunken women drove there; one night a woman was dragged into the house, tearing her clothes in the struggle." One night he returned home to find two men—"One man was black"—with two white women trying to enter his house. When the men refused to believe that this was not the desired address, "there was a row, and Latimer used a whip freely upon one of the men."[32]

One Mrs. Stewart, a "brazen female," annoyed the wife of Councilman Currie when she circulated her business cards.

> Upon this card the woman gave as the location of her low den the "corner of Baltic and Rhode Island avenues." Her house is not on the corner at all, but only near to it, a vacant lot coming in between. But the Currie mansion is on a corner of Baltic and Rhode Island avenues, and to the horror of the

Currie family, disreputable visitors, gay young men, and intoxicated persons . . . have frequently tried to gain admission to their house.[33]

Another lady, "highly esteemed in the city," resided at 20 South Massachusetts Avenue. At Number 20 North stood the "pestilential hole" of Mabel Haines, one of the larger and more established brothels in the city. The confusion caused the house of the unfortunate woman to be "invaded at all hours by drunken loafers; her door bell is rung late in the night, and scandalous inquiries are put to her."[34] The problem was, of course, that most of the clientele were strangers to the city and unfamiliar with the streets.

Playing expertly on the deepest fears and prejudices of the middle classes, the exposé achieved the desired effect. Only once did the *Bulletin* report access to the interior of a brothel, at Kittie Weigle's Sea Breeze Cottage on Maine Avenue, where the following scene was recorded: "In the general drinking room, amid men and women drinking—some half intoxicated, others more or less in the same condition—stood last night, or rather early this morning, a little boy. He was perhaps about nine years old. There he stood singing for the amusement of the patrons of the place. Where was his mother?"[35] We can only imagine the debaucheries the boy was exposed to or "the depth of disgracefulness" attained on Bella Thomas's porch "on a recent Sunday when in broad daylight . . . a scene was enacted so disgusting in character that it is beyond description."

Frequent reference to the racial identities of the vice participants and the location of brothels in the Northside also fanned the flames of indignation. Harry Smith's saloon, "a den for blacks and whites," stood on Arctic Avenue, as did Mrs. Burnett's cottage, "the vilest of the vile and a death trap for girls and boys of tender age." On the same street, "Mrs. Baker, [alias] Mrs. J. Collins," ran a brothel. "She has a white man for a husband, and her house is for black and white." On Baltic Avenue, Mrs. Taylor, a respectable resident of twenty-three years, complained of "Mrs. Smith's or [Mrs. Johnson's]" interracial house where on a Sunday evening after a fight, a woman was thrown from the house screaming for the police. Race mixing was one of the primary pitfalls of the underworld in Atlantic City.[36]

In addition to the twenty-four brothels, the *Bulletin* saw fit to list sixty-seven "saloons with Ladies Entrance signs." Actually, most of these were small hotels scattered widely about the city. Ladies' entrances, as well as back rooms, as the *Bulletin* admitted, existed to shield women from the male-dominated atmosphere of the bar. While "some of these drinking resorts" were conducted in a respectable manner, others tolerated and solicited "the custom of the lowest kind of people." Sheer numbers indicated that "Ladies" were "very steady and profitable customers of liquor saloons."[37] Readers could draw their own conclusions.

The *Bulletin* frequently castigated Mayor Hoffman as cowardly, weak-kneed, and derelict in his duty, but on the question of a more intimate association between the city and the purveyors of vice, it was more circumspect: "In several cases the protection was mentioned as secured for cash down: in other instances it was said to be obtained through house rent: then again patronage and influence were suggested as that which purchased unlawful toleration of crime and disgrace."[38] "Cash down" can have only one meaning, but bribery is difficult to prove. A reporter observed Chief of Police Harry Eldridge and a member of city council on Delaware Avenue in earnest conversation with Dutchy Muhlrad and overheard the councilman say that "he would try to make matters all right." Mrs. Burnett, "the polluter of girlish modesty" on Arctic Avenue, boldly assured both her employees and customers that they were safe. They had only to "keep quiet for a little while." Mr. Levy's house was also quiet after a "mysterious tip" of an impending raid.[39]

The protection of vice became an issue two years later when one Amanda Blitz, the keeper of a "ladies boarding house," told the unlikely story that Chief Eldredge collected protection money by selling copies of "The Life of Harrison" for $200. A hearing before city council revealed that Eldredge had arrested the woman three times in the past five years and, on the most recent occasion, had detained a group of women overnight for twelve hours with nothing to eat. Democratic committeeman Clarence Cole seemed a reluctant prosecutor, and Mayor Wright, also a Democrat, had nothing but praise for the police department. But even a highly sanitized procedure can be revealing. In summing up the defense, ex-judge Westcott blurted out a succinct summary of the city's policy toward commercial vice. "These places, run within proper limits, are pronounced necessary by all wise men." Over the entire procedure hung the not very tacit understanding that gamblers and prostitutes did indeed have a place within the liberal policy.[40]

Although the *Bulletin* shed more heat than light on commercial vice in Atlantic City in 1890, some facts do emerge. Gambling and prostitution enjoyed official sanction of one sort or another, and, if not rampant, were widespread and available in roughly equal proportions to all classes of visitors, both black and white. The notable absence of any complaint from the area of the Boardwalk except in the excursion district indicates an effort at containment somewhat effective insofar as the major hotel interests of the city were concerned. Gauging the extent of commercial vice on the basis of a vengeful and sensational newspaper probe has its limits. But the strongest indication that we may accept the *Bulletin's* facts, if not its interpretation of the evidence, is that none of the allegations were denied. Finally, the source of most of Atlantic City's vice was the source of most of its revenue: Philadelphia.

Commercial vice did not suddenly spring into existence in Atlantic City in 1890, but indications are that its origins can be traced to events in Philadelphia two years earlier. In 1887 that city attacked its own vice problem through a high license law, police raids, and careful scrutiny of liquor license applications during the spring of 1888. The result was dramatic. The city reduced liquor licenses by more than three-fourths, and miscreants fled the city in droves.[41]

The *Bulletin* made frequent reference to the Philadelphia backgrounds of the underworld figures. Minnie Weigle, "the former high kicker at the Fox Theatre fifteen years ago," along with her sister, Kittie, owned the notorious Sea Breeze Cottage. Mrs. Schellinger was "an old-timer, well known to the authorities in Philadelphia," as was Harry Smith, the gambler whose den was also a haven for prostitutes. Proprietors of disreputable saloons, denied liquor licenses in Philadelphia, came to Atlantic City, bringing with them "the scum of Race and Vine streets." The *Bulletin* provided no background on the inscrutable Mr. Levy, but Maria Weed, Mary French, Hattie Brown, Lottie Wilson, Lavinia Thomas, and Kate Davis had been indicted in Philadelphia for prostitution the previous February. Lavinia Thomas was now Bella Thomas, the notorious neighbor of the Methodist pastor on Delaware Avenue. Like Dutchy and the rest of the refugees of the Philadelphia vice wars, she had apparently found the business climate in Atlantic City more congenial.[42]

The *Bulletin* attacked the liberal policy, but fully accepted its most basic premise. A statement prefacing each of its one-hundred odd columns on the city declared:

> It is generally conceded that drinking saloons are necessary adjuncts to a popular summer resort; a certain element of the floating and resident population of the place demands them, and the law allows them. There are many here conducted with propriety; they have quiet, well-behaved patrons, and

no disturbance of the peace can be traced to them. These are open on Sunday, but that is apparently in touch with the sentiment of the town and its visitors.

To corroborate its assessment of conditions, it frequently drew upon the wisdom of "honest" and "square jawed" "Squire" John Gouldey, county recorder, former alderman, and distinguished resident of forty years. Gouldey allowed: "I would like Atlantic City to be a place where mothers could send their daughters and husband send their wives without fear. . . . There are two classes that can never rule this city—the extreme temperance people and the extreme rum people. There must be a happy medium. It would be as damaging to the city's prosperity to allow one to control as the other."[43] For both the *Bulletin* and Gouldey, as for Mayor Belisle twenty-five years earlier, the liberal policy served both the interests of decency and profit, shared as it presumably was, by the vast majority of middle- and upper-class Americans.

On September 5, the *Bulletin* concluded its probe with the declaration, "The Evening Bulletin Scores Great Victory," and assured its readers that things were now on the mend in Atlantic City. During the spring of 1891, in weekly and biweekly columns, the *Bulletin* boomed the city as the "Queen of Resorts" and as the ideal place for the "respectable families of Philadelphia." On June 7, Chief Eldredge raided three gambling dens, a barbershop in the excursion district, and two black houses in the Northside. At the white establishment, "the proprietors and frequenters of the place were gone, but a lot of chips, cards, and other paraphernalia were captured." The blacks were less fortunate. The proprietors, Charles Coleman and Joshua Foreman, reputed political powers in the Northside, were fined and spent six days in jail. No mention was made of Dutchy Muhlrad or Mr. Levy, but the *Bulletin* did comment that "a number of places have yet to be attended to." Later that month, police arrested "the notorious Dolly Shaw and Mrs. Burnett," but fined them $150 each for selling liquor without a license. To some it may have seemed that the city's newfound probity was selective. But the *Bulletin* declared that its "seed had been sown on good ground," and that Chief Eldredge deserved credit for his "energetic treatment of the social disorders." No more was heard of gamblers or prostitutes that year.[44]

In November, Editor Hall rejoiced at the cleansing of the city and predicted a bright future, for the excursion trade was "gone forever": "Never again probably will Atlantic City be what it has largely been in the past, a great excursion town. Ten years ago the Narrow Gauge brought down thousands of people on fifty cent and dollar excursions, factory hands and working people in large numbers. But these people can now go to other places."[45] Other places included Gloucester, the sin-filled river domain of James B. Thompson, located just south of Camden. In 1890 Thompson, a Democratic power in Camden County who was styled "The Duke of Gloucester," built a racetrack, and the town quickly became a wide-open resort for the working classes of Camden and Philadelphia.[46] Atlantic City would now achieve its true destiny as a "first class cottage and hotel town instead of a Coney Island." Cheap excursions would now go to "cheaper places not so far from the great cities."

The *Bulletin* exposé had a chastening effect on the city, but the excursion trade continued to grow. During the 1890s, the population of Atlantic City more than doubled, and the crowds grew proportionately, placing even more severe strains on the liberal policy. In 1892 amusement operators tested the Democratic administration of Mayor Wright by opening on a Sunday. Wright swiftly ended the brief protest, threatening the entire group with arrest. The protesters spitefully vowed that on the following Sunday they would close every saloon in the city and even stop the trains, but nothing came of the threat.[47] Sunday amusements posed increasing challenges to the liberal policy during the seasons of 1893 and 1894, but the issue reached crisis proportions during the "Amusement War" of 1895.

By 1895 Sunday closing had become a national issue. Newark and New York were embroiled in conflicts, and in July six Hebrew butchers were arrested in Philadelphia. August found the issue more heated as a group of Philadelphia bakers and ice cream sellers decided to test the Pennsylvania blue law in the courts.[48] Surrounded on all sides by the conflict, it is unlikely that Atlantic City's Sunday traffic could escape notice. But matters quickly came to a head in July when a delegation of amusement men approached Wright's Republican successor, Franklin P. Stoy, requesting that they be accorded the same privilege as the saloons. Stoy's adamant refusal set the stage for a major confrontation between the amusement men and the city.[49]

On the following Sunday, all of the Boardwalk amusements opened in direct defiance of the mayor and city ordinances. Stoy promptly responded with mass arrests and the threat of stiff fines and jail sentences. The amusement men countered by filing formal complaints against a number of other resort businesses including Mayor Stoy's Union Transfer Company, charging him with keeping a disorderly house by operating transfer wagons on Sunday. When the proprietor of the "Haunted Forest" was ordered to shut down, he replied: "They can't close us. . . . If the mayor wants to close us on Sunday, let him close the drinking places as well." He did on one Sunday, but howls of protest made short work of that tactic, and the stalemate continued through the rest of the season. The resort was threatened with paralysis, held hostage, as Mayor Stoy declared, "by a group of migratory birds who cared nothing for the welfare of the city." The resolution of the Sunday conflict was a victory for the mayor and the liberal policy, but the means of the settlement remain obscure. By September all of the charges on both sides had been dropped, including a $20,000 lawsuit against the mayor and the city.[50]

In the midst of the crisis, another bombshell burst with the publication on August 4 of a lengthy and sensational piece in the *Philadelphia Inquirer* entitled "Atlantic City's Foul Blots." Speaking for the heavily taxed but unrepresented cottage community of Philadelphia, the paper portrayed the city more as a victim of criminal elements and of its own lethargy than as the perpetrator of evil and warned that the place was quickly degenerating into a Coney Island: "The elements of low life have been allowed to gain what may be truthfully termed a dangerous ascendancy, and notorious women are free to lure their victims to their gilded dens. Disreputable houses and low drinking resorts are thick in many parts of the town, and to their sorrow many visiting parents have learned that the fast life of the place is filled with danger to their dear ones."[51] The *Inquirer* praised the mayor's efforts to maintain a semblance of the Sabbath but pointed out that the dilemma was of the city's own making. No attempt had been made to curtail the Sunday liquor traffic and now the city was reaping a whirlwind, "struggling with this open defiance of the law" and "in a quandary as to how to stave off what Mayor Stoy has declared means ruin for the resort." The delineation of municipally sanctioned and unsanctioned lawbreaking had always been the most precarious aspect of the liberal policy, but as the city grew the balance became more difficult to maintain.

Shows and amusements that would have been summarily shut down in the 1880s, or as late as 1892, now ran rampant in the excursion district. "Here," said the *Inquirer*, "everything goes, and it is not one whit better than Coney Island." A variety show featured "negro minstrels whose old jokes are varied by indecencies" and "a female singer whose success not infrequently depends on the amount of double meaning in her songs and the suggestiveness of her gestures." At Guvernator's Mammoth Pavilion and at Doyle's and the Oceanic, beer and music mixed, attracting innocent youths to vulgar shows and vicious company. Thieves and pickpockets posing as barkers for the exhibits preyed upon the drunk or otherwise unwary excursionists, and vendors of obscene postcards conducted a loud and rushing business. It was "Gloucester glorified . . . reminiscent of the days when mothers wept for the fate of their sons and daughters."

Nor was the social disorder confined to the excursion district. At the Inlet, the extreme opposite end of the city, Atlantic City's tribute to the Chicago World's Fair consisted of a rather shabby version of "The Streets of Cairo," the lascivious exhibit which two years before had scandalized the Midway and, in various forms, had reappeared in unsavory resorts throughout the country. For ten cents patrons observed the "grotesque antics of several clumsy performers in Oriental attire" accompanied by exotic drummers and pipe players. But for an additional quarter, they followed a procession of horses and camels into an inner sanctum and witnessed the performance of six women: "One, a big ugly female, apparently 60 years old, it is claimed is from Chicago; another, about 40 is not prepossessing, is from Morocco. Two of the Eastern dancers might hail from East Newark, N.J., while the fifth, a negress, is alleged to be Nubian. The sixth is a very fat, good looking young woman with raven hair and of undoubted Eastern origin." The women were accompanied by a fiddler, a harp player, and a "big gross man in a Turkish costume" who twanged a stringed instrument but made no music. The *Inquirer* pronounced the whole spectacle ridiculous but nonetheless demoralizing and outrageous. Apparently the audience felt more cheated than outraged and laughed at the "screech-owl" singing of the raven-haired woman, but "forbore to annoy her further, for she was good-looking." Now the issue clearly transcended the Sunday question, for under the liberal policy such amusements were intolerable on any day.

Not everyone who viewed Atlantic City during the summer of 1895 found it an expression of the vulgar aspects of mass culture. The *Bulletin*, as a former crusader, now had a stake in the resort's wholesomeness.

> Atlantic City today with its summer population of 100,000, most of whom are in search of pleasure, is one of the most remarkable manifestations of American life. . . . The Boardwalk is one of the greatest illustrations of "Triumphant Democracy" in this country. . . . The rich and the poor, the millionaire and the bootblack, the owner of the luxurious cottage, and the denizens of the excursions houses all meet on common ground in Atlantic

City. The wonder of it is that it is so nearly free of offence to men and women of good sense.[52]

The *Philadelphia Press* praised the efficiency of the police department and evinced a sympathetic understanding of the difficulties of managing a huge resort.

> No other community in this country presents such peculiar social problems for a city government to wrestle with. These scores of thousands of people flock to the seaside for relaxation from the cares that must be borne through the long year and they are essentially a pleasure-seeking class. Of course a large proportion of them wish to see more "life" than the sea and the sky and the breezes impart, and the authorities must strive to keep within the bounds of good order the inclination to undue hilarity and raucous pleasure.[53]

A more explicit statement of the liberal policy could not have been made by the mayor himself who, oddly enough, found himself defending a stricter standard than most of the regional press. Even the staid *Trenton Times* ridiculed the "Laws of Puritans," finding them out of touch with the modern public sentiment of the nineteenth century.[54] Joseph Pulitzer's *New York World* predictably blamed Theodore Roosevelt for the wave of Puritan zealotry "sweeping away the chewing gum business at Asbury Park" . . . and now flinging "its white caps in the face of Atlantic City."[55]

If the city had lost its grip on the Boardwalk, by 1895 it exerted a firmer hand on the more serious problems of gambling and prostitution. Gambling was not an issue for the *Inquirer*, yet its continued existence was never in doubt. Dutchy Muhlrad still held forth at the Lochiel, and the Extra Dry Cafe had prospered since its exposure in 1890, having evolved from a low gambling den into "a saloon and restaurant of fairly good class" although "frequented by men and women of rapid inclinations." In the Northside, black gaming establishments such as Coleman's and Joshua Foreman's continued to provide the city with the means for periodic symbolic crackdowns. For gamblers in Atlantic City, the watchword was discretion. Vice unseen did not excite moral outrage as did the presumably less serious but more flagrant evidence of social disorder as risqué amusements and Sabbath desecration.

The same was true of prostitution, which, however, had had more of a checkered progress since 1890. In the fall of 1894, the "infamous trio"—

Minnie Weigle, Dolly Shaw, and Minnie Burnett—spent thirty days in the county jail as a result of raids conducted by a handful of local clergymen known as the "Civic Federation." The reform effort went decidedly unapplauded in local circles, and the clergymen were encouraged to "mind their own business." In 1895 the leader of the group, Dr. Aikman, was in Detroit, and the secretary, the Reverend Dr. Cross, was suffering from nervous prostration and declined either to be interviewed by the *Inquirer* correspondent or to identify other group members.[56]

By 1895 the infamous trio held sway in "the tenderloin," a strip of North Carolina Avenue between Atlantic and Baltic. Here stood the residences of Minnie Weigle, Dolly Shaw, and Minnie Burnett, and also Kittie Weigle's Sea Breeze Cottage, all much enlarged and refined from the modest edifices described in 1890. Despite their brief brush with the law, the women had prospered considerably. All four of these places were described by the *Inquirer* as large caravansaries of the first class. The Shaw cottage was one of the "finest in town," and just down the street Minnie Weigle's cottage had evolved into "almost a mansion." Just across the street, Minnie Burnett occupied another substantial cottage and at the time was negotiating to buy the property next door. A profusion of "furnished room" signs hung from the street's boardinghouses, a sure indication that the entire strip was given over to the same attractions.

In the Inlet, on Massachusetts Avenue, stood "Mom Fisa's," "one of the swellest places of ill-repute in town." Frequented by "gilded youth and politicians of note," Fisa's was a handsome cottage surrounded by well-kept grounds. Nearby, another large cottage housed the "Blazing Rag" which, like Fisa's, was licensed by the city to sell liquor. The sporting crowd could also revel at the less elegant but more notorious Charley Smith's hotel located across the inlet in Brigantine, then known as Peter's Beach. Business there was brisk, and local boatmen reaped an annual harvest, but this was not the city's problem. Although the *Inquirer* said that there were a number of such places and that they catered to "men of every stamp" from wealthy politicians to hoodlums and crooks, it described a situation considerably more constricted and controlled than it was in 1890.[57]

Recent studies have suggested that the Victorian attitude toward prostitution was one of "quiet toleration." So long as places of assignation were located away from respectable areas or otherwise hidden from view, they did not excite public indignation.[58] In 1890 things were out of hand, and the sinister quality of the *Bulletin* probe was notably absent from the tone of the *Inquirer*. Minnie Burnett, the "vile creature" of 1890, had become almost matronly by 1895: "Minnie has a gentle, conciliatory manner, and addresses her visitors as 'boys,' but if the 'boys' speak of the 'girls,' she will say archly, 'You mean the ladies . . . .' Minnie Burnett has a humorous vein, for in a response to a call for beer, she declared that she would serve nothing but ginger ale. . . . The 'ginger ale' was very properly iced and suspiciously like beer, and the visitors drink and smile and the landlady laughs."[59] Minnie spoke frankly about her business difficulties, but "became solemn" when police matters were touched upon and "doesn't forget her thirty days in jail." Minnie was no saint, but by 1895 she had become a human being and a known quantity.

Except for Smith's, control was evident everywhere, from the Extra Dry Cafe where patrons reveled "under the careful surveillance of sturdy looking waiters who are instructed to 'stand no monkey business,' " to North Carolina Avenue where visitors were instructed to make no loud noises and the pianists were forbidden to play after 12 o'clock on orders from the police. Apparently the arrangement satisfied most resort residents, as we find no evidence of local protest in the *Inquirer* probe.

Nonetheless, the events of 1895 spurred further reforms. After a brief show of resistance by amusement operators in July of 1896, the amusements ceased to operate on Sundays. The city had enlarged and rebuilt the Boardwalk that year, and the process, as well as soaring land prices, eliminated many of the older pavilions and amusement apparatus. Interestingly, in 1896 the mayor and city council viewed a performance of the "Streets of Cairo" and, having purged it of an "objectionable feature" (the Houche-Couche dance), pronounced it wholesome. That exhibit would survive in the Inlet at least through the 1899 season.

In the summer of 1897 a correspondent for the *New York Journal* found the Sabbath a "day of absolute quiet, so far as public entertainments and amusements are concerned," and noted that this precaution saved the city from a great deal of rowdyism. He even marveled at the strenuous silent gestures of hackmen restrained from barking on Sunday. At the end of the season, Mayor Stoy received a delegation of local clergy who congratulated municipal authorities for their success in breaking up Sunday amusements. That delegation, said Walter Evans Edge, now editor of the *Atlantic City Press*, "voiced the sentiments of the entire religious community and those of the vast majority of citizens."[60]

By 1898 Editor Hall, who in 1894 and 1895 had begun to have second thoughts about the wisdom of the liberal policy, was entirely gratified at the result of the mayor's firmness. Four years ago, from Florida to Rhode Island avenues, "a panorama of living freaks" crowded out legitimate enterprise. "The fat woman, the lean man, stuffed and unstuffed animals, gypsies, fortune tellers of all nations and creeds, cheap pictures called works of art, merry go rounds, toboggan slides, weighing and lifting machines," the "endless variety of catch-pennies that should never have been tolerated," were now confined to the excursion district, which Hall conceded "will always harbor the bonhomme of the working class who prefer to separate themselves from the wealthier visitors."[61] Democracy in Atlantic City had now come to mean segregation of the working classes.

The 1899 season went off without major conflict, and the liberal policy seemed on firm ground. But events beginning that fall portended new, more serious threats to the resort equilibrium. In October, Robert A. Elwood, the young and aggressive pastor of the Absecon Presbyterian Church, issued a call for the formation of the Atlantic County Law and Order Society to attack gambling, prostitution, and Sabbath desecration, which he declared to be "wide open" in the county. For him, "the county" really meant "the city." On the mainland, there were bicycle races on Sunday, and the Egg Harbor Fair was open, but the real objective of the league was to reform Atlantic City, where there was no Sunday and vice flourished under the very noses of ordinary citizens and officials alike.[62]

Elwood laid his plans carefully and gathered forces from throughout the county. He also enlisted the aid of lawyers and clergy from the Gloucester and Philadelphia societies who were to offer ongoing advice and counsel. Yet his first public meeting turned out to be an embarrassment as a Dr. Mundy and other members of the Atlantic City clergy wanted to know by what authority Elwood had issued the call and moved for an immediate adjournment. Mundy and his supporters no doubt saw the whole movement as a very unsubtle reflection on their own lack of vigor on these matters and were also piqued at not being consulted. Mundy objected to the presence of the press at the meeting and to the public nature of the movement, which he said had "failure written across its face." He knew from experience that cash would be needed and that reform would require "the low down tactics" of the opposition. Elwood had naively tipped his hand, and the saloon men were already at work to defeat his effort.[63]

As Elwood would soon learn, it was one thing to close the fair in Egg

Harbor but quite another to tilt at the windmills of vice in the great American resort. Encouraged by recent reform successes in Chicago and Philadelphia, he reasoned that a moral reawakening in Atlantic County would similarly cleanse the city. Even wicked Gloucester had been shut down by the Gloucester Law and Order Society, and if Atlantic City could not be reformed by moral means, there was always the law. In Gloucester the law worked in favor of the reformers, for James B. Thompson presided over a Democratic enclave in Republican Camden County, and the instrument of reform was the county grand jury. A Democrat, Joseph Thompson, served as mayor, but as Elwood would also learn, politics on the island stopped at the water's edge.

Like his only Democratic predecessor, Willard Wright, Mayor Thompson was a distinguished local personage of impeccable reputation and committed to the liberal policy. He flatly declared that "ninety five percent of the property owners in the city want an open Sunday." The city solicitor, Clarence Cole, consented to address the group, but offered only a classic statement of official equivocation.

> The subject of the enforcement of the law has given me much concern. . . . I am not here to discourage the members of this league, but there has been an almost absolute failure from Sinai down . . . in driving man to an observance of the law. We cannot close our eyes to conditions as they exist. We cannot make man better than he really is by law. God has given us a will and he forces no man's will. He has given the law for man's good. The trouble is not with God's law, but with man who violates His law. Men must be taught that violated law bears a penalty here and hereafter. I am in accord with the movement which has for its object the suppression of Sabbath desecration. I question if we can hope to do much by insisting on an enforcement of the law.[64]

Elwood declared that the members would "agitate, agitate, agitate," but even Judge Ashman of the Philadelphia society counseled moderation: "I don't believe in denunciation. Visit the Sunday lawbreakers and show them the error of their ways. You can't legislate men into religion. The Word of Infinite Truth must touch the heart. You must make religion attractive to men. If you want to reform Atlantic City go out among the men—not with denunciation—but with brotherly love."[65] Even coming from a Philadelphia lawyer, a tactic of brotherly love must have seemed incredibly naive to the impetuous Elwood who was becoming quickly acquainted with the obstacles to reform in Atlantic City. Actually, of the

"A healthful and pristine wilderness." A scene taken in the 1890s of a yet undeveloped portion of Absecon Island suggests the landscape as it looked to Jonathan Pitney during the 1830s. (Courtesy, Atlantic County Historical Society, Somers Point, N.J.)

The founding triumvirate: *(upper left)* Jonathan Pitney (courtesy, Atlantic County Historical Society); *(upper right)* Samuel Richards; *(left)* Richard Osborne (John Hall, *A Daily Union History*).

"A puff of rosy optimism." The *Roanoke*, the Camden and Atlantic's first engine, was carried to the island by boat. (Courtesy, Atlantic County Historical Society)

Atlantic City Hotels in 1857. (Courtesy, Atlantic City Public Library)

Facing page: This picture *(top)* of the beachfront at Virginia Avenue taken in 1866 contrasts sharply with the photograph *(bottom)* of the same spot taken thirty years later, in 1896. (Courtesy, Atlantic County Historical Society)

(top left) "Seabathing," 1867. *(top right)* A beach scene in 1886. *(bottom left)* Woman on the beach, 1914. *(bottom right)* Woman bathing, 1904. (All courtesy, Atlantic County Historical Society)

(facing page, top) "Tiny, wooden planks." The first Boardwalk as it appeared in 1867 (Hall, *A Daily Union History*). *(facing page, bottom)* The Boardwalk in 1870 (courtesy, Atlantic County Historical Society). *(top)* The Boardwalk in 1885 (courtesy, Atlantic City Public Library). *(bottom)* Roughly, the same scene in 1895 (courtesy, Atlantic County Historical Society).

(top) The beach in 1895 (courtesy, Atlantic County Historical Society). *(bottom)* A busy beach, 1915 (courtesy, Atlantic City Public Library).

"Every time a keg was tapped, the gong was struck." Schaufler's Hotel as it appeared in 1885. (Courtesy, Atlantic City Public Library)

"Frequented by men and women of rapid inclinations." The Extra Dry Cafe in 1900. (Courtesy, Atlantic City Public Library)

"The Corner." Kuehnle's Hotel in 1900. (Courtesy, Atlantic County Historical Society)

Grand Marshall Louis Kuehnle of the Golden Jubilee Parade, 1904. At right, on horseback, is Mayor Franklin P. Stoy. (Courtesy, Atlantic County Historical Society)

Louis Kuehnle, sitting in the rear with Sheriff Smith E. Johnson on his right. At the wheel is John Mahoney with county leader Lewis P. Scott to his left. (Courtesy, Atlantic County Historical Society)

By 1900, the Chalfonte House, pictured above in 1875 *(top)*, had evolved into Chalfonte-Haddon Hall *(bottom)*. This structure would later house the first legal gambling casino. (Courtesy, Atlantic City Public Library)

The Traymore Hotel, designed by noted architect Sanford White and completed in 1915, began as a ten-room cottage in 1879. It also evolved in stages, as these pictures, taken in 1895 *(facing page, top)*, 1910 *(facing page, bottom)*, and 1915 *(above)* show. (Courtesy, Atlantic City Public Library)

"Then, as now, Atlantic City was a study in contrasts," as this photograph of the Northside taken in 1912 makes clear. (*Survey*, June 1912)

Black excursionists, 1895. (Courtesy, Atlantic County Historical Society)

"A Saturnalia of Vice." This unsigned postcard was sent to Governor Fort during the summer of 1908. The message read: "The same effect most generally noticed when the lid is off." The writing in the lower left reads: "We're lost, but we are on the way. The Boardwalk's surely gone astray. What fearsome things this night befell, if we get home, we'll never tell." (Courtesy, New Jersey State Archives, Trenton, N.J.)

Harry Bacharach defeated Daniel S. White for mayor of Atlantic City in 1911 and again became mayor in 1916 with the defeat of William Riddle. (*Atlantic City Commission Government*, 1916)

The Kuehnle fortress under siege. (*Atlantic City Review*, January 16, 1912)

This photograph of Louis Kuehnle was probably taken during the 1890s when Kuehnle was in his thirties. It appeared in the *Review* on the day after Kuehnle was sentenced to a year at hard labor in the state prison. (*Atlantic City Review*, January 25, 1912)

William Riddle. (*Atlantic City Commission Government*, 1916)

two, Ashman as a Philadelphian probably was more familiar with conditions in the resort than the country parson, who though living but six miles away was socially as far removed from the city as one could get. The dimensions of the task were perhaps best expressed by a local policeman who said that reformers "might just as well try to stop the ebb and flow of the Atlantic tides as to try to reform this town."[66]

The Atlantic County Law and Order Society died aborning. But however much the local press might sneer at "long-haired cranks and short-haired women," Sabbath reform constantly posed a serious threat to the moral equilibrium of the liberal policy. The announcement, in February 1900, that the Reverend H. Fitzwilliams, Pittsburgh's "fighting parson," had assumed the pastorate of the First Baptist Church, was not taken lightly by the *Atlantic City Sunday Gazette*, which frankly warned that he promised to "make it warm for us." Interviewed by the *Pittsburgh Leader*, Fitzwilliams declared:

> As soon as I become settled and get the lay of the land, I will keep an eye out for Sunday desecration and corruption of all kinds. . . . There are plenty of dives and gambling joints. . . . The saloons run all day wide open. . . . I think this is a violation of New Jersey state laws. . . . My course will be fearless and outspoken. . . . It would be a herculean task to clean out Atlantic City, but something can be done at least.[67]

Fitzwilliams prudently pointed out that the visitors, not the citizens, brought in the sin. But despite this positive assessment, a cleansing of the city did not promise to win the hearts of many residents, except, perhaps, for a few among his new flock.

A visiting member of his Pittsburgh congregation, defending Fitzwilliams, only made his arrival more ominous.

> He is not a "fighting parson" nor a Parkhurst. He pushed a reform in the region known to us as "the Scarlet Slums." He visited 100 poolrooms where gambling was carried on and frequented by several hundred boys five years of age and upward. . . . Armed with this evidence, he secured the passage of an ordinance prohibiting boys under the age of sixteen of age in such places. . . . He works quietly but persistently, without the bombastic speeches of Parkhurst or the gaudy display of the Law and Order League. . . . He is also a lecturer of note . . . a member of the Grand Army of the Republic and an Odd Fellow.[68]

As there were no poolrooms in Atlantic City, city officials "need not shake in their boots." Fitzwilliams was precisely what the city feared most. Not easily dismissed as a crank or a fanatic, he was just the sort to invite the kind of scrutiny that the liberal policy sought to avoid.

Although by 1900 the liberal policy, including the quiet toleration of gambling and prostitution, enjoyed the support of the majority of the voting population. When things periodically got out of hand, as they were wont to do, citizens were willing to break the conspiracy of silence to bring the management of vice back to acceptable proportions. But as vice could get out of hand, so could reform—and threaten the Sunday liquor traffic. Most resort residents had no more use for gamblers and prostitutes than people generally, but to shake the rickety structure of vice equilibrium was to threaten its collapse and bring about the unthinkable result of a Puritan Sunday. This situation also made reformers unwelcome even to many in the city who might otherwise sympathize with their goals. The effect of this condition was to mute the reform impulse generally and to confine its direction to the more flagrant and noisy evidences of disorder.

In July 1900, Editor Hall declared in a sensational headline: "Dens of Iniquity Cannot Exist Here. The People Will Not Tolerate Inaction Any Longer." "The people" referred to a Citizens' League recently formed, at least ostensibly, to take up the abortive struggle of the Law and Order Society. Hall went on to warn that if the mayor did not act, the League would take matters into its own hands. If Fitzwilliams was the leader of the movement, his name never appeared in print, nor did the names of any of the other members whom Hall vaguely described as a group of prominent hotel keepers, citizens, and clergy. Anonymously financed, the group employed private detectives and was poised to carry out raids if the mayor did not act to improve conditions.[69]

The *Washington Post* observed that the "storm broke" when a music hall announced that a full-fledged theatrical performance would be given on a Sunday night. The week before saw a riotous Sunday replete with theatricals, catch-penny shows, menageries, and other loud amusements. Also that summer, a number of saloons had introduced nickel slot machines that evidently were heavily patronized by excursionists. In short, the limits had been breached.[70]

Even the *Review*, normally quiescent on vice matters, exclaimed: "There are just about half about as many more houses of ill fame in this town this year as there have been any summer for the past ten years. This is stated on the authority of a police officer who ought to know and who says the patrolmen have no orders to interfere with the 'joints.' The denizens of the Whitechapel district were never so shameless in their operations."[71] The controlling adjective in the protest was "shameless." Whitechapel had existed in London as a sanctioned red-light district for a score of years, and the North Carolina Avenue strip had been devoted to that use at least since 1895. The problem was not that prostitution existed but that it had proliferated. Even the *Sunday Gazette*, normally hostile to reform, felt that the time had come to "put the brakes on" and that the town would be well rid of gamblers, streetwalkers, and other crooks which were giving the resort a bad name.[72]

In July, Chief Eldridge staged a general raid on gambling dens but succeeded in closing only Joshua Foreman's establishment on Baltic Avenue. Foreman escaped his usual fate of being the first victim of reform movements by jumping out of a window. His partner, one Robert Johnson, was spared a thirty-day jail sentence by Recorder Stephany who declared that there were others of greater means who deserved the maximum penalty. Obviously, the white establishments had been tipped. Sneered the *Washington Post*, "Even the police authorities laughed at the farcical attempt at a general raid, and within an hour after the colored men were arrested, they had been bailed out by white politicians and all the dens opened up again."[73]

After a stormy meeting in a church basement, the reformers took matters into their own hands, conducting a series of private raids against the brothels, and the *Bulletin* noted that "for the first time in years the tenderloin district was closed all night." The city learned that the reformers meant business when they raided Dutchy Muhlrad's Lochiel Hotel and caught a dozen men playing poker in an upstairs room. Dutchy, "cool, nervy, and smiling," hastened to settle the matter with the prosecutor. His guests were "respectable millionaires" who did not want their names made public. They also raided several hotels and saloons, but charged the proprietors with selling after hours, not with Sunday violations.[74]

Of interest here is the limited scope of the raids. The *Sunday Gazette* offered the following analysis: "The Citizens' Committee does not bother about open saloons [on Sunday] or the operation of businesses which do not offend the moral sensibilities of themselves or the visitors, but they have decided to fight any opposition that is not liberal enough to grant some consideration of their opinions, since they are willing to overlook some things which are not in accordance with the law."[75] In other words, the price of a liberal Sunday was the suppression of gambling and prostitution.

Although the local press constantly fretted that a "Dry Sunday" was near at hand, the tides of reform, though lapping at its base, never quite reached that citadel of the liberal policy. The slot machines were pulled, gamblers and prostitutes ceased operations for a time, and the city council passed a new ordinance against Sunday amusements. Reformers were once again quiet, and Atlantic City returned to its old ways. The city fined a number of prostitutes for selling liquor without a license, but none spent time in jail. But the benign fate of Dutchy Muhlrad provides a clearer insight as to how things were settled. The September session of the county grand jury found that body liberally sprinkled with Atlantic City residents, and the foreman was congressman and former mayor John Gardner. They returned no bill against Dutchy, but indicted three of the League's private detectives for conspiracy.[76]

Between 1890, when gambling and prostitution first became a serious problem, and 1900, when they became a source of serious discontent within the city, the evidence points to a problem of management, not graft. The *Philadelphia Public Ledger* noted: "As a result of the raid on the 'White Chapel' district last night, all the disreputable houses are closed, and inmates, Chief of Police Eldredge states, are scattered all over town and liable to cause the authorities much trouble. The Citizens' Committee defends its raid on the ground that the houses sell liquor illegally and should be obliged to contribute to the city treasury."[77] The problem of controlling vice, once driven underground, vexed police and city officials everywhere. In a city where strangers vastly outnumbered local inhabitants, the resulting anonymity and the absence of the normal constraints of neighborhood and familiarity compounded the difficulty of keeping order. Numbers alone created problems that would have taxed the wisdom and resources of the most enlightened administration. Controlling huge crowds and dealing with amusement violations and petty crimes strained its resources to the limit. The added burden of pursuing streetwalkers and breaking up gambling operations created another incentive to maintain the status quo.

Finally, the surest indication that the liberal policy met with the approval of the voting population of Atlantic City is the fact that throughout this period the issue of vice and Sunday closing did not intrude in local politics. During the 1890s, local elections were matters of personal rivalries and petty differences over such issues as tax assessments, and one looks in vain for any connection between politics and reform. The election of Democratic mayors in the normally Republican town in 1892 and 1898 signaled no change in the management of its affairs, at least in the areas most critical to its prosperity.

Throughout the nineteenth century, Atlantic City functioned at the very edge of conduct acceptable to the Victorian sense of order and propriety. On balance, the liberal policy had served the city well. Atlantic City's meteoric rise to prosperity and prominence during the 1880s and 1890s, a period that saw the relative decline of sister resorts such as Cape May and Long Branch, testified to its effectiveness as a management and censorship device.

Among evangelicals, the resort might evoke images of a modern-day Babylon, but it enjoyed the constant advantage that its policy met with the approval of the vast majority of its patrons. Existing as a recreational appendage to the industrial centers of the Northeast, Atlantic City during this period reflected the myriad nuances of social change, including the growing social and intellectual gap between Protestant churches and the masses of working-and middle-class Americans. The growing distance between the clergy and even their own communicants generated a proportional increase in church militance and caused the churches themselves to assume a more secular and scientific approach toward the problems of sin and social disorder. As the new century brought to Atlantic City new forms of popular entertainment and even greater prosperity, it also invited closer scrutiny from evangelical reformers, a process that would place more severe strains on the liberal policy and culminate in the conflict of Progressive reform.

CHAPTER FIVE

A Saturnalia of Vice

"I love Atlantic City," declared newly elected governor John Franklin Fort in February 1908. The guest of the Atlantic City Board of Trade, he added: "Atlantic City lives all the time. One comes to this place, walks on the Boardwalk, . . . meets fine women, and goes back only to return again. . . . Tonight I say that everything you want which I can give you, after, of course, you have first applied to the legislature, everything you want which is in the best interests of business . . . I promise I will give you."[1] Allowing for the flight of a banquet speech, Fort's remarks could not have been more reassuring. Although he carried the city by only a thousand votes in the November election, Fort had been endorsed by all four of the city's newspapers, by now all Republican, and had received the support of the local Republican organization. Party stalwart Isaac Bacharach explained his relatively poor showing in this normally Republican stronghold by saying that many voters felt him "unsafe" on the Sunday question.[2]

As it turned out, Fort was indeed unsafe. Only six months later he proclaimed the resort a "Saturnalia of Vice" and threatened to impose martial law. What had intervened, of course, was the Excise and Crimes commissions' probes revealing that liquor was sold on Sunday in defiance of the statutes and that the rules governing the liquor traffic were promulgated by the Royal Arch, a body of local license holders. More damaging was the credibility Fort lent to reports that the city was overrun with gamblers and prostitutes and that commercial vice was protected by city officialdom. Not surprisingly, a Trenton clergyman condemned the resort as a "sinkhole of iniquity" and suggested that bayonets were a proper remedy, and the Methodist Conference labeled the city as "the Sodom and Gomorrah of New Jersey."[3]

The city's defense took the form of an open letter to the governor drafted by a committee composed of members of the Board of Trade, the Business League, and the Hotel Men's Association. Predictably, the "Saturnalia Resolution" seized upon Fort's previous praise of the city and proclaimed that to its millions of visitors, vice was practically unknown. From time to time, evils had "crept in," but this was to be expected in the nation's foremost resort, and the city had dealt with them firmly. On the Sunday issue, the letter made a virtue of necessity by portraying the resort as a victim of its own honesty. For fifty-four years Atlantic City sold liquor on Sunday "frankly and openly . . . with the almost universal acquiescence of the entire community and state, official and otherwise." Other cities had done the same thing surreptitiously. To its authors, the Saturnalia resolution made a "fair statement of Atlantic City's excise controversy."[4]

But to many, the Regulations of June 1, 1907, stood as patent evidence that the city was controlled by the liquor interests. Given the findings of the Excise and Crimes commissions on conditions throughout the state, it was easy to believe that the resort was in the grip of sin and that the Royal Arch was a shadow government of gamblers and saloon keepers bent on wringing the last dollars out of the resort economy. Actually, the Royal Arch was an organization of hotelmen and restaurateurs, not saloon keepers. By 1908 its membership constituted 130 of the 212 license holders in the city and was led by such men as the Whites, Charles Spiedel, Louis Kuehnle, and other pillars of the business community.[5] But more importantly, the regulations represented a compromise between hotelmen and evangelical reformers within the city that was forged in stages over a six-year period beginning in 1901.

The process whereby the liberal policy came to be embodied in the regulations of the Royal Arch revealed the changing moral and social tensions implicit in the management of a commercial resort city at the beginning of the century. It also provides evidence of the significant growth in power and influence of the evangelical community within the state during this period as seen in the Sabbatarian and Prohibition movements. From the point of view of Atlantic City, the process illustrated the difficulty of controlling commercial vice and the effect of Sunday laws on the moral equilibrium of the city.

As early as 1891, Mayor Hoffman observed: "I think the time will come when the law governing the sale of liquor will have to be obeyed. For a long time the saloons have been open on Sunday and nothing was said about it. . . . Yet I am of the opinion that the tendency of the times on the liquor question will eventually close the saloons on Sunday."[6] Hoffman's offhand remark may have been a factor in the close municipal elections of 1892 which cost the Republicans the mayoralty. Yet his observation proved to be prophetic. During the following decade the Sabbatarian and Prohibition movements in New Jersey gathered focus and momentum, and by 1901 combined to make the liberal policy increasingly untenable, bringing the power of state government to bear on the affairs of Atlantic City.

Left to their own devices, the political and commercial leaders of Atlantic City would have continued to deal in traditional fashion with the legal and moral questions raised in the operation of a popular summer resort. But in June 1901, Supreme Court Justice Hendrickson, citing the Vorhees Act, broke the equilibrium when he ordered Mayor Stoy to close the bars on Sunday. The Hendrickson decision came as a complete surprise to Atlantic City residents, including Senator Lewis Evans who declared: "My understanding and that of all the other senators, was that the law . . . was to reach gambling houses in Jersey City and Long Branch. Every senator voted for it, and but two spoke a word against it. They were from Hudson and Monmouth, but they voted for the act. The employment of it to close up Atlantic City or any other coast resort was never contemplated or thought of while it was before the Senate."[7] After a lengthy conference with Hendrickson in Trenton during the following week, Stoy returned and assembled the entire police force, ordering it to close all the bars in the city on Sundays.[8]

June 30, 1901, noted the *New York Times*, was the first dry Sunday in the history of Atlantic City. In his sermon that morning, the Reverend Charles Fitzwilliams of the First Baptist Church declared: "That which was said to be impossible has been brought to pass . . . by one man, who having respect for his oath, demanded that the law should be enforced." At the Inlet, patrons washed down clams and oysters with fifteen-cent lemonades, while at one pavilion the band repeatedly played the refrain, "How Dry I Am." On Saturday, local breweries and liquor suppliers, swamped with orders, worked feverishly into the night to deliver bottled goods to cottages and boardinghouses before the Sunday deadline, and hotel guests prudently ordered cocktails to be delivered to their rooms on the next day. Saloons throughout the city locked their doors, and public drinking occurred only at the lower end of the beach, where excursionists brought their own beer and whiskey and drank it with their lunch. This, said Chief Eldridge, ought to be stopped as "it did not look well."[9]

Actually, Stoy had reason to be pleased with the crisis. By 1901 the city had begun to do a brisk spring trade, and the perennial amusement controversy surfaced early that year when, on an April Sunday, the Old Mill at the foot of Tennessee Avenue opened for business. Interestingly, the Old Mill was probably the least offensive of the Boardwalk amusements. Located in the heart of the hotel district, it consisted of a wheel-driven sluice that propelled boats through grottoes and tunnels decorated with scenes of oriental splendor. Although the local press found the ride "charming" and "well worth the price," the mayor, fearing a precedent, had the proprietor, Edward C. Boice, arrested. Boice pled guilty, paid the fine and court costs, which amounted to $3.30, and, bowing to public opinion, agreed not to open again on Sundays. Said the *Press*, "This ends the first chapter of the Sunday amusement question for the present season."[10]

The state courts had invalidated the 1892 amusement ordinance on a technicality, and the city prosecuted Boice under the old blue law which provided for only a one-dollar fine. Stoy prepared another ordinance providing for a $200 fine and a thirty-day jail sentence and sent it to council for approval. Despite Stoy's repeated urgings, the council had failed to act on the measure, and there the matter lay at the time of Hendrickson's order in June.[11]

Although the first dry Sunday passed without incident, the license holders quietly organized to fight the ruling. On the following Sunday, police arrested the proprietor of an open saloon in the excursion district. Two Boardwalk hotels serving drinks to guests who had purchased tickets the night before were not charged.[12] Evidently the mayor was prepared to recognize that loophole and provide at least for an upper-class evasion of the law. The practice might have blossomed into an Atlantic City hotel tradition, but it was quickly squelched by other forces.

The Old Town hotelmen and the saloon keepers were now in the position of the amusement operators. On the following Sunday, all opened for business. Louis Kuehnle, having emerged as the spokesman for the license holders, stated: "We don't want any publicity; its only a test as to the intentions of the officials, and we think we have a right to know just where we stand." The protest took on an ominously familiar tone as Kuehnle added: "Of course this means one of two things. The hotels and bath houses must close with us or we stay open together and make common cause against the law which is against local sentiment and (that of) a vast majority of visitors, and their opinions should be considered in this matter, as in the point of keeping the hotels open for their entertainment."[13] Kuehnle had not threatened to stop the trains, but neither the mayor nor the Boardwalk hotelmen could miss the point. The Old Town interests would accomplish what the amusement men had failed to do. They would close the city.

To make matters worse, the amusements opened, and from two dry and quiet Sundays, the Boardwalk was transformed into a carnival of Sabbath revelry. Things were now out of control. In a series of front-page editorials, Walter Evans Edge excoriated council members for their failure to pass the amusement ordinance. To permit the Boardwalk to become a "Midway of the Coney Island type" would be disastrous to the interests of the city. On August 12, council finally responded with another "Ordinance for the Suppression of Vice and Immorality," the new law providing for a $200 fine and a thirty-day jail sentence.[14]

Cafes, saloons, and hotels continued to sell liquor on Sunday, and city license holders were buoyed by court decisions in Essex and Monmouth which appeared to indicate that Hendrickson had gone too far in applying the Vorhees Act to Sunday selling. Governor Vorhees declined to comment on the Hendrickson ruling. Mayor Stoy found it prudent to spend Sundays during July and August on his mainland farm as the city awaited Hendrickson's next move.[15]

Carrie Nation added a colorful dimension to the liquor question in Atlantic City with her arrival on August 18. In the *Press*, Walter Evans Edge declared her "The Queen of all the Fakirs," and added: "Mrs. Nation is short, stout, almost to the point of obesity, is decidedly homely, tanned to a dark brown as though she had been summering at a seaside resort, and is unprepossessing when seen at close range."[16] Unable to secure accommodations at a hotel, she was taken to a boardinghouse, swam in the ocean, and that afternoon delivered "the wildest kind of tirade against saloons and liquor in general." She returned a week later to be "hissed by thousands" as she denounced William McKinley because he was "owned by the rummies." Nation departed the city on a dramatic note amid rumors that she planned to smash the windows of Kuehnle's hotel. Kuehnle hastily shuttered the hotel and declared that if Nation came to his place he would have her arrested.[17]

Carrie Nation left Atlantic City as she found it, but Judge Hendrickson was not amused that the bars remained open on Sunday. He sent Mayor Stoy a sharply worded note that the practice would have to cease. Meanwhile, seizing the opportunity, a group of local clergy organized yet another Citizens' League and prepared to mount a campaign against Sabbath desecration. They secured the services of several private detectives, and the Reverend Samuel H. Hann of the Camden County Law and Order Society took personal charge of the operation. Hann's agents gathered evidence against over eighty saloons and cafes and filed thirty-four complaints to be heard at the September session of the Atlantic County Grand Jury.[18]

The reformers secured no evidence against the Boardwalk hotels although they had continually served liquor to guests throughout August. The distance between the Boardwalk hotelmen and the other license holders was accentuated on September 6 with the appearance of a public statement signed by one hundred "leading citizens" declaring themselves in sympathy with the work of the Law and Order League and denouncing the reckless defiance of the law. The memorial, careful not to denounce Sunday liquor sales in principle, read like a *Who's Who* of the wealthy beachfront interests, cottagers, and local clergy and condemned the indiscriminate granting of liquor licenses.[19]

When the grand jury convened on September 10, Hendrickson let it be known in no uncertain terms that he expected indictments on the Sunday sellers, and the news from the surrounding counties was not good. The Cape May County Grand Jury handed down sixty-nine indictments for Sunday selling, and a Camden jury sentenced a saloon keeper to two years in prison. Rumors circulated that if there were no indictments, Hendrickson would either keep the members empaneled indefinitely or cite them for contempt, or he might even cite the mayor, council members, and the police for dereliction of duty under the provisions of the Vorhees Act. In the absence of a ruling by the full Supreme Court, an air of uncertainty hung over the proceedings.

Apparently, these pressures were enough, and on September 15 the liquor interests capitulated. Said Kuehnle:

> So far as my place is concerned, it will be closed. . . . What other license holders will do, I am not prepared to state. Some of them have told me they will not open, while others have expressed no opinion. . . . The members at the meeting yesterday were quite sure that it would do no good to prolong the fight. The court has fixed opinions on this matter, and it is useless to struggle against what is sure to come in the end.[20]

On Sunday, September 15, all of the saloons closed and remained so on Sundays for the entire winter. The *Sunday Gazette* declared: "The crusaders have won the battle for dry Sundays," and outwardly it appeared that the matter was settled.

The grand jury handed down no indictments for Sunday selling, but, as the defendants were now in compliance, Hendrickson released the panel with a mild admonition, a settlement that smacked of a deal. At the annual meeting of the Camden County Law and Order Society, Secretary Hann revealed that the body spent $698.59 gathering evidence in Atlantic City and strongly censured the grand jury for its failure to indict the Sunday sellers. Of the twenty-four members of the panel picked by Sheriff Smith E. Johnson, at least ten were Atlantic City residents and the foreman was once again Congressman John Gardner. But if the jury was stacked, it was not disposed to test the resolve of Hendrickson. The season was over anyway and there remained the entire winter to set things right.[21]

The Boardwalk hotels and the exclusive restaurants had no less an interest in Sunday liquor sales than the working-class saloons in the excursion district, and, ironically, Sunday closing fell most heavily on the upper-class interests. After September, the excursion trade dried up, and most of the saloons closed for the winter. The large hotels and some of the more exclusive restaurants stayed open, and it was not long before they experienced a sharp reduction in business. In November a restaurateur announced that in view of Sunday closing he would renew his lease only with a substantial reduction in rent. Plans to enlarge the Windsor and Islesworth hotels were canceled, and real estate agents reported that property values had fallen and mortgage money for city properties was becoming scarce. By January, railroad travel was down 30 percent, and the talk among all segments of the business community was of impending doom.[22]

Beginning in January, a series of meetings took place in various Boardwalk hotels to discuss the effects of Sunday closing. Participants included members of the Citizens' League, city officials, Boardwalk hotelmen, and representatives of the small hotel and saloon interests. By March they hammered out a compromise. Sunday liquor sales would resume, but saloons would do business through side doors. In the Boardwalk concert gardens, orchestras were eliminated altogether, the Citizens' League objecting to "the results that frequently followed when rum and music mixed."[23]

A Saturnalia of Vice • 123

"Music at the Inlet but None in the Grottos" ran a lead to a March item in the *Sunday Gazette*, a succinct comment on the class-conscious nature of the reform agreement. Concert gardens had long been a staple of upper-class night life in Atlantic City. But now Wagner and Strauss were no longer in vogue. Popular music at the turn of the century consisted of such numbers as "Sweet Adeline," and vaudeville and minstrel shows were now the mainstay of Boardwalk entertainment. In 1902 John Philip Sousa played daily on Tilyou's Pier, but in addition to his regular concerts he provided the music for the "Floradora Sextette of Lovely Dancers."[24]

The liberal policy now categorized popular music with mechanical amusements, unwelcome in the hotel district and banned on Sunday. When the Boardwalk concert gardens, now reduced to the status of cafes, experienced a sharp decline in business, a conference was quickly called with the Citizens' League and city officials, and "the word was quietly passed that music would now find favor." However, only "sacred concerts" could be played on Sundays and none of the concert gardens would be permitted an orchestra of fewer than six pieces.[25]

The negotiations that produced the revisions of the liberal policy were conducted secretly. Except in the comments of the *Sunday Gazette* or perhaps in some long-lost journal or diary, it is doubtful that the regulations were ever recorded. If they were, the ink would barely have been dry when the Great Boardwalk Fire of April 1902 occurred and produced an embarrassing incident revealing more of the accord and the role that the Reverend Hann and the Sunday laws played in its formulation. When the flames threatened a posh hotel gambling operation at Robert Delaney's Dunlop Hotel, workers hauled out the furnishings for a quick deposit in a warehouse. There on the beach for all to see were faro tables, a roulette wheel, and assorted other gambling paraphernalia.

The *Press* immediately began a front-page crusade against gamblers in Atlantic City. Alluding darkly to "rumors of protection," Edge described the Boardwalk operation in detail. The operators had sent agents as far west as Pittsburgh to advertise the room to wealthy gamblers. The room itself was entirely in keeping with the ambience of the Boardwalk hotel in which it was located. "The place is furnished in a luxurious manner. The floor is carpeted in heavy velvet carpet and the walls are adorned with costly oil paintings. There is a bar, but no drinks are sold. Any player can call for a drink at any time and colored waiters hasten to serve it. The 'stock,' that is a pile of chips, is sold at five dollars and is the least sum that one can commence to play with."²⁶ To Edge, it seemed bad enough that gambling went on in the back parts of the city, "but when a small sized Monte Carlo makes its appearance in the center of the city, the time has arrived to act."

Although the operation was alleged to have been conducted in secrecy, discretion is a better word. It is doubtful that Edge or anyone else well posted in the city learned of its existence through the fire. But morality was not the issue, with Edge warning: "If this is permitted to continue, citizens may see the Boardwalk filled with gambling places, and maybe Monte Carlo occurrences of some heavy loser departing this earth suddenly by his own hand. It is a dangerous thing to allow to exist. . . . Saratoga and Long Branch tried to cater to this class of people, but their end is only too fresh in the minds of the people to need refreshing."²⁷ Gambling had played a role in the flagging fortunes of Long Branch, but it posed more than just a threat to the reputation of Atlantic City. In July the *Press* reported that the Reverend Hann was "here on business." Hann and his detectives were "gunning" for certain places that not only violated the laws, but "also the compact that was made between the hotelmen and the local Citizens' League in regard to Sunday selling." In this context, "hotelmen" referred to the entire range of license holders in the city, most of whom, like Louis Kuehnle, operated a food and liquor business in connection with a hotel. Few members of the Citizens' League shared Hann's Sabbatarian views, and he was not a party to the agreement to permit Sunday selling. Yet Hann had "friends in town" and stood poised as an avenging angel to insure compliance with the compact.²⁸

For Edge, as well as the Boardwalk hotelmen, an invitation to the Law and Order League was a tactic of last resort. The fate of the Boardwalk Monte Carlo is uncertain, but by the end of July the *Press* crusade ceased as suddenly as it started. By the second week of August, Edge had returned to his customary policy of booming the city and ridiculing reformers. That weekend had been the biggest in the city's history, and, citing railroad figures, he estimated that 300,000 people had visited the resort. The hotels were filled, and Captain John L. Young reported that 45,623 people had paid admission to his pier. Next to this article appeared the lead, "Reformers Strike at Ocean City." The implication could not be missed. Authorities had closed candy and cigar stores and prevented drugstores from selling ginger ale. Ocean City was a nearby temperance resort, and the liberal policy had spared Atlantic City a similar fate.

Reverend Hann's valiant band of earnest workers thought that the resort needed "reforming" . . . and succeeded beautifully in throwing a quiet resort into great excitement and getting themselves thoroughly talked about. . . . And now Ocean City residents are discussing the probability of their Sunday bathing being cut off. The selling of Sunday papers will be stopped and omnibuses and other conveyances will also cease doing business on future Sabbath days. Probably the trolley will be stopped, and from present indications, it would not be at all surprising to see the Law and Order League endeavor to stop the tide.[29]

For Edge and the Citizens' League, Hann had his uses, but he was clearly no friend of Atlantic City.

If it appeared that the agreement of 1902 merely reaffirmed the liberal policy, there were two significant changes, the regulation of music at the beachfront and the elevation of the Citizens' League to a voice in the censorship policy of the city. Both reflected the class consciousness of the reform impulse within the city and the role that Sunday laws played in effecting reforms in other areas. As a *Gazette* correspondent ruefully noted, before 1901 "reformers were looked upon as mere clamor."[30]

The compromise of 1902 began the final revisions of the liberal policy. Now lacking a reform constituency within the city, neither Hendrickson nor Hann were inclined to roil the waters, and for the next six years citizen censors trod a broad middle ground between profits and propriety. In this situation it remained for the city in the persons of Mayor Stoy and the police department, under the watchful eye of the Citizens' League, to deal with the ebb and flow of vice and disorder.

During the summer of 1903, the mayor bannned dancing and vaudeville on Sundays throughout the city, and had the police instructed in the refrains and lyrics of religious music so that they could prevent Sunday musicals held in the guise of "sacred concerts." In 1905 Everett Meher gave up his lease on the popular Inlet Pavilion were for years he had presented concerts and vaudeville acts because Sunday closing had made the operation unprofitable. The *Gazette* declared that the mayor was an "autocrat" in these matters and that there was "no appeal from his ruling." The mayor had won out after a long fight because public sentiment had supported him. Vaudeville as a Sunday entertainment never made much headway, concluded the editorial, and its absence "was never an injury." That June, Judge Enoch A. Hibee enjoined a Sunday bicycle race to have been held on the Meadow Road in what was then an undeveloped portion of the city northeast of the excursion district. Local clergy had appealed to Higbee to "enforce the laws of the state." Said Higbee: "Perhaps we can be indulgent occasionally, but Sunday racing of any kind in my estimation, is not to be encouraged."[31] Poker and prostitution quietly continued in their usual places, but police dealt firmly with streetwalkers and brothels outside of the tenderloin.

When things got out of hand, as they periodically did, a word to the wise was sufficient, and backsliders were brought into line. Rumors of "promiscuous dancing" in Boardwalk cafes brought counterrumors of a renewal of the Law and Order Society and an announcement from the Citizens' League that "certain resorts had better mend their habits." "One hears of the formation of a Law and Order League," grumbled the *Sunday Gazette*, "with a feeling of resignation. Many persons are of the opinion that if there was not the restraining influence of the cranks, things would go to the dogs." Yet even the *Gazette* had to admit the positive influence of the Citizens' League on the tone of the city.

> Those in power and every property owner realizes that Atlantic City cannot afford to have its reputation suffer from any cause. . . . With the "lid" off and the resort wide open, Atlantic City would suffer for reasons of the pocketbook and investments in property, and the government of the resort would be forced to respond to the sentiment to "keep good. . . ." The governing force of the resort cannot please everyone, and it is trying to please the majority, and in doing so, gives offense to some, but the results up to date of existing methods and management seems to have justified their course. Atlantic City never stood better in the estimation of the public, never had more patrons, and never had as much business and money.[32]

The new censorship not only took into account changes in popular entertainment, particularly music, dancing, and vaudeville, but also reflected the growing evangelical influence within the state. Held in place by these conflicting tensions and buttressed by the prosperity of the city, the liberal policy by 1905 was, in the eyes of its architects, if not thoroughly "respectable," at least a modern response to changing conditions that enjoyed the sanction of a half-century of usage.

The passage of the Bishops' Act in 1906 signaled little change in the management of the resort. In May, Hann and the Law and Order League closed the bars in Hammonton, Egg Harbor, and Mays Landing, but the *Review* was not alarmed. Atlantic City was a "place unto herself." Stringent laws had been passed by legislatures all over the country and had been "quietly ignored." The resort would continue to do as it and other cities in the state had always done, "interpret the law to suit her own people." The *Sunday Gazette* predicted that instead of correcting evils, the law would only aggravate them. In July, amid rumors that "trouble breeder" Hann had targeted the resort, Mayor Stoy declared that "outsiders" were not needed to run the town and anyway the saloons were now so quiet on Sunday that "one would not even know they were open." As far as County Prosecutor Abbot was concerned, the new regulations made Sunday selling no more illegal than it ever was.[33]

The Citizens' League, whose membership was "yet secret," complained that there were at least a dozen gambling establishments "running full blast" within the city and threatened to call out the Law and Order League to make the liquor interests "come to their senses." The police seized thirty slot machines, and Mayor Stoy, declaring, "The gamblers don't own me," smashed them with a hammer.[34] Councilman Riddle, never reconciled to the Sunday proscription of music and amusements, threatened that he too could "raise the Sunday issue" unless the Citizens' League "acted reasonably." A League spokesman replied that its members liked their liquor "quite as much as anyone else" and that reports that the League would dry up the town were a "political canard." In Atlantic City the Bishops' Law created only a stronger incentive to maintain the middle course. To all but a very few of the parties to the liberal policy, calling out the dogs of reform was a tactic of last resort.[35]

Prostitution was not an issue in 1906. In April, Chief Eldridge died suddenly, and after an elaborate civic funeral, was mourned by the *Union*, his harshest critic, as "a man who preferred honesty to wealth." "There is no one to hint," said the *Sunday Gazette*, "that he 'got his' for the Chief died a comparatively poor man, although he held a position which could have yielded him a fortune."[36] That summer, Anna Steelman of the WCTU organized a local chapter of the Florence Crittendon Circle and set up a shelter for fallen women. They quietly went about the business of relocating and rehabilitating prostitutes, an approach to reform that met with the warm approval of both the Citizens' League and city officialdom.[37]

Later, Malcomb Woodruff, Eldridge's successor, revealed the arrangement the city had with sanctioned prostitutes in a "frank talk" to the local YMCA. Woodruff stated that he exercised a "close supervision over every disorderly house in town," he knew where each was located, was "personally acquainted with the women who conduct these places and with many of the inmates in them," and that in each liquor was sold in violation of the law. Each October he ritually arrested the proprietresses for excise violations and fined them $200 each, annually enriching the city treasury by "more than $2500."[38] While we may doubt that this was the only "tax" the women paid, Woodruff's statement placed the number of sanctioned brothels in the city at probably thirteen.

Between 1902 and 1906, "respectability" in a cosmopolitan resort meant more than concessions to the Protestant ethic. It was in the summer of 1904 that blacks were barred from amusements. In 1906 the beachfront interests announced that blacks were no longer welcome to bathe in the ocean except in the designated spot.[39] Although the latter edict proved difficult to enforce, it is clear that the interests of the Citizens' League extended beyond morality. With the working-class amusements and saloons confined to the excursion district and the Inlet, the blacks relegated to the Northside, the prostitutes and gamblers in the tenderloin or clandestinely operating elsewhere, and the semblance of a quiet Sabbath, Atlantic City during this period presents an interesting social tableau. It is also an incisive comment on middle-class values at the beginning of the twentieth century.

In January 1907, Anna Steelman, representing the WCTU and the Florence Crittendon Circle at municipal license hearings, complained of the presence of women in Boardwalk cafes. Louis Kuehnle agreed that cafes were worse than saloons because of the temptations for women. The mayor responded by banning "unescorted women" from the Boardwalk cafes. In April the Reverend Sherman Pitt asked the mayor to stop Sunday paving because it gave visitors the impression that the city had no regard for the Sabbath. Stoy, fearing another Sunday war, complied. In a city anxious to complete the work before summer, this was no small concession.[40]

By 1907 the liberal policy had become more stringent than it had ever been. But Atlantic City with the "lid down" did not satisfy everyone. In April a group of clergy and a handful of local citizens formed the Good Citizenship League. Said W. L. Garrison, the League's president, "This means war on hotelmen. . . . This thing of keeping open on Sunday has been going on for years. For years we have been promised by City Council that they would abolish the Boardwalk saloons in the Bowery [excursion district], but nothing has been done yet. Its a shame. A Christian man cannot walk along the Boardwalk on Sunday but what he sees saloons wide open."[41] The Royal Arch offered to meet the reformers under a "flag of truce," but Garrison said there would be no compromise, and the city braced for a resumption of the Sunday wars.

The local press was at a loss to explain this development. Conditions had never been better. To the *Union*, it seemed strange that a body of citizens, "representative in a sense," and "not altogether lacking in good judgement," should without any apparent reason plunge the city into a conflict that could only mean disaster. The *Gazette* was more defiant, issuing a polite invitation to the reformers to move to Ocean City. Actually, it would appear that the source of renewed discontent lay in the recent discovery by the Reverend Sinkenson of eighteen youths gambling in a saloon, some of whom were the sons of prominent members of his congregation.[42] Yet the formation of the Good Citizenship League suggests the continued existence of a residual body of local opinion that would never reconcile to the liberal policy even in its most stringent form.

The war commenced as the reformers, within the week, secured ten warrants for Sunday selling. The conflict escalated when the Good Citizenship League met with Samuel Hann and representatives of the Anti-Saloon League. J. Frank Burke, the president of the New Jersey Anti-Saloon League, journeyed from Newark to address the locals and gave the movement an even more severe agenda. In doing so, he placed Atlantic City, from the temperance point of view, in the context of the Prohibition movement: "This is not merely a move against the violation of the Sunday law, but a step toward the total abolition of the dram shop. You seem to think that conditions here are singular, but the only singularity about it is that the campaign is being made in Atlantic City, known the world over as 'liberal.' "[43] On May 3 the Royal Arch announced that on the following Sunday the bars would be closed, but that this was a "special Sunday" to give the community a taste of the effects of Sunday closing. Sunday closing continued for the rest of the month, but the movement came to a crashing halt on May 29 when the county grand jury indicted six saloon keepers for selling to minors but declined to indict Sunday sellers.[44]

The spirit of compromise was once again in the air, and the Good Citizenship League agreed to meet with members of the business community. The result was the Regulations of June 1, 1907, promulgated by the Royal Arch, the last of the compromises making up the liberal policy.[45] With this final adjustment to the liberal policy, the Citizens' League went quietly out of existence. The burden of reform was now carried by the

Good Citizenship League whose agenda was far too severe for the Boardwalk hotelmen, who now found themselves in a middle position—to the left, as it were, of the evangelicals, but well to the right of men like Kuehnle and Riddle whose vision for the city was more tolerant of the working classes.

Article Ten of the Regulations read: "Gambling is to be absolutely suppressed in Atlantic City." Gambling was a sensitive issue, not only because of the objections of evangelicals, but also because of the widespread belief that the "sporting crowd" had destroyed the fortunes of Long Branch and Saratoga. The scandals of 1901 in Long Branch remained fresh in the minds of resort businessmen, and the resulting Vorhees Act had meant nothing but trouble for coast resorts. Now with the passage of the Bishops' Act, the evangelicals' hand was further strengthened and the incentive to eliminate gambling was stronger.

Between 1901 and 1908, we find numerous press accounts of police raids on saloons and barbershops keeping nickel slot machines and similar devices. While there is no definite pattern, most of the raids took place on Atlantic Avenue, particularly in the excursion district, and were more frequent during periods of agitation. Although periodic headlines indicated evangelical discontent, the local press regarded them as more of a nuisance than a danger to the city, and grand juries freely indicted the culprits.

The same was true of small poker and dice games run by blacks in the Northside. Shortly after the Regulations went into effect, W. L. Garrison gave Justice Trenchard of the Supreme Court a list of nine gambling establishments in the city. Trenchard sharply ordered Mayor Stoy to close them at once. Three were run by Joseph Ford, the "King of Negro Gamblers" and, according to press reports, a refugee of vice wars in Hot Springs, Arkansas, and Richmond, Virginia. A week later, a "Colored Ministerial Union" joined the movement against gambling, and the *Union* featured a picture of Bud Griffin's "notorious gambling place" on North Kentucky Avenue with a huge bar across the door.[46]

But the *Review*, having grown impatient with reform, exclaimed: "First it was Sunday closing, now it is gambling. . . . The fact is that most of these places are crap joints and ten-cent poker parlors. There are two or three exceptions and these establishments are so conducted that few people know of them and the neighbors speak of them as the quietest kind of neighbors."[47] This comment suggests that, despite the Regulations of 1907, the city tolerated two classes of gamblers, and for different reasons.

A Saturnalia of Vice • 131

The tolerance of petty operations in the Northside reflected the racist conviction that blacks had a special propensity for cards and dice. This could not be eliminated, only contained. Men like Dutchy Muhlrad and Robert Delaney catered to a wealthy clientele, and it is safe to assume that they paid for protection in some form, probably to councilmen and police officers, with the proviso that the games be conducted quietly.

Bud Griffin stayed on, but the glare of publicity was enough to end the Atlantic City career of Joseph Ford. The exclusive white establishments proved more elusive. At least since 1901, the "King of the (white) Gambling Fraternity" was Robert Delaney, the proprietor of the upscale Dunlop Hotel at Ocean Avenue and the Boardwalk. Generally regarded within the town as a lovable scamp, there can be little doubt that he was behind the "Boardwalk Monte Carlo" in 1902. Delaney was the nemesis of the Boardwalk hotelmen and the Citizens' League, and at one point Henry Leeds hired one of Hann's detectives to get evidence on Delaney, but the effort was unsuccessful. Leeds charged that Delaney annually paid $1,000 each to "certain councilmen" to insure his license renewal. This seems likely, but whether the sums took the form of bribes or "campaign contributions" is unclear.[48]

Delaney was "exposed" in 1905 when a Trenton man charged that he was fleeced out of $600 in the Dunlop by two men using loaded dice. Delaney went surety for the men in the amount of $8,000, but the culprits fled to their native Baltimore and could not be located. When Judge Trenchard and the county demanded the balance of the bond money, Delaney pled poverty and claimed that anyway he was drunk when the incident occurred and should not be held responsible. The legal maneuverings that followed gave the town a chuckle, and eventually Delaney was forced to come up with the money.[49]

"Drunken Bail Bond Bob Delaney," as he became known, was one of a small number of "big time" gamblers who operated with near impunity in Atlantic City between 1901 and 1908. Another was William "Dutchy" Muhlrad, who still operated the Lochiel Hotel on Delaware Avenue in the Inlet section of the First Ward. To many, it was a mystery that Dutchy, the chief villain of the 1890 scandals, had generally managed to escape notice during the recent vice crusades. Later it was explained that he "catered to the big contractors and politicians of Philadelphia," no locals were admitted, and "only men who are wealthy and able to stand their losses are allowed inside his doors."[50] It is probably also safe to assume that Dutchy's games were honest. But another, more cogent reason for Dutchy's impunity was that the Lochiel, tucked away on Delaware Avenue, like the tenderloin, did not excite the ire of the Citizens' League as did Delaney, who had the effrontery to operate on the Boardwalk, practically in the shadow of the great hotels, and also had the misfortune of getting caught.

By 1908 Dutchy Muhlrad was a citizen of some twenty years standing in the community and the Lochiel, an institution in the Inlet. This was not the case with "the leading gambling men of New York" who set up operations in a "palatial cottage" on South Illinois Avenue in 1907 and were shortly raided. Reportedly, the gamblers scoffed at reports that they were in a panic. "That is all rot," said one, "It'll all blow over and we'll be open in a week." If they did reopen, it was not on Illinois Avenue. The place was closed and the gamblers were indicted.[51] The pattern of police activity during this period indicates clearly that New Yorkers and Baltimoreans were not welcome to set up gambling operations in Atlantic City.

The crusade against gambling received a boost in March 1908 with Governor Fort's appointment of Clarence Goldenberg as county prosecutor. Goldenberg had done legal work for the now defunct Citizens' League, but he was not the choice of the Boardwalk hotelmen for the position. Nor was he favored by Senator Wilson and the Republican organization who endorsed City Solicitor Wooten. Both sides urged their choices on the governor, but Fort, ignoring senatorial courtesy, appointed Goldenberg. A compromise appointment, he was clearly "the governor's man" and under strict orders to eliminate gambling in the city.[52]

A series of raids commenced shortly after Goldenberg took office. County detectives, along with city police, closed a number of "dives" in the Northside and, on April 22, raided the "Manhattan Club" in Chelsea, seizing $7,500 worth of gambling apparatus. In August, the New Yorkers were indicted, and the *Union* reported that the gamblers were again "in panic."[53] On August 13, in the midst of the excise revelations, Goldenberg published a list of a dozen establishments still operating, including the Lochiel, and complained that his efforts were nullified by the "political powers at the head of the city administration. . . . The only reason these gamblers have not been arrested is because there is no use dragging them to police headquarters' cells when they would escape either by the payment of a small fine or by the failure of the grand jury to indict them." The police were "honest," but in view of the political situation, Goldenberg would now play a "lone hand," aided only by the press and the public. Publishing the list was only the first move. "County Detective Baitzel, connected with my office, has absolute evidence against every one of the places and people that I mention, and the only reason that they have not been openly raided is that we know positively that there was no use."[54] This evidence, along with the reports from the Excise and Crimes commissions, formed the basis for Fort's Saturnalia proclamation.

Fort had sent Assistant Attorney Nelson B. Gaskill to Mays Landing to assist Goldenberg in obtaining indictments. At the August session of the Grand Jury, the following exchange took place between Gaskill and Foreman Salus. Complained Salus: "We have time and again asked the assistant attorney general and the prosecutor to present to us evidence which they said they had against gamblers and other lawbreakers. They have refused to give us such evidence. We have not been treated fairly as citizens and grand jurors." Gaskill replied: "I have found that the prosecutor was not in possession of sufficient evidence against gamblers, but I do believe that the prosecutor submitted ample evidence of the open and notorious violation of the excise laws."[55] The exchange between Salus and Gaskill hardly let the city off the hook, but it did point up the difficulty of controlling gambling, especially in an urban resort environment. Gamblers, shut down in one place, could simply rent space in another and resume operations. In the resort economy, there was no shortage of available rental properties, and, given a good lease, owners would not be inclined to scrutinize their customers. There was usually a distance between the backers of the games and the people who actually ran them and were caught in the raids. This was the case with Delaney and also with one R. H. Goff, the New Yorker who actually held the lease on the Manhattan Club. Indicted, Goff escaped conviction, presumably because he was not caught in the raid.[56]

Beginning with Hann's Law and Order League in 1901, the Citizens' League, the Good Citizenship League, the local police, from time to time, and finally Goldenberg in 1908 all employed professional detectives to root out gambling. All experienced some success in apprehending working-class gamblers but never succeeded in corralling locally run upper-class white establishments.[57] Both Trenchard's list in 1907 and Goldenberg's list of 1908 appeared after intense sweeps of gamblers in the resort and presumably represented the "protected establishments." Dutchy Muhlrad appeared on both, but Delaney was on neither. Trenchard's list contained nine names, Goldenberg's an even dozen. Combining the lists, only four establishments aside from the Lochiel were located south of Atlantic Avenue.[58] The evidence suggests an upper-class gambling situation in Atlantic City similar to the management of prostitution, only a little less structured, and probably about half as large.

Aside from gambling, prostitution, and Sunday selling, other activities threatened the moral status of Atlantic City. In the summer of 1908 the police arrested "The Wild Man From Borneo," who, as it turned out, was a "swarthy white man" named Jim Sullivan who worked for a black concessionaire in the excursion district. Dressed in a primitive costume, he grunted and cavorted in a cage surrounded by chunks of raw meat. "Although under orders not to use the English language, he asked the time about ten o'clock as his time was up." Sullivan was arrested, but a year later the hotelmen were "again up in arms." In the "same pit," on the Boardwalk near Arkansas Avenue, danced the "Black Salome," an "exhibit for men only." "The newest disciple of Salome is a big and muscular Negro woman whose dance is said to be almost appalling in its brutal sensuality." To the *Review*, the burden of censorship had become too onerous for the police and the city had a "pressing need for an Official Censor."[59]

But even an official censor would have found life difficult in Atlantic City in 1908. In June a delegation from the WCTU and the Crittendon Circle reviewed the motion pictures being shown on the Boardwalk that summer. One Mrs. Balliot pronounced the collection wholesome, finding "nothing objectionable." While some agreed, others, reported the *Union*, "turned pale" at the thought of lending their names to the films.[60] A year later Anthony Comstock visited the Boardwalk with a federal marshall in tow and confiscated a number of "obscene" postcards. But prosecuting the culprit promised to be difficult because there was some question as to whether the postcards were obscene, suggestive, or merely inappropriate for young people.[61]

At the close of the 1908 season, and well into the spring of 1909, observers of Atlantic City could assess its moral status from a host of sources. These ranged from Fort's proclamation and the Methodist Conference, to whom it remained "the chief ulcer in the state," to the following, almost Menckenesque, assessment offered by Irving Lewis in the *New York Telegraph*. "Atlantic City has always drawn heavily from the peaceful yeomanry of the Middle West, for the abundant reason that it was a place of harmless and continuous gaiety, a relief from the dull monotone of life in an interior citylet, and yet free from disorder and vice. It is about as wicked as an Ohio church picnic. Its innocuousness is not the least of its assets."⁶² It was impossible to calculate, concluded Howe, the harm that Fort had done to Atlantic City. But we may doubt this final point.

A. Maurice Low, a British writer, devoted a lengthy section of his treatment of American manners and mores to Atlantic City, and agreed with Howe that the resort essentially expressed the values of the American middle class, but that part of its appeal was that it held out the allure of the forbidden.

> One may do in Atlantic City what one would not be permitted to do anywhere else; and although occasionally a highly respectable and middle-aged matron from the West is shocked and watches with jealous care over her husband to see that he does not stray from the well-trod path of narrow routine, the middle-aged matron is in the minority, and the great majority, old and young, men and women, go to Atlantic City enjoying all that they see, even though they are virtuously thankful that such dreadful goings on would not be tolerated in the less rarified atmosphere of their homes. They have much the same feeling that English people have when they go to a Paris music-hall. There is fascination for most persons to be within hand-stretch of the prohibited, and to know that they are immune from its danger.⁶³

"Atlantic City is all on the surface," said Low, and it is doubtful that he observed much of the city north of Pacific Avenue.

But the beachfront was the badge of the city's respectability, and, as Heston had done in the 1880s, Low placed Mrs. Grundy in the midst of the rollicking throng to denounce it as "sinful and demoralizing." But such were the dangers of life on the precipices of morality, and when the scales tipped in the wrong direction, the city could find immunity in its own insouciance.

> It has the unaffected innocence of a little child that is unabashed in the presence of its own nakedness. Like a little child it romps and plays before the whole world and affects a pretty unconsciousness of the attention of doting admirers. It is too essentially middle class for its folly to degenerate into wickedness; and the tone of middle-class America is distinctly healthy. . . . Atlantic City is free and easy, unceremonious and undignified, good-naturedly boisterous, and unnecessarily loud, but it is respectable; it must maintain its respectability, otherwise it would cease to be the playground of the middle-class.

If the preceding reads suspiciously as though Low obtained some of his copy from the Atlantic City Publicity Bureau, the piece provides insight into the moral ambivalence of middle America at the turn of the century and the problems it created in managing a popular summer resort. "To women—mostly young, usually good-looking, and not averse to attracting attention—who delight in doing audacious things and pushing propriety to the verge without quite stepping across it, Atlantic City offers the opportunity they desire, because there the boundary line between the conventional and the unconventional has never been delimited." The prospect of sexual contact, both licit and illicit, was a powerful drawing card for the resort, and it is doubtful that the boundary line in 1908 was delimited in any but a very few places. This presented serious practical problems for the city, particularly in the management of the Boardwalk cafes, dance pavilions, and music halls. But if Mrs. Grundy, in the persons of the evangelicals, was the fly in the ointment, she was also an asset, an important restraining force and a continuing and convenient foil against which the city could create mystery out of the innocent wares on the Boardwalk.[64]

Finally, aside from Sunday selling, it does not appear that Atlantic City, even at its worst, suffered by comparison with other cities in the state. Among its staunchest defenders was the *Hoboken Observer*, probably because that city had vice and image problems of its own. According to the *Observer*, conditions in the resort were little if any worse than conditions in Paterson, an industrial city of similar size: "North Carolina Avenue and Natters Alley in the former city is no worse than Ryerson Street or River Street in the latter, and in the matter of gambling, Delaney is no worse than a well-known politician of Paterson who has ceased his horse racing and legislative activities and is content to run his faro-bank and poker games unmolested in his home city."[65] Paterson provided a good comparison in other ways. Crimes Commission detectives reported "a well defined system of licensing houses of prostitution of which there are at least twelve in the city, one of which is in a brick building built especially for the purpose." Police fined keepers of disorderly houses "seventy-five dollars every three months."[66] This, incidentally, amounted to one and one-half the annual assessment that prostitutes paid in Atlantic City.

Crimes Commission detectives who visited Atlantic City discovered a show on the Boardwalk (in the excursion district) marked "Just From Paris" featuring a woman who "undressed completely" and were solicited at least twice by streetwalkers, once on the Boardwalk and once on Atlantic Avenue. The "plain-clothes" men made a thorough canvas of the city and turned up thirty-eight illegalities within a two-day period, July 30 and 31, 1908. In addition to the film and the streetwalkers, these included ten picture shows and amusements, including Young's Pier, where there were children between eight and sixteen years old, three cigar stands where children bought cigarettes, and twenty-one saloons with back rooms. With the exception of two on the Northside, all of the saloons were on Atlantic Avenue in the excursion district. In three of the saloons, one in the Northside, men were throwing dice. In another, "three girls about 17 came from upstairs very much under the influence of liquor," and from another, "two boys about 18 came out very much intoxicated." At 721 Atlantic Avenue, there were "two back rooms, women drinking." The detectives also tested nine drug stores, but could not buy cocaine without a doctor's prescription.[67]

Asbury Park was a temperance resort. To obtain evidence here, the Crimes Commission relied not on detectives but on Charles A. Rosenwasser, M.D., who was present in the city for six days between July 16 and July 26, 1908, and agreed to "keep his eyes open for violations of the law which would interest the Crimes Commission." As in Atlantic City, city officials had made no attempt to enforce the provisions of the Theatre Act, and children under age 16 were playing billiards. When he advised Mayor Appleby, a member of the Excise Commission, Appleby replied that neither he nor the chief of police "had studied the Theatre Act but were willing to enforce it."

He also found in the stands of both Asbury Park and Ocean Grove many postcards, "which while they might not come within the law as obscene and indecent, they were of a highly suggestive character to be placed before children." But the following advertisement that appeared morning and night in the *Asbury Park Press* suggested to Rosenwasser another "line of inquiry" for the Commission:

> NOTICE: Signs bearing these words have been put up on Deal Lake at the Athletic Grounds: "No boats will be allowed to land here after nightfall." Fathers and mothers of daughters who go boating on Deal Lake should seek to know the significance of these signs.

"Much evidence was found in the canoes when they were returned." At Lochharbor, on the other side of the lake, "hundreds of canoes" were rented each night, and "not one of a hundred is rented by a man alone." On one night, Rosenwasser accompanied Officer Truax, an Asbury Park policeman, in a speedy launch equipped with a powerful searchlight and flushed out "eight pair, six white and two black." But, explained Truax, the young men and women who frequented the sands at Lochharbor were those who were driven from Asbury Park and simply crossed the bridge to find seclusion.[68]

Commission evidence indicates that Atlantic City also had safety valves in Brigantine, across the inlet, and in South Atlantic City (now Margate), by 1908, a short trolley ride away. But if the commission turned up more evil in Atlantic City than it did in Asbury Park, the crowds were larger, the scrutiny more intense, and certainly more hostile, and, of course, the latter was a temperance resort to begin with.

Perhaps the moral crisis of Atlantic City was put into its most accurate perspective by the Crimes Commission in the brief and prosaic section of the Secretary's Report dealing with fornication. Immediately after concluding that "much crime could be avoided by the repeal of the blue laws," it offered the following:

> Another law which is a dead letter upon the statute books is that section of the Crimes Act which prohibits fornication. *Seldom is a conviction for fornication recorded unless in a case where there is some other motive than a desire to enforce the criminal statutes back of the prosecution by the complaining witness.* . . . [italics added] While fornication is a crime, our reports show that the authorities in several municipalities, notably Atlantic City, Burlington, Trenton, and Paterson countenance houses of prostitution, which exist because of fornication.[69]

But in cities without houses of prostitution, "a condition which is even worse is found; young girls and old women plying the trade of street walkers. Observation has shown an alarming prevalence of syphilis and other venereal diseases among this class of women."

It is doubtful that many people read the proceedings of the Excise and Crimes commissions with any care. It is even more doubtful that, among those who did, many, with the exception of the Atlantic City press or the editor of the *Hoboken Observer*, concluded that, at least in the management of the social evil, Atlantic City was classed with Burlington, Paterson, and Trenton among the better-run cities of the state.

Although city publicists would continue to tout the liberal policy, the summer of 1908 marked the last year that the compact was actually in effect. Outwardly, civic unity found expression in the boosterism that was common to all American cities at the turn of the century. All would agree that Atlantic City was the world's greatest resort and that it was a place where rich and poor, though not black and white, could mingle freely in gaiety and relaxation.

In 1915 Mayor William Riddle referred bitterly but nostalgically to "the policy of liberality" and the "spirit of one for all and all for one" that had made the city great: "It was never a rowdy resort, nor was it ever a prudish resort. There was good fellowship among the citizens, a glad welcome for the visitors, with amusements for all tastes and temperaments that did not offend decency or good order. . . . Those were the days of equal opportunity. Practically every man made money."[70] Actually, Riddle described the halcyon days in the resort when he first arrived in 1888. But his memory was selective. As Riddle, if anyone, surely knew, class tensions among the white entrepreneurs were already in evidence and increased with the growth and prosperity of the city.

Between 1901 and 1908 the beachfront was represented in council by the likes of Walter Buzby and Daniel S. White, and in 1908 Henry W. Leeds became council president. Even during periods of internal conflict, the local press exhibited discretion by not referring to the protagonists by name. For example, Walter Edge knew very well that Robert Delaney ran the Boardwalk Monte Carlo, but never said so. The Boardwalk hotelmen found anonymity in the Citizens' League. The *Gazette* might excoriate the "Cits," but never personally attacked William F. Wahl or Henry Leeds.

The local press fondly referred to Kuehnle's hotel as "the corner," and at the conclusion of primary elections, which within the city were tantamount to general elections, the call would go out to close ranks and fight for the state ticket. There appears to have been little in the way of political retaliation. This probably is the source of Kuehnle's reputation as the "easy boss." William Riddle, the exception who proved the rule, had continually been fair game for all of the local papers. But Riddle was a maverick and firmly ensconced in the Fourth Ward, where the Republican organization had never made much headway. Continual disputes over license renewals caused internal dissension, but a certain chivalry governed political discourse in the one-party town.

In 1907 the *Review* described "Old Brains" John Gardner as the leader of the county Republican organization.

> He has had some close calls in his thirty or forty years of leadership, but it would be well to remember that he has never been beaten. . . . Perhaps

there are men in the city and county today who are equally bright in this regard, but no one has appeared as yet. . . . Furthermore he commands in politics what might be termed ultimate power in that he can call on a cohort of men of influence who[m] he has befriended in one way or another. Commodore Louis Kuehnle has the same sort of political power through his business connections, and County Clerk Scott, Senator Edward S. Lee, and Sheriff Johnson, through their personal affiliations which are political units.[71]

If these were not the sort of men with whom the Boardwalk hotelmen preferred to deal, they made no effort to challenge that leadership. They had prospered under the liberal policy, and carried a powerful voice in city affairs.

In 1908, many signs indicated that the political system in Atlantic City was beginning to unravel, but none surer than a letter contained in Fort's files written by John F. Hall in response to the Saturnalia proclamation. Hall, recently retired as editor of the *Union*, congratulated the governor for his "Message to Garcia" and went on to denounce "the gang" that had looted and demoralized the city for thirty years. They had had done so with impunity because the sheriff had put "his own kind" on grand juries. "This is a regular league of crime," said Hall, controlled and encouraged by the Royal Arch. The people "take gamblers' dollars and vote the wrong way." Drunkenness, misery, crime, and corruption—Hall laid all at the door of "the gang," Sheriff Smith E. Johnson, and the open Sunday. To make matters worse, the organization had nominated for sheriff Enoch L. Johnson, the son of the man who had controlled that office for twenty-four years.[72]

Hall was one of the distinguished citizens chosen by the city to draft the Saturnalia resolution one week later. He composed the letter in longhand and obviously wrote it in haste. Had Fort used the letter, Hall would probably have been run out of town. But Hall was right in at least one respect. The commission probes and the Saturnalia proclamation had a devastating effect on Atlantic City. They had exacerbated long-simmering tensions between the beachfront and the Old Town interests, and both sides had begun to mobilize for a political conflict that by this time had become almost inevitable.

CHAPTER SIX

The Reason: The Rise and Fall of Boss Kuehnle

In May 1909, Louis Kuehnle and Edward L. Bader of the Atlantic City Athletic Association announced that their baseball team, the Atlantics, would play Connie Mack's Philadelphia Athletics at the Inlet Field on the first Sunday in June. Kuehnle and Bader had visions of a major league franchise, and spared no expense to secure the best talent. Despite protests and demonstrations by the newly formed Lord's Day Alliance, Sunday baseball was drawing huge crowds in Jersey City, in the nearby farm community of Egg Harbor, and in other parts of the state. In the city council, William Riddle introduced a revision of the Vice and Immorality ordinance to allow the games, and "the Baseball War" of 1909 began.[1]

The Reverend Birney S. Hudson of the First Baptist Church formed a local chapter of the Lord's Day Alliance and appeared in council at the head of a large delegation of clergy and representatives of the WCTU. After a heated debate, the ordinance passed the first reading by a vote of eleven to five. "This means war," said Hudson. If the ordinance became law, the Alliance would "shut up the town."[2]

"There is no difference between baseball and golf," argued Riddle, who attempted to turn the debate into a philosophical discussion of the Sunday question. But that was not the issue. Henry Leeds warned that Sunday baseball would have a detrimental effect on property values and would "be a step toward the standards of Coney Island." The entire beachfront agreed. Daniel Myers and Joseph Thompson of the Chelsea

Hotel spoke against it, and to Daniel White of the Traymore it looked like a direct challenge to the church people, and "the license holders would be the victim of the struggle." Charles Myers of the Rudolf said: "We must take these reformers at their word. They said they would fight and we may expect a battle."[3]

The opposition shaped up quickly, as both the Lord's Day Alliance and the Boardwalk hotelmen sent delegations to the mayor. After a lengthy debate, the Business League demanded that Stoy put a stop to the move. Said Stoy: "We are monkeying with a buzzsaw." Charles Evans, president of the Atlantic City National Bank, saw nothing but disaster and wondered why "anyone should want to stir up a controversy when you can't tell where it will end."[4]

Riddle had long championed both the working classes and the liberal Sunday. As a member of council since 1901, he had consistently opposed the banning of Sunday amusements.[5] He defined the issue in a classic exchange of views with the editor of the *Review:* "If the ministers would stop the golf playing at the golf links on Sunday, that would show their sincerity. If the Christian Endeavor would also do this, it would show sincerity. But because the people who attend the ball games are clad in old clothes, and love the great American game better than the Scotch game of golf, it is considered a sin." From a practical point of view, the evangelicals had greatly hindered the "progress of the city": There are thirty-five hundred employees in Luna Park, Dreamland, and Steeplechase Park at Coney Island. One of these enterprises wanted to come to Atlantic City if they could be assured that innocent amusements would run on Sunday, the same as they run in Willow Grove and Woodside Park in Philadelphia. But no, our narrow minded Sixteenth Century bigots won't permit it."[6] The *Review* saw the progress of the city in a different light:

> Sunday baseball promises to bring on the collision so long held in check. Ball playing on Sunday has no defense. It is condemned by property owners, the hotel men, the clergy and the great body of citizens who believe in, outwardly at least, observing some respect for the Sabbath. Those whom the ball games would induce to come to the shore are not the class that is desired, as a rule, and those whom it drives from the resort, are the class we are anxious to retain as friends and visitors.[7]

Kuehnle was not given to philosophical musings. Sunday baseball was a bold stroke, and he was breaking the compact that had long held the

Republican organization intact. We can only assume that defying the evangelicals gave him the opportunity to settle the Sunday question once and for all, and the time appeared ripe for doing so. The Crimes Commission had urged the repeal of the Sunday laws, and Sunday games were being played in many parts of the state. Efforts in the legislature to liberalize the Sunday laws had failed amid a growing chorus of opposition to restrictions on Sunday recreation throughout the state, and Sabbatarians found themselves increasingly on the defensive.[8]

On June 6, 1909, over four thousand people paid the fifty-cent admission to watch the Atlantics go down to defeat before Connie Mack's Athletics by a score of eleven to five. Petitions both for and against the game had flooded the city by the time Mack had arrived. The city made no attempt to stop the game, but Mack and owner Shibe were clearly worried. Each who entered the grounds was handed a card saying: "All persons are respectfully requested to conduct themselves in such a manner that the Athletic Club will not be censured by the public."[9] From all accounts, the people complied. But on the following Tuesday, Recorder Keffer fined Bader $200, and Riddle's ordinance never saw a second reading in council.[10]

Kuehnle saw the event as a mandate for Sunday baseball and now felt compelled to answer his critics publicly: "I have very large interests in Atlantic City and flatter myself that my civic pride is as strong as that of any other resident. I have spent my whole life here, living in harmony with my neighbors, and, at this late date, I do not propose to make any move that would injure the city or annoy my neighbors, or that would disturb the good feeling which now exists between myself and fellow citizens."[11] The statement was clever; Kuehnle was at once a leader and merely a fellow citizen. Nonetheless there seemed to be a "fixed and stubborn opposition," and, in view of that sentiment, he would cancel the remainder of the games scheduled for June. Hudson and the Alliance interpreted the statement as a victory, but Kuehnle left the door open by concluding that "the people will decide." Kuehnle reportedly had over four thousand signatures on petitions, but the Lord's Day Alliance claimed an equal amount, and Joseph Salus told the Royal Arch that "even one game of baseball was a mistake."[12]

Hence, it came as a complete surprise to residents and visitors alike when, on July 3, the Athletic Association suddenly announced a game for the following day, Sunday the Fourth, at the Inlet Field. Even on such short notice, over fifteen hundred people attended. Hudson and the

Alliance claimed that Kuehnle had broken his word and this meant war. Exclaimed Riddle to council, as he introduced a resolution in support of the games: "Why should you let a dozen clergymen blackmail this town?" But Councilman Moore, who had voted in favor of Riddle's amusement ordinance, now denounced the resolution as "foolish and dangerous," and it never reached a vote.[13]

Samuel Hann once again assumed command of the operation, but this time with the heavy financial backing of the beachfront. The raids began on the second Sunday in August when William Winter obtained warrants for all of the motion picture shows on the Boardwalk, a sure indication of the escalation of the conflict, because in previous crusades the films were exempt. The reformers also secured fifty warrants for the Sunday sale of liquor, but Hudson declared: "We will not stop with saloons. We will go after everything that is unlawful, including the tenderloin."[14]

For the second August in a row, headlines and editorials proclaimed the city's iniquity. The *Trenton True American* saw Atlantic City as a "moral sewer" and a "rebel city," and recomended martial law to resolve the crisis:

> It bids defiance to the authority of the commonwealth, and flings contempt into the teeth of every law abiding citizen of the state. It has seceded from New Jersey. . . . Arguments, persuasion, and threats have no effect on Atlantic City. Its civic conscience is apparently dead, and it knows no such word as shame. It has embraced outlawry and is therefore outlawed. It can no longer claim sisterhood with the other communities of the state.[15]

Governor Fort declared that the situation amounted to anarchy and the *Newark Evening News* agreed, saying that the authority of the state was being "flouted, ignored, despised and defied by a mere municipality."[16]

In Burlington, a community recently cleansed of brothels and speakeasies by Hann and the Law and Order League, a local pastor declared that Atlantic City had "banished God": "Like the swineherds of old . . . the rum sellers whose business is the most unclean in existence today, and the gamblers, who are their partners in vileness, have virtually said through the city government they control: 'Jesus Christ, you are not wanted here. Depart from these shores.'"[17] As in the previous year, the city found defenders among the Philadelphia press and in upstate papers such as the *Bergen County Record*, which suggested that Fort investigate the saloons of Trenton and Paterson and called for a repeal of the Sunday laws.[18]

The local press exhibited an air of resignation. The *Atlantic City Press* remained above the fray and greeted the opening of the conflict with a sigh: "Once again the Sunday-closing agitation is with us. Like the circus it seems to pay a visit every year. As the circus brings with it the same old canvas, the same old acts, and the same old side show, so the annual recurring agitation seems to be ever characterized by the same features."[19] By the end of August, the *Review* had also grown accustomed to reform. The publicity was bad, but business was good. Anyway, the season was nearly over, "and no one is going to worry very much." By this time scores of warrants had been issued, but the unspoken end to the crisis would again be the county grand jury; no one expected indictments for Sunday sellers.[20]

Neither Hann nor Hudson ventured into the tenderloin, but both journeyed to Trenton for a meeting with Governor Fort, asserting that it was unfair that the clergy should bear the burden and expense of reform for upholding the laws of the state. Anticipating that the September grand jury would again nullify their efforts, they persuaded Fort to invoke the dormant Vorhees Act of 1901 and compel Mayor Stoy to enforce the laws. Assistant Attorney General Gaskill sent Stoy the necessary letter. Stoy ignored it; and on September 5 was arrested under a warrant issued by a special magistrate.[21]

This time the reformers had gone too far. The entire city rose in his defense, and a neutral observer declared that the arrest had made Stoy "the biggest man in the city." The unlikely combination of Louis Kuehnle, Carlton Godfrey, and Joseph B. Thompson, directors of the Marine Trust Company, the Guarantee Bank and Trust Company, and the Chelsea National Bank, three of the largest financial institutions in the city, immediately posted a $5,000 bond.[22] But Stoy's heroism was short lived.

A chancery court resolved the Sunday baseball issue on September 14 when it ruled against the Athletic Association and enjoined the games. But an incident that night irrevocably polarized the city. A group of Goldenberg's hired detectives, all from Newark, went into the Northside and drew a crowd of hooting and jeering citizens, some white, but mostly black. Some in the crowd carried clubs, and, according to at least two accounts, knives and pistols. Fearing for their lives, the detectives drew their guns, and began a retreat. By the time they had made good their escape across Atlantic Avenue to their hotel on South Carolina Avenue, the crowd had swelled into a mob of over a thousand. Trapped in the

Algonquin Hotel, they fired their pistols in the air and wounded a woman bystander on a balcony across the street. The police arrived, dispersed the crowd, and arrested the detectives for inciting a riot.[23]

The recriminations that followed were predictable. Charles D. White of the Marlboro-Blenheim and the president of the Hotel Men's Association blamed the politicians and the police who were "openly and directly responsible for the riot and the shooting of a woman":

> The business element of this city, not those so-called reformers, have been for some time trying to close the gambling houses in the negro section in the back part of town. . . . When the gambling expose came some time ago these resorts were closed, but we found that they were reopening lately one by one, and that all out appeals to the police were in vain. On bringing state detectives here we found they were hampered and harassed.[24]

To White, the riot was a deliberate effort to discredit the detectives in their efforts to halt gambling. The *Review* agreed: The actions of the "organization's heelers verged on murder." When Kuehnle arrived on the riot scene, Goldenberg greeted him with the question, "Are you satisfied now, Commodore?" Kuehnle replied, "What have I to do with this?"[25]

The *Trenton True American* saw the confrontation as the "First Bloodshed in the Atlantic City Rebellion" and the riot as "a desperate attempt by the followers of the Kuehnle political ring" to thwart Goldenberg's efforts to eliminate gambling. Local police in plain clothes had shadowed the detectives. "These men have gone further and have done their best to incite the negro habitues' of the gambling dens go after the detectives who are on patrol. . . . At Natter's Alley [a small street running to Baltic Avenue near the tenderloin] the county detective and his men discovered that they had been trapped by two crowds of negroes numbering between two and three hundred."[26] Woodruff's police, knowing the probable ramifications of Goldenberg's operation, were indeed present, but incitement to riot by the local police is unlikely. According to the *Union*, Woodruff believed that the majority of businessmen were satisfied that the "rear of the city joints should not be made sensational issues at critical times."[27]

According to the *Atlantic City Press*, the "disgraceful scene" occurred because the detectives lost their composure and pulled their revolvers on a "curious crowd" of onlookers who "hooted and jeered" when the detectives attempted to raid a place that was already closed.[28] This also is unlikely. Obviously, the imported detectives knew little of what they were getting into. If, on the one hand, the riot was not police inspired, on the other, "composure" would have been difficult to maintain by eight white detectives faced with hundreds of hostile blacks in an enclave long recognized as their own territory.

Goldenberg, under strict orders from the governor to eliminate gambling, had been raiding places in the Northside throughout the spring and summer. The May grand jury had indicted fifteen blacks for gambling, but over the summer some of these and other places had reopened. In September, a frustrated Goldenberg appealed to the governor for reinforcements. They came in the form of eight private detectives from a Newark agency who arrived in the resort at the end of August looking to a reporter from the *Baltimore Sun* like a "gang of steamboat roustabouts."[29]

Goldenberg instructed the detectives to "root out gambling in Atlantic City," and after a raid on a "Negro Monte Carlo," the *True American* reported triumphantly that Goldenberg had finally broken the resort gamblers and thwarted the local police and politicians: "His detail of eight imported detectives, armed with axes and crowbars, patrolled the negro district all last night following the raids on the 'Negro Monte Carlo' when tables and other paraphernalia were smashed to splinters." No one was captured, the gamblers having "smashed through the windows," but "for the first time in years, said the *True American*, Atlantic City is absolutely free of gambling tonight." For the first two weeks in September, Goldenberg's detectives roamed freely through the Northside community.[30]

The local press constantly sneered at Goldenberg's successes in breaking up "negro resorts" and "petty negro crap games," expressing the attitude of the white community that, given the blacks' "inclination for vice of all kinds," the best solution for the Northside was to contain it. The Reverend G. Howard Fletcher had expressed the inevitable effect of this policy in a letter to Governor Stokes in July 1907, just after the Royal Arch regulations went into effect. Fletcher, a founder of the Black Ministerial Alliance, had lived in the city since 1875, but of course had no part in forming the regulations. He did not identify himself by race, but his isolation as a black reformer in a city controlled by whites was evident. "Only about twenty-five percent [of Northside saloon keepers] keep a place halfway respectable, and a great many have attached or annexed assignation attics and gambling joints, paying protection of twenty-five to one hundred dollars per week."³¹ "Assignation attics" is an interesting term. They no doubt provided an opportunity for privacy otherwise denied young black men and women living and working in the seasonal and unsettled conditions of the resort economy. In a situation where stable and familial relationships would have been impossible for all but the very few, outside of the Church, the Northside saloon provided practically the only means of socialization for the majority of black people in Atlantic City.

Fletcher went on to describe the violence and degradation that flourished in these "Devil's freight trains," and his letter comes down to us as the only thoughtful account of conditions in Northside saloons. It also provides the only statement of protection money, but given the frequency of police raids on Northside saloons, its accuracy is in some doubt. The reform press quickly seized upon the Northside as evidence of the city's iniquity. The terms "Northside" and "tenderloin" often became confused, and Fort and Goldenberg were determined to eradicate evils in the only accessible target in the city.

Fletcher and the rest of the black clergy constituted one of the few anchors that existed in the Northside. Surely they had a greater incentive than Fort or anyone else within the city to improve conditions within their community. But it is doubtful that even Fletcher was pleased at the sight of a group of white Newark toughs armed with badges, warrants, axes, crowbars, blackjacks, and guns patrolling the streets and entering places at will. The Reverend A. L. Murray, one of Fletcher's black colleagues, saw the connection between Goldenberg and the riot as follows:

> I am not condoning gambling, but I do say that it is as fair for the black man to gamble or be a saloon keeper as it is for the white man, and the white man's place has just as much right to be raided. . . . I do not care if he is backed by his millions and the colored man has not a penny. . . . [If he] must be the target of this latter weeks' reform campaign, and an army of "strong arm" men must be imported to carry out the "dirty work," the time is here when every negro who has even one-eighth of negro blood coursing in his veins should resist this inhuman punishment perpetrated upon his race.³²

Racial discrimination formed one of the pillars of the liberal policy, but it had created a set of expectations throughout the city. If in the Northside those expectations were the products of racism and neglect, they were nonetheless in force, and as powerfully in force in the Northside as they were in the rest of the city.

In the days immediately following the riot, Mayor Stoy, Chief Woodruff, Prosecutor Goldenberg, and Assistant Attorney General Gaskill conducted hearings, but they were inconclusive. Charges brought denials and countercharges, and the only new information to emerge was that Stoy, anticipating violence, had alerted a local military company, and one of Goldenberg's hired detectives had a police record. Nonetheless, blame was heaped upon Kuehnle and Stoy, setting the stage for an intense political conflict between the beachfront and the Old Town factions of the Republican organization.[33]

In that struggle, Kuehnle, to outside observers, assumed the role described by the *Philadelphia North American* in a lengthy analysis of the riot. "Kuehnleism" was "the menace of political domination through terrorism and vice." But "protection was granted to the dives, not for money, but for votes," and "the machine" drew its sustenance from Northside voters.

> The large colored male population is very susceptible to the blandishments of the gambling house and the resort of evil. The balance of political power rests with the negro and the vicious white element in the Third Ward. This is Kuehnle's stronghold. It is the tenderloin of Atlantic City as McNicols' Tenth Ward is the tenderloin of Philadelphia. From this source, Kuehnle and his partners get the political strength to control the government of Atlantic City. From this lair marched the arrogant mob of thugs and crooks which the other night defied the law, broke into the regions of respectability, from which they had hitherto been excluded, and ended a riot with potential murder.[34]

Joseph Salus further clarified the boundaries of the conflict and the identities of the protagonists as he denounced Kuehnle and bossism in the same breath. The reformers were "satisfied" and there would have been no crusade without Sunday baseball. Sunday baseball was "harmless in itself," but would lead to a situation in which the "undesirable pleasures of the rabble would be engaged in; excursion features of amusement would predominate . . . making the Boardwalk a Midway from the excursion district, past Michigan Avenue, to the Royal Palace Hotel in the Inlet."[35] In the riot and Sunday baseball lay both the symbols and the substance of Progressive reform in Atlantic City.

The tensions between the beachfront and the Old Town interests so precisely described by Salus had simmered within the city and within the Republican organization for some time. They surfaced during the 1890s during the Riddle attempt to impose higher assessments on beachfront properties, and were present to some extent in Kuehnle's movement to pave Atlantic Avenue and in other organization efforts to effect municipal improvements for the benefit of the Old Town interests. But the social and economic divisions within the city appeared in sharpest relief in the give and take of the negotiations that produced the final revisions of the liberal policy between 1901 and 1907. The divisions appeared most clearly in the formation of the Citizens' League by the Boardwalk interests in 1901. The creation of the Ministerial Union, the Good Citizenship League, and, later, the local Lord's Day Alliance by the evangelicals with a more severe social agenda split the reform movement and further testifies to the accuracy of Salus's analysis of the conflict.

Fort's Saturnalia proclamation, particularly his threat to use troops, and Stoy's arrest a year later resulted in brief closings of ranks between the Boardwalk and the Old Town interests. In the reply to Fort and the defense of Stoy, the city seemed to speak with one voice. But ultimately, these events served only to exacerbate the tensions between the two factions and to destroy the liberal policy insofar as that policy was a compromise among conflicting groups within the city. The conflict began in 1908 as an attempt by Republican insurgents to replace Stoy. As such, it amounted to no more than a factional fight within the organization. The failure of that effort, along with Sunday baseball and the riot, intensified the beachfront opposition to the organization, led to the reform movement, and began the career of "Boss Kuehnle."

The year 1908 began inauspiciously for the political fortunes of Louis Kuehnle. In March he lost a bid for the county clerkship to Edward S. Lee, who, next to Gardner, was seen to hold the leadership reins of the county organization within the city.[36] That summer, in the wake of the Excise and Crimes commissions revelations, various factions of the Republican organization moved to replace Mayor Stoy. Joseph Salus saw in the crisis an opportunity to become mayor and emerged as the first and most active of the insurgents. On the day after the Saturnalia proclamation, he wrote the governor assuring him that "no extreme measures would be necessary." If Fort would meet him at Sea Girt the following week, Salus could be "of some service in satisfactorily shaping the whole matter." There is no record of a meeting, or even of a reply, and Salus, as foreman of the September grand jury, had to be satisfied with denouncing the governor for the "damndest lies ever put out."[37]

Although, by 1908, the New Idea movement in New Jersey was in full flower, opposition to Stoy and Kuehnle hardly took the shape of Progressive reform. Stoy's chief rival was Gus Parker, described by the *True American* as "a First Ward councilman who had grown rich in office." Parker was backed by Edward S. Lee and the Boardwalk hotelmen, but also by Robert Delaney, who had political ambitions of his own. The Boardwalk faction also suggested Walter Edge as a compromise candidate, but Edge, citing the press of business, declined to run. But Louis Kuehnle doomed all attempts to unify the Republican organization by dumping Stoy when he declared: "I am for Stoy to the end."[38]

Kuehnle proclaimed, "We will take care of our friends," and took charge of the Stoy campaign. The inability of the opposition to settle on a candidate made the September primaries easy, but Stoy won the November election by only 1,520 votes over Democrat John Murtland. There was a serious split in Republican ranks, but as the city government reorganized in January 1909, the organization, now in control, made a clean sweep of the insurgents. The *New York Times* declared that Kuehnle was now "boss in fact and will practically be the dictator of the policies during the coming year."[39]

If the election of 1908 began the career of "Boss Kuehnle," it was, according to the *True American*, "the cleanest and most orderly election known for years." The Boardwalk faction was still represented by Councilmen Buzby, White, Gale, and Parker and Alderman Henry Leeds. Attempts by black leaders to organize the Northside on their own behalf had been continually rebuffed by all factions of the Republican organization. In 1909, Gus Parker put together a plan to redistrict the city in order to give the beachfront better representation in council, but he quickly withdrew it when he discovered that it would have given blacks a fifteen to one majority in two precincts. Said Parker, "There was no thought of making the colored vote supreme in the uptown division."[40]

In January 1908, A. L. Murray and Isaac Nutter, a British-born attorney and the first black member of the Atlantic County Bar Association, organized the Atlantic City Progressive Club, an organization of black voters dedicated to the "elimination of the ward heeler." Nutter met with Governor Fort, who pledged his support, and by March Nutter claimed a thousand members. But Nutter was understandably cautious, declaring that either Stoy or Parker would be acceptable, and the black vote had apparently little impact on the fall primaries. Nonetheless, Stoy's slim margin in November left no doubt that with the split in the party, the balance of power in the city lay in the Northside. By the end of 1908, for the first time, the black vote became critical.[41]

The split in the party became formalized in August 1909 when Daniel S. White filed for reelection to his council seat in the Third Ward. On the following day Kuehnle announced that the organization would support William Malia and Victor Friesinger, not White. On August 30, J. Haines Lippincott announced for the Second Ward, and on September 20, the Boardwalk hotelmen formed the People's Republican Organization and fielded a full ticket in the council races in opposition to the organization candidates. Everett Colby, the leader of the New Idea movement, traveled from Newark to inaugurate the campaign, as the People's Republican Organization took on the colors of Progressive reform.[42]

The primary elections, held but two weeks after the riot, and the November elections found most of the white population already polarized between the Kuehnle faction and the beachfront. The loyalties of the blacks remained uncertain. Hence, the races, particularly in the Second and Third wards where White and Lippincott were running, centered on the Northside. At the outset of the campaign, Joseph Salus publicly suggested that the way to beat Kuehnle was for the Boardwalk hotelmen to discharge their three thousand waiters and other employees and "thus deprive Kuehnle of the greater part of the force which enables him to control the city elections."[43]

To the white electorate, the People's Organization stressed Kuehnle and Sunday baseball. But in the Northside they made more practical points. The *Review* began the campaign by urging that "every colored voter must realize that his welfare depends upon the welfare of the hotel men," who annually paid $1.5 million in wages to their black employees, mostly male waiters. The city employed but forty-five blacks. The Headwaiters' Association was more blunt. Hotelmen could "employ white waiters and waitresses just as cheaply as they could colored men." Said one Lawrence N. McCoy: "Some are saying that this is a white man's fight only. This is one time in local politics when it is a black man's fight as well." It was "a business proposition pure and simple"; blacks should support the hotelmen who were "the bedrock and substrata of our being."[44] Headwaiters were the aristocracy of black "hotelmen," the instruments of authority and discipline in hotel dining rooms, and probably altogether less popular among the rank and file than the owners themselves.

White complained that "the gang" had threatened city employees with dismissal. The Reverend Samuel W. Robinson and Isaac Nutter fell in with the beachfront, and, in keeping with the Progressive tone of the campaign, Nutter urged black voters to throw off the onus of vote buying and "political serfdom" by rising up against the machine.[45]

A. L. Murray saw serfdom in the Northside in a different light. The Boardwalk hotelmen had said in very plain language that the black waiter would either "vote right" or "be kicked out to starve." If the city employed but sixty blacks, there was at least no discrimination in salaries. Why were there no black clerks in hotels? "Have we not men with capabilities to fill such positions?" But the employment practices and racial policies of the hotelmen were well known. To Murray, another issue cut even more deeply against them: "It has been said that the Organization gives protection to the gamblers and saloonkeepers, and by this forces them to vote as they dictate. Does this mean that the men and women who are employed . . . [by the city and in the public schools] are gamblers, thieves, and cutthroats because they support the organization that supports them, that they are to be dubbed as 'thugs of the town'?"[46] In the Northside, Goldenberg and the reformers were the issue no less than employment although, given the recent strike in White's hotel and the bathing edict, many blacks were frightened at the prospect of a wholesale repudiation of the beachfront. When Murray asked, "Is Atlantic City the only place where a black man can make a living?" more than a few answered in the affirmative.

The People's candidates were all defeated, although White ran strongly in the Third Ward.[47] After the primaries, the *Review* saw the defeat as a victory. All told, three thousand votes were cast against the organization, and "much credit" was due to "the independent colored voters." The fact that they were evenly divided, as the *Review* surmised, constituted in itself "a rebellion against Kuehnle." Later the *Review* conducted a private investigation of the primary vote in the Third Ward and found a number of illegal votes. But these were cast by white repeaters from Philadelphia at a cost of "ten dollars each plus carfare." "Three fistfights" marred the November election, but this time, according to the *Review*, repeaters were not numerous.[48]

Nineteen hundred and nine was not a good year for Progressives statewide, and 1910, even with the candidacy of Woodrow Wilson, promised to be no better. The elections of 1909 saw New Idea candidates beaten by regular organizations at every turn, and the talk within Progressive circles in New Jersey was of a focus on national issues. Even the name "New Idea" was dropped in favor of the more national term, "Progressive."[49] Despite sporadic efforts by such men as Fort, Colby, and Record to cultivate like-minded politicians in the resort, the New Idea movement never made much headway in Atlantic City. Resort voters were just as concerned as their counterparts in Newark or Jersey City over equal taxation, railroad and utility regulation, workmen's compensation, and election reform, issues that dominated the agendas of Progressives in the industrial cities to the north. But the overriding issue in Atlantic City since 1901 had been Sunday closing, and the New Idea had consistently borne the burden of evangelical reform on the excise and Sunday issues, particularly since the passage of the Bishops' Law in 1906.

But the defeats of 1909 served to feed the groundswell of popular discontent with the old order in New Jersey and galvanized Progressives of both parties in their efforts to curb corporate monopoly and machine politics. The rising tide of discontent was reflected earlier in the near identical Progressive platforms of Fort and Katzenbach in 1907, but became more evident in 1910 with the Progressive candidacies of Vivian Lewis and Woodrow Wilson.

By 1910 Louis Kuehnle was at the height of his power and influence in Atlantic City. After the previous November elections, supporters tendered Kuehnle a huge civic banquet signifying his leadership in the Republican organization and his preeminence in the city. Of course, the Boardwalk hotelmen did not attend. The Reverend Francis McShane of St. Nicholas' Catholic Church was also unable to attend but sent the following regrets: "I yield to no one in my esteem and respect for Commodore Kuehnle and his manly qualities and his modest bearing toward his fellow citizens. From all I can learn from reliable sources, he is easily the first benefactor of Atlantic City."[50] The out-of-town press might vilify "Boss Kuehnle," but it served to increase his stature among residents and businessmen grown hotly resentful at sensational and often unwarranted attacks on the city. In the masculine circles in which he moved, loyalty and comradeship were prime virtues, and Kuehnle's loyalty to Stoy was a symbol of the siege mentality that pervaded the city after 1908. Nothing in his career indicates that he was a brilliant manipulator of men. But attacks on his bossism only fed the myth of Kuehnle's invincibility within the city and created an aura of absolute leadership that further cemented him to his Old Town constituency.

The defeat of the People's Organization put a temporary quietus on social and political agitation in the city. Goldenberg continued his forays against gamblers in the Northside, but the Lord's Day Alliance was silent. The biggest political event of the summer was the Republican picnic in July. Never one to lose the common touch, Kuehnle became a main attraction for the gathering when he challenged all comers in the fat man's race and won the event with a headlong slide in the mud. In August, fresh from his victory over Jim Jefferies, heavyweight champion of the world Jack Johnson arrived in the city to be received by an adoring throng at Ben Allen's Northside hotel. His reception portended Joe Louis's triumphant tour of Harlem a generation later, but, after some controversy, the city banned films of the fight on the Boardwalk.[51]

Sunday visitors to Atlantic City in 1910 neither saw baseball nor rode the amusements. With Kuehnle at the height of his power, there can be no surer indication that his clutch on the city was overestimated. Nonetheless, discontent within the Boardwalk faction remained deep. In August, the *Review* quietly changed hands, and, on September 1, announced the appointment of Harvey Thomas as president and editor in chief of the Review Publishing Company.[52]

The legend "The Truth Shall Make You Free" now appeared on the masthead of each issue of the *Review*, as Thomas opened a "new chapter" in the life of the paper: "From this day forward the *Review* will be particularly for Atlantic City against the world. . . . It will fight no battle for any one man or for any clique. . . . Politically the *Review* will be Republican, but independently Republican. It will stand for those reforms which will tend always to give Atlantic City and Atlantic County clean, honest, efficient business governments."[53] Having no "political ambitions to achieve," the *Review* would be the "people's paper" and "nothing more."

Few in the city took Thomas at his word. A nephew of Governor Fort, Thomas had been a political writer for the *Newark Evening News*, and was handpicked by Daniel S. White, Henry Leeds, and a syndicate of Boardwalk hotelmen who had purchased the *Review*. The purchase of the paper was part of a well-laid plan by the beachfront interests to wrest control of the city and its government from Kuehnle and the Old Town interests, an effort that began in the midst of Woodrow Wilson's campaign for governor of New Jersey.[54]

Initially, Wilson and the Democratic campaign for the State House did not figure in the plans of the Boardwalk hotelmen to reform Atlantic City. Progressives in both parties, such as Joseph P. Tumulty, James Kerney, and George L. Record, were highly suspicious of Wilson at the outset. But in October, the Wilson campaign caught fire, inspiring the forces of reform throughout the state. During the campaign, Wilson flayed the bosses of both parties, but he never took notice of Kuehnle. He appeared in Atlantic City only once. Speaking at the Steeple Chase Pier, he made the case for the Democratic party as better placed to carry into fruition the Progressive reforms of the New Idea Republicans and attacked the legislative record of Walter Evans Edge, then running for the state senate.[55]

During the campaign, and later as governor, Wilson adroitly avoided the liquor question, much to the satisfaction of the leaders of the Democratic campaign committee. He was against Prohibition but in favor of local option; he saw the liquor issue as a social, not a political, matter, a red herring that distracted the voters from the real issue, the alliance of the political bosses with the corporations.[56]

The meaning of Wilson's candidacy to Atlantic City was expressed by Edge and Isaac Bacharach, the Republican assembly candidate, to a black audience at Ben Allen's hotel. "Think of what form of government we would have in this city," said Edge, "if Clarence L. Cole was city leader instead of Louis Kuehnle." Between his days as attorney for the Citizens' League and the advent of Goldenberg, Cole had personified the antigambling crusade of the Boardwalk hotelmen. The prospect of Cole as county prosecutor did not appeal to Northside voters, nor for that matter, to many others in the city. Kuehnle was not given to long speeches. At a Northside appearance with Edge and Bacharach he drew a larger ovation than either candidate but merely said, "You know where to find a friend when you need one."[57]

Neither Edge nor Bacharach was in any danger; nor was there any doubt that Atlantic City would roll up a sizable vote for Vivian Lewis. But, at a meeting of the Republican State Committee, Kuehnle had guaranteed a majority of seven thousand votes from the county, two thousand more than would normally be expected. As the election neared, Cole warned that Republican workers were padding registration lists. The city election board registered 2,725 people in one day, and by the election the registration books listed 1,944 more voters in Atlantic City than they had in 1909. State Democratic Chairman James R. Nugent hired Frank Halliday, a Newark private detective, to investigate election activities in Atlantic County, and by election day Halliday and a host of investigators were on hand to document what turned out to be the most violent and corrupt election in the city's history.[58]

The Wilson landslide had produced a Democratic majority in the assembly. Halliday turned over reams of evidence to Nugent, and the assembly Democrats wasted little time in setting up a commission to investigate election frauds in Atlantic County. Headed by William P. Macksey of Essex County, the commission organized on Monday, January 16, and by the following Friday was seated in council chambers ready to hear the parade of witnesses subpoenaed by commission attorney Clarence Cole.[59]

Structured around evidence gathered by Halliday and a score of private detectives hired by the Democratic State Committee, the Macksey Commission hearings consisted of Democratic legislators and their attorneys grilling citizens and voters. But if it was, like the Riddle probe of 1893, a partisan effort, the evidence clearly pointed to an election marked by practically every form of ballot abuse and shows a clear conspiracy to roll up a large majority against Woodrow Wilson.

Hundreds of nonresident or nonexistent voters were registered at the homes of policemen, firemen, and other city employees. Boardinghouse and hotel keepers had conveniently destroyed old registers for the new year and could not recall the names of men who were registered to vote at their addresses. A proprietress of a boardinghouse in the tenderloin must have elicited laughter from knowing onlookers. When asked about the identity of several men registered at her place, she replied, "Why, this is a boardinghouse for ladies only."[60]

To help vote the names, an interracial group of 105 repeaters had been put together in Philadelphia and put on the train for Atlantic City. Halliday described the system as it was confessed to him by one of the "captains," a white man named Phillip Stinson.

> Why, he said that when they got off at the station they divided into groups and were taken around in a bus—or taken in a bus to a particular place, and the next morning, after breakfast, they divided in groups and went throughout the city, that they would meet certain individuals in each precinct who would hand them a slip with a name on it which they were to vote; that they so voted; after coming out of that place, as captain of that

one squad, he would take them to another place, where they would meet another worker, who would hand them a white slip where they would vote.[61]

Another captain, interviewed by Halliday in Wilson's office, told the governor that his party of eleven had voted a total of 117 times at the rate of two dollars per vote. One man had voted sixteen times, and "the poorest record was three." Stinson had voted thirteen times, and seven of these votes were cast in the Fourth Precinct of the Fourth Ward.[62]

That polling station was assigned to Democratic election officer James Jones, an employee of the Atlantic City Electric Company. At 3 A.M. the night before, Jones's supervisor called him out of bed, told him of trouble on the lines, and took him by car to the wilds of the county some fifteen miles from the city. Jones managed to escape, walked to Mays Landing, and boarded a morning train for the city. But by the time he arrived, the damage had been done.[63]

Democratic election officers complained of intimidation by groups of toughs who stole their registry books, and on one occasion, committed an outright assault. They also complained that local police stationed at the polls made no effort to prevent illegal activity. In defense of his men, Chief Woodruff testified that they were instructed to stand outside of the polling stations and that scuffles resulted from Democratic efforts to obstruct the vote.[64] Frank Smathers, Democratic election officer and a candidate for the assembly, told of a more bizzare incident. On duty that afternoon, Smathers was offered a drink of water containing "shoofly," a colorless, odorless chemical emetic which, taken internally, caused simultaneous vomiting and purging of the bowels. The ruse effectively eliminated Smathers as well as his Democratic colleague from his station at the Second Precinct of the Third Ward. Frank Steelman, a Prohibition official, counted 220 illegal votes cast at that station.[65]

The principals in the election frauds appear to have been Fourth Ward councilman John Murtland; Frank Majane, a saloon keeper; Thomas McDevitt, a hardware dealer; Bud Griffin and Ben Allen, Northside hotel owners; Thomas Mahoney, a small-hotel proprietor; Alfred Gillison, the city building inspector; and Robert Delaney. Murtland, a Democrat turned Republican, conducted operations at Jones's precinct, plying voters with drinks at a nearby barbershop; Majane was arrested three times on that day for buying votes; McDevitt paid off voters in the basement of his store; Allen and Griffin paid off voters on the street;

Mahoney, an election judge, presided over a carnival of irregularities, and Republican as well as Democratic election officials testified that they were bribed both directly and indirectly by Gillison.[66] But the list is by no means complete. Halliday had targeted ten of the twenty-six voting districts where the canvass of local Democrats had indicated that illegal registration was highest. The evidence given to the commission based on these districts alone indicated an illegal vote of approximately eight hundred. If the proportion in the other districts were the same, Halliday estimated, repeaters cast at least twenty-five hundred illegal votes.[67]

In the face of overwhelming and damaging evidence given by Democrats and Republicans alike, Kuehnle could not deny that "it happened." But he said, "My instructions to the workers were that we didn't want any padded lists, because we had enough Republican votes in Atlantic City and county to win the election any time."[68] Kuehnle's demurrer makes a certain amount of sense but at the same time raises troublesome questions. From Kuehnle's standpoint, aside from his boast to the state committee that he would deliver the county to Lewis by seven thousand votes, there was little at stake in 1910. Lewis was in the Fort faction of the state organization and presumably less safe on excise and Sunday matters.

But the Wilson candidacy had galvanized Democratic county committees across the state, including the long-moribund organization in Atlantic County. Was the threat of a revived county Democracy sufficient for Kuehnle to have masterminded, or at least sanctioned, the gross irregularities? Prosecutors eventually charged Kuehnle with conspiracy but never connected him personally with any of the election frauds. It is unlikely that the scheme could have been organized and carried out without his knowledge, but equally unlikely that he could have prevented it. Kuehnle "bossed" an organization that had never held firm control at the ward level. Given the rancor that remained between the Old Town and the beachfront, it is also unlikely that Kuehnle would have taken large steps to purify the process. He was not known to mollify his enemies by antagonizing his friends. He could prove a stubborn and implacable political foe, but none of his local adversaries ever knew him as mean, vindictive, or even dishonest. The Macksey Commission hearings produced 1,439 pages of transcribed evidence, and all of it that pertains to Louis Kuehnle points to a boss in name more than fact, one with little control over the activities, political or otherwise, of his so-called minions in the wards.[69]

According to Halliday, Stinson had been gathering repeaters in Philadelphia for Atlantic City elections for "three or four years." Three years would have meant that the ballot fraud system was in place in 1908, the year that marked the end of the liberal policy and the beginning of the struggle between Kuehnle and the beachfront. That year also saw the brief alliance between Robert Delaney and the Boardwalk hotelmen against Stoy and Kuehnle. On election day in 1910, Simon Faber, a People's Organization detective, approached Harry Bacharach, the brother of Isaac Bacharach, complaining of stolen registry books. Bacharach immediately sent Faber to Robert Delaney with instructions to return them. According to Faber, Delaney said: "Tell Harry Bacharach to go to hell, I don't take orders from him."[70] By this time Delaney had been jettisoned by the Independents and was back in the regular organization. Bacharach apparently knew the source, or at least one source, of election irregularities. Among the would-be "bosses" in the city, Delaney had the least local following. Were repeaters the source of his influence?

The Macksey Commission revelations marked the beginning of the end for "Boss Kuehnle and the machine." They burst upon the city with all the fury of the riot and the Excise and Crimes commissions scandals. This time the city had few defenders. Even the *Gazette* held its nose at the "corruption and rowdyism" of the recent election but remained confident that the investigation would "clear the party of those sins which may have been committed by thoughtless individuals who were led astray by party enthusiasm." Halliday had assembled over eight hundred witnesses, and the hearings dragged on through February and March, each one creating a new sensation.[71]

As the Macksey proceedings went on, the prosecutors delivered evidence to the county grand jury drawn by Sheriff Enoch L. Johnson. The panel indicted only a few minor figures, all of whom had disappeared, and persons connected with the White campaign in 1909. It did indict Harvey Thomas for libel on a complaint made by Frank Bowman, the manager of Robert Delaney's hotel. Bowman's name appeared twice on the registry lists, and a Democratic election officer had testified that Bowman voted twice. Making the most of Bowman's connection with Bob Delaney, Thomas trumpeted the case on the front pages of the *Review*, and Bowman charged him with libel. To make matters worse, the check mark indicating the illegal vote had been erased, or appeared to have been erased; the election books, in the possession of Sheriff Johnson, had been removed from the vaults; and Bowman had been a member of the grand jury.[72]

What had been a minor outrage in the catalog of election abuses grew into a major issue involving the sheriff and the grand jury system in Atlantic County. The plot thickened when Bowman sued Thomas and the *Review* for $50,000. The *Trenton Times* saw the criminal indictments and the civil suit as "conceived by the machine with the endorsement of Boss Kuehnle." In the one instance the machine would put Thomas in jail, and in the other, Bowman would force the *Review* into bankruptcy.[73]

By March 1911, Kuehnle and "the machine" were caught in the web of a trap well laid by James R. Nugent of the state Democratic Committee and the Boardwalk hotelmen. Both had anticipated election irregularities and had employed detectives to gain evidence. The connection between the two groups was Harvey Thomas, who actually wrote the resolution that created the Macksey Commission.[74] During the election of 1910, the reformers had given the organization more than enough rope to hang itself, and the actions of Johnson's grand jury only drew the noose tighter. On March 9, Supreme Court Justice Thomas Trenchard gave the city what the *Trenton Times* called "Atlantic's Last Chance." He reconvened the grand jury specifically to investigate the election of 1910. At Trenchard's request, Goldenberg stepped down from prosecuting the cases in favor of state Attorney General Edmund Wilson. But again the grand jury, to the "shame of Atlantic City," failed to return a single indictment.[75]

Harvey Thomas saw the grand jury's action as "an open blow at the attorney general as well as a challenge to the state to do its worst": "As a result, nothing more will be submitted to the grand jury at this time. There is nothing more to be hoped from this body of inquisitors. But there is machinery beyond the twenty-three that can cripple all they have hoped to support. That machinery will be set in motion now that the chance this county has had has been rejected."[76] To the *Trenton Times*, it was inconceivable that the state should remain helpless at the hands of "a little gang of political bosses . . . under the influence of lawbreakers." Perhaps, said the *Times*, it would be necessary for Wilson to call out the militia, or "it may be, as the *Review* suggests, that the Attorney General's visit was intended to give the county authorities a last chance to deal with the situation before the state sets in motion the machinery that will wipe out the stain that has been put upon the fame of New Jersey."[77]

County grand juries had long been the refuge of political lawbreakers in New Jersey, particularly in Hudson County, where Robert Davis was heard to say, "Give me the grand jury and you can have the rest of the county." Efforts by Republican legislatures to replace sheriff-picked grand juries with panels chosen by jury commissions dated from 1888 but had not been successful. The legislature had aimed the Vorhees Act of 1902 specifically at this abuse, but a succession of governors had been reluctant to employ it since it was an attack on home rule and invaded the traditional sanctuary of judicial independence.[78] But the scandals in Atlantic County made it propitious for Wilson to act decisively. He appointed Samuel Kalisch, a progressive Newark attorney, to a vacancy on the Supreme Court. A rearranging of assignments brought Kalisch to the Atlantic County circuit.

At the request of Attorney General Wilson, Kalisch drew upon a long-neglected practice in English common law that provided for elisors or "disinterested citizens" to be picked to draw a grand jury when the sheriff was under a legal disability. Johnson's father had controlled the sheriff's office since 1884, but if this were not enough of a disability, Johnson himself was accused of tampering with the election books. The device survived an immediate court challenge, and, with Johnson set aside, paved the way for a judicial resolution of the conflict in Atlantic City.[79]

Kalisch picked William Clevenger of Atlantic City and William Black of Hammonton as the elisors. Clevenger, an Independent Republican, served as the legal counsel for the Review Publishing Company. Black was an active Democrat and an unsuccessful candidate for county freeholder. Charles S. Moore, a Democratic attorney who did legal work for the Macksey Commission, became foreman of the elisor grand jury. Kalisch picked the remaining twenty-three members, a mixture of Democrats, Republicans, and Prohibitionists, from a carefully chosen list of citizens given him by Clarence Cole.[80]

With the tables so turned, indictments came quickly. The panel indicted Louis Kuehnle, Enoch Johnson, Robert Delaney, Councilmen John Murtland and Thomas McDevitt, Frank Majane, City Clerk E. R. Donnelly, Postmaster Harry Bacharach, and a host of lesser organization figures, including Bud Griffin and Ben Allen, for election frauds, and on August 6 the *New York Times* reported that graft rule was broken in Atlantic City. At the next session, they indicted five freeholders and the county engineer for grafting on road contracts, Alderman James Carmony and Councilman Henry Bolte for liquor license payoffs, and, finally, they indicted Water Commissioner Louis Kuehnle for conflict of interest in a water main contract. All told, the elisor grand jury handed down 138 indictments on sixty-two individuals, eight of whom were city or county officials.[81]

The elisor grand jury provided other opportunities for reform in Atlantic City. As soon as they had been empaneled, the Good Citizenship League announced: "The decent people in Atlantic City who believe in keeping the Sabbath day holy have waited for this opportunity for years. Now that we have it, rest assured it is not our intention to let it slip by. Atlantic City wants to be rid of lawlessness—not partially so, but altogether." By the end of the month Samuel Hann and the Law and Order League were again in the city gathering evidence, and by October the panel handed down eighty-nine indictments against Sunday liquor sellers. The Sunday wars finally ceased on October 15, when the city went dry on the Sabbath.[82]

The *New York Times*, already booming Wilson for president, reported: "Governor Wilson's Cleansing Process Is Being Carried Out With a Vengeance": "Wilson's boast that he intended to give the city clean government if possible was looked upon as mere political buncombe at first . . . scarcely a handful of citizens took the governor seriously. . . . Public spirited citizens have sprung up on every side . . . and where a week ago the whole crusade looked like a hopelessly lost cause, today even the sturdiest Kuehnlean man is trembling.[83] Wilson was no puritan but was going "stoically on with his crusade" to wipe out "one of the worst political blots in the history of the State."

Kuehnle's world was indeed crumbling. Mayor Stoy was saved from indictment by his death on July 22. The passing of the "Dandy Mayor" brought an outpouring of grief and tribute from the citizens of Atlantic City. However, the pageant of his funeral provided but a brief interlude in the drama of Progressive reform.[84]

To William Davenport of the Philadelphia *Public Ledger*, Atlantic City was under siege:

> The present cleansing process that is being applied to this protesting child of New Jersey is either a political scheme to stamp out the present Republican organization and open some aperture in the Kuehnle fortress through which the Democratic party can enter, or it is the culmination of a slow but steady growth of righteousness and a desire to reform. It all depends on how you look at it and where your affiliations are.[85]

But Atlantic City had never welcomed the "civic salvationist," and reform, if it came, would be due to the "invasion of outside forces."

164 • *The Reason: The Rise and Fall of Boss Kuehnle*

Actually, the Kuehnle fortress was besieged by a combination of forces from within and without, each of whom had reasons to destroy the power of the Republican organization. Daniel S. White and the Boardwalk hotelmen who, along with Harvey Thomas, had begun the movement, were bent on redeeming the city from the likes of Delaney, Riddle, Kuehnle and the Old Town interests, and the Northside. For James Nugent and the Democratic State Committee, the movement was an attack on a Republican stronghold in South Jersey and provided an opportunity to even up perennial charges of vote fraud in Essex and Hudson counties. For Nugent, the election of a Democratic assembly was a godsend. The Macksey sensations reverberated throughout the state and caused severe embarrassment to New Jersey Republicans. Local Democrats such as Smathers, Cole, and Moore, long on the outs, were able to revive their organization. Evangelicals in the persons of the Good Citizenship League, the Lord's Day Alliance, and Samuel Hann and the Law and Order League were able to close the bars on Sunday.

Finally, there was Woodrow Wilson who declared, "I am behind the movement for all there is in it." For Wilson, running for president and battling the bosses of both parties, the situation in Atlantic City was "made to order." The "thieving politicians were Republicans, and he had been making great efforts to convince Republican voters that their party was boss-dominated."[86]

The disparate army of reformers found unity only in their opposition to the Republican organization, a fact cleverly, and often viciously, exploited by Harvey Thomas. As the titular head of the organization, the Commodore presented a likely target. As Thomas seized upon the Macksey sensations, Kuehnle became the symbol of all the ills that had plagued the resort for a generation.

By attacking Kuehnle, Thomas confronted the "machine" head on. By July, at the head of each sensational revelation there appeared a picture of an overweight, disheveled, and confused-looking Kuehnle with his little dog Jerry, captioned simply by "The Reason." Thomas explained the reason at some length on August 4.

What the *Review* has tried to show by the publication of Mr. Kuehnle's picture, which is a perfect likeness, is just exactly what its critics are harping on—the facial and physical characteristics of the man whose reign is rapidly and surely decaying and who has for a decade of years held the people of this municipality in the hollow of his big fat hand, to be crushed at will, or to have their money blood squeezed from them to aid him in his nefarious political practices—practices which are . . . "The Reason" for the present slough of despondency through which Atlantic City is presently being dragged.

Mr. Kuehnle may be all his friends say he is, jolly, good natured, generous, and jovial, . . . but . . . look at his picture and see who and what he is.

Observe the bull doggish attitude, the Simon Legree pose, the heavy headed build, the sinister eyes, and then ask yourself: "Are you proud of this man as your owner?" for he owns the town as absolutely as if he held a mortgage on every man, woman and child in it.

That is the object of "The Reason." It is to show a man who has fattened off the profits bled from the citizens . . . a man who has ordered indictments and again ordered them quashed; . . . a man who has furnished "the reason" for almost all of what is transpiring now to the shame of this city.[87]

Twenty years ago, said Thomas, Kuehnle might have been a benefit to the city. But politics had ruined him. He was now "Atlantic County's evil genius, . . . debauching the consciences of men he might have led to decent careers."

The pages of the *Review* for 1911 and 1912 provide as sanguinary an example of muckraking journalism as could be found during the Progressive era. Thomas's theme was picked up by his colleagues in Philadelphia, New York, and throughout the state, particularly by the *Philadelphia North American*, the *New York Times*, and the Wilson papers in New Jersey, the *Trenton True American*, the *Trenton Times*, and the *Newark Evening News*. By September 1, 1911, the *News*, in an editorial entitled "The Passing of a Boss," was already writing Kuehnle's political obituary:

> For years he has been the head and front of the Republican machine in Atlantic County . . . the most successful of any county organization in the state. . . . It has stood for all forms of crookedness. It has prospered through bribery, thuggery, ballot box stuffing and kindred crimes. It has gathered sinews of warfare from degraded and degrading sources. Under its rule gambling and prostitution have been permitted for the benefit of the Republican party.[88]

That era, said the *News*, was now drawing to a close.

By September 1911, Kuehnle's career as boss of the city was over. But reports of the organization's demise were greatly exaggerated. Stoy's death meant that a successor would be chosen in November, providing

LOUIS KUEHNLE

"The Reason," Louis Kuehnle with Jerry. (*Atlantic City Review*, December 23, 1911. Courtesy, Wilson Papers, Princeton University Library)

the first political test of the reform movement. Alderman Carmony succeeded as mayor, but his was among the first indictments. The organization turned to Harry Bacharach, but soon after the endorsement, he too was indicted. Daniel White announced as an Independent Republican and, after some wrangling with local Democrats, emerged as a fusion candidate representing both Democrats and Independent Republicans.[89]

During the bitterly fought election of 1911, the flurry of indictments gave Thomas more than enough ammunition. Toward the end of the campaign he summed up the issue as follows: "Your leaders, the men who are in control, are conspicuous alone for their cupidity, their infamies and their crass ignorance. They are the vermin of society, the corrupters of good manners, and because of their example, are active agents in debauching the youth of the city."[90] To the *Gazette*, reform meant nothing more than a power grab by White on behalf of the Boardwalk hotel interests: "While everyone respects his personal honor, he is frigid, unapproachable and solely committed to the interests of the beachfront. It is doubtful if he has ever been North of Atlantic Avenue except when he has passed through it in a parlor car or his automobile. He was put in Council in answer to the claim of the beachfront for recognition in that body. And he never pretended to represent any other interest."[91] White did little personal campaigning. He presented his candidacy in terms of the national Progressive movement: "An independent movement has started on the Pacific Coast and is sweeping eastward to the Atlantic. Seattle, San Francisco, Boston, Pittsburgh and other cities have felt the strength of this mighty movement towards betterment in civic government, and there is every reason to believe that Philadelphia and Atlantic City will feel it next Tuesday."[92] Although Bacharach, like Edge, managed to keep a prudent distance between himself and Kuehnle, he worked strenuously to keep the Northside and the Old Town intact for the organization.

Isaac Nutter, who had worked for the Independents in 1909, now supported Bacharach. A cartoon appearing on the front page of the *Review* a week before the election gave clear indication that Thomas had written off the black vote. James Ottery, Ben Allen, and Bud Griffin, Northside saloon keepers who were indicted for gambling and election frauds, were drawn in racist caricature cheering for Bacharach. Their pockets stuffed with playing cards, they each held a string of repeaters in tow.[93]

Meanwhile, as the elisor grand jury sat, Johnson drew a regular grand jury, and on October 26 it indicted White along with other Indepen-

168 • *The Reason: The Rise and Fall of Boss Kuehnle*

A Progressive view of African-American voters. (*Atlantic City Review*, October 31, 1911. Courtesy, Wilson Papers, Princeton University Library)

dents—Walter Buzby, Charles Mathis, and Overseer of the Poor Risley Barlow—for election frauds allegedly committed during the 1909 primary. A private investigation had produced phony rent receipts said to have been used by the Independents in a scheme to "colonize" black voters in the hotly contested Third Ward. Said the *Sunday Gazette*, that campaign was the most "notoriously corrupt in the city's history" and had been a "stench in the nostrils of the community" for two years. To the *Review*, the White indictment was a "desperate act of political retaliation." In either case, as the campaign drew to a close, the voters, living under an indicted mayor, could choose between candidates for his successor who were also indicted.[94]

The White campaign culminated with an appearance by Woodrow Wilson on November 1. In fighting trim, Wilson made "one of the most swashbuckling speeches of his career":

> As I have stood here tonight and looked into your faces I have wondered how it feels to live under a reign of terror. How does it feel? How does

your self respect fare in the circumstances? Atlantic City is famous all over the United States and over a greater part of the world for its charm and for its shame . . . a place to which all the continent comes and of which all the continent thinks with condescension and pity because you have submitted—you have not done the thing; you have stood cowed and submissive and seen the thing done . . . . I invite you to tell me on the seventh of November—not tonight; there are policemen at the door and they would lay their hands on me if they dared because I have come here and told you what you know, but perhaps would not like to stand on this stage and say it. It is not a question of party politics; it is a question of emancipation from everything that is disgraceful and rotten.[95]

Wilson gave the White campaign a splendid dose of political revivalism, inviting the voters of Atlantic City to join the ranks of American manhood by throwing off the yoke of bossism. But despite his eloquence, White and the rest of the fusion candidates were soundly defeated.[96]

To the *Press*, the result was "Vindication" for the Republican organization. To Thomas it was "Vice Triumphant." "We are a city controlled by gamblers, guided by rascals, devoid of conscience, and the people do not want it otherwise." The "deplorable result" had three causes: apathy, repeaters and "the willingness of colored voters to swing with the side that offered the profit. It was settled yesterday that the colored vote is as purchasable as it has been in the past years of degradation."[97] The *Newark Evening Call* agreed: "Atlantic City elected some bad men to public office last Tuesday because there are a majority of men in that town who want bad conditions to rule on account of the money there is in it. . . . The city seems to choose to be indecent. Very well then, let it stew in its own filth. Decent people will stay away and the city will go bankrupt."[98] Neither gloating nor recrimination explained the political failure of reform in Atlantic City. In Bacharach and Robert Ingersoll, the Republican candidate for sheriff, the organization had presented fresh faces. Neither had ever been associated with the Kuehnle faction, and Bacharach was later cleared of election violations. Despite the rantings of the reform press, the election was not a mandate for graft, election frauds, and commercial vice. Nor was it a mandate for Kuehnle. Class conflict, censorship, and Sunday closing were the vital issues for the white electorate in the election of 1911. Black voters, having been written off by the White ticket, merely chose between the lesser of two evils. The divisions in the city remained essentially as they had been since 1908. The result was a repudiation of Harvey Thomas and the beachfront.

Despite the defeat, trials for graft and election frauds kept the reform pot boiling. On December 23 a struck jury convicted Kuehnle of conflict of interest in a water main project, and in January he was fined a thousand dollars and sentenced to a year at hard labor at the state prison. Kuehnle was the chairman of the water commission and a stockholder and vice president of the United Paving Company. For five years that company had a practical monopoly on paving contracts in the city. The president of the company, William Cherry, came to the city from Tennessee in 1906 as an agent of the Warren Brothers Company, a firm holding the patent on the "bitulithic process" for street paving, then seen as an alternative to dealing with the "Asphalt Trust." The United Paving Company was formed locally, and a number of local people held stock, including Kuehnle and Walter Evans Edge. All of the city's contracts specified bitulithic, and under this arrangement, Cherry secured the material cheaply from Warren Brothers and United underbid its competitors for the street contracts.[99]

In November 1909, the city awarded the water main contract to one Frank Lockwood, a New York contractor who later assigned it to the United Paving Company. The trial revealed that Lockwood and Cherry were connected and that Lockwood's bills were paid by United. Kuehnle denied any knowledge of the subterfuge, but there could be no doubt that, at least technically, he was in conflict of interest. On that basis he was convicted and sent to prison.

Cherry was a known gambler and a high liver. To Thomas, Kuehnle was a common thief, but many in the city believed that Kuehnle, ever a trusting soul, was the victim of Cherry's greed. The United Paving Company quickly collapsed, and Cherry left town. Kuehnle personally made good all of the company's notes which, according to Thomas, cost him $75,000. With his conviction, Kuehnle resigned as director of the Marine Trust Company, but the board refused to accept it. Said the editor of the *Gazette*, "Kuehnle convicted and sentenced is a bigger man today than his little enemies who are crowing over his misfortune."[100]

In March, Kuehnle, awaiting the results of an appeal, was tendered a testimonial banquet by the Young Men's Republican League. Over six hundred people attended, including some of the city's most reputable citizens. Kuehnle's former adversary, Joseph Salus, brought the audience to its feet with the following: "When the roll of fame of the most sturdy among us is unfolded, the name of Kuehnle must lead all the rest. He is the peer among the pioneers of our town. . . . I question if the resort ever needed more men of his type than she does today." To complete the flowery tribute, they presented Kuehnle an album, embossed in gold, which was curiously apologetic in tone.

> You have always been a sincere friend, ever ready to sacrifice your personal interests in the sacred cause of friendship. Yet friendship, like gold may be tested. Though clouds may hover and lightning flash and storms rage that would malignantly menace your well dressed reputation for Truth and Honesty, we would still regard your honor and integrity as being above reproach. . . . As you read our signatures on the following pages, kindly forget our shortcomings and try to recall even some little act that would entitle us to subscribe ourselves Your Sincere Friends.[101]

Was this a banquet of thieves or was Kuehnle a martyr? The gathering included individuals who were later convicted of graft and election frauds but also many who survived the intensive investigations of the reform movement with their reputations intact. The two Bacharachs and Walter Evans Edge were conspicuous by their absence from the tribute. To a number of local Republicans, the Commodore had become a pariah.

Meanwhile, in 1912, reform proceeded along other lines. Soon after his election, Mayor Bacharach closed the gambling houses in the city which, including the Northside establishments, came to forty-six in number. But somehow Dutchy Muhlrad, Bob Delaney, and one Al Marsten, another who catered to an exclusive clientele, escaped the sweep. In July, the mayor quickly squelched a plan for Sunday baseball, warning that the police would close the game and arrest everyone concerned. The bars remained closed on Sunday as seventy-two hotelmen pled guilty to Sunday sales and paid fines of $200 each.[102]

The reform movement had little effect on the tenderloin. An incident in January revealed a close working relationship between the police and prostitutes. Approached by a white slaver, a tenderloin proprietress went to the police and Detective Herbert set a trap for the culprit. The case created a national sensation, and the department received a commendation from the Justice Department in Washington. Later, the federal authorities offered Herbert a position setting up similar systems in cities where "vice conditions were horrible and traffickers in White Slavery flourished unmolested."[103]

The passage of the Walsh Act, in April 1911, gave New Jersey cities the opportunity to adopt the commission form of government. Commission government promised to eliminate the boss and the ward healer from city politics and put municipal affairs on a sound businesslike basis. A number of cities, most notably Trenton, had adopted the plan, and, by 1912, many in Atlantic City saw commission government as an answer to the city's problems.

While the Walsh Act was being debated in the legislature, Kuehnle spoke in favor of it. A survey of leading business and hotelmen, including Kuehnle, done by the *Press* in August 1911 found none opposed. Immediately after his endorsement for mayor by the organization, Harry Bacharach made a strong statement in favor of the plan. The *Press* agreed: "This plan of placing municipal machinery on a business-like basis making it entirely responsible to the people and wiping out factionalism which has made this resort a hotbed of sensationalism for years, will likely be received today with general enthusiasm."[104]

It took only one day to obtain the required two thousand signatures on a petition to hold the referendum. But on May 14, in a low turnout, the city adopted commission government by a scant 122 votes. Thomas charged that Kuehnle had quietly tried to kill it and that its opponents "had the backing of every colored gambler and blackleg in the city with their white allies who abound in the back section." The *Gazette* reported that the organization had supported the plan and, in doing so, may have "dug its own grave."[105]

By June, fifty-four candidates had filed to become one of the five commissioners. One P. J. Hawkins, a black physician, polled 2,354 votes in the primary, providing an accurate statistic of black voting strength in the city.[106] In the general election, in July, the voters elected five commissioners: William Riddle, Dr. J. B. Thompson, Harry Bacharach, William H. Bartlett, and Albert Beyer. Riddle, Bartlett, and Beyer had been endorsed by the organization, but none were organization men as such. The body elected Riddle as mayor, and the city prepared for a new era in municipal government.

But there remained the final, most sensational phase of the reform movement. On the eve of the primary elections, Councilmen Phoebus, Malia, Kessler, and Lane confessed to taking bribes, and all resigned in disgrace. The four had been caught in an elaborate sting operation conducted by the famed detective William J. Burns. "Atlantic City is the most corrupt municipality I ever worked in," said Burns. It was "easy, almost amusing" the way the grafters went after the bait. "I want to make it plain that the people behind this movement are in deadly earnest and they are going to wipe out all forms of corruption that exist in Atlantic City."[107]

By 1912 Burns enjoyed an international reputation, and he did not work cheaply. He had collared the McNamara brothers, the Los Angeles dynamiters, and gotten the goods on Abraham Ruef in San Francisco and on municipal grafters in Seattle, St. Louis, Pittsburgh, and a score of other cities. The Boardwalk hotelmen had hired Burns in April 1910 to, in Thomas's words, "make a thorough probe of Atlantic City's political corruption and municipal thievery." After a year's investigation, Burns had nothing more than rumors.[108]

In July 1911, at a meeting with Harvey Thomas and Attorney General Wilson, Burns proposed the scheme that entrapped the councilmen. They secured the services of James K. Howard, the noted New York architect and engineer, to draw up plans for a concrete esplanade to replace the wooden Boardwalk. The project, worth more than a million dollars, was easily the biggest thing the city had ever contemplated and constituted lucrative bait for small-town politicians. Burns sent to San Francisco for James Harris, one of his detectives who had posed as a contractor in trapping Ruef. Harris, now of the fictitious New York firm of Harris and Henderson, set up sumptuous headquarters in the Marlboro-Blenheim and at the Waldorf Astoria and had each room wired with a dictaphone that led to a concealed stenographer. Harris broadcast the scheme, let it be known that there was $5,000 in it for each councilman, and arranged the payoffs through a bogus millionaire backer named Francklyn, who was really one Frank Smiley, another Burns detective.[109]

Harris first contacted W. J. Palmer, a local realtor whom he plied with drinks and dinners and who boasted of his friendship with Kuehnle, Edge, and Mayor Bacharach. Palmer said that the right money could easily push the scheme through council. But Kuehnle, said Palmer, was "an expensive piece of furniture" and was anyway under indictment. Harris could save a great deal by going directly to the councilmen. Palmer led Harris to Councilman Samuel Phoebus, who ran a small hotel and chaired the Boardwalk Committee. From Burns's standpoint, the operation went off without a hitch. Phoebus jumped at the bait and Howard made a number of appearances before the Boardwalk Committee. At least nine councilmen received bribes in numbered gold certificates, and in the following March, the ordinance passed Council by a vote of thirteen to three. But Mayor Bacharach, having no knowledge of the scam, vetoed it. Phoebus told Harris that the veto would cost him at least an additional thousand dollars, but by now Burns had all the evidence he needed.[110]

The recorded interviews that Harris had with Palmer, Phoebus, Kessler, and others made sensational reading but provided conflicting and often contradictory evidence, not only as to levels of graft in the city, but also its sources, particularly in regard to Louis Kuehnle. From the beginning Harris repeatedly steered the conversation toward Kuehnle but was told either that Kuehnle was too expensive or that he had lost his power. According to Palmer, "the boys" were glad that Kuehnle had been convicted because he had been "hoggish and the boys got very little." "That fact" (Kuehnle's conviction), said Harris, "seemed to please Phoebus immensely" because it "kept Kuehnle out of the divvy." Said Phoebus, "He is worse than Croker. . . . If Kuehnle got a line on this Boardwalk thing—like on all the others—he would tell the boys what to do, and it would go through without taking care of those who do the voting." Kuehnle and the United Paving Company supposedly reaped $100,000 on a storm drain project—an astronomical sum—but, again according to Phoebus, "Kuehnle got his, but they haven't shown us a nickel."[111]

On another occasion, Phoebus told Harris that Councilman William Malia was "a clever grafter and generally framed up all the deals in the past years where money was needed to pass bills." According to a sworn affidavit given to Burns by Kessler, Kuehnle's cousin, Malia had sent Kessler to Kuehnle to see about graft payments on the storm drain project, but Kuehnle said, "That is up to Cherry."[112] Harris's own investigation revealed the following about Kuehnle, Cherry, and the storm drain project:

> I had been told that certain work done for the city by the United Paving Company and Cherry has been unsatisfactory and payment has been refused. Cherry owes $30,000 to a man named Comiskey for material and has been pressed for it.
>
> Comiskey, being anxious for his money, decided to go to Kuehnle and was told, so I learn from good authority, that he, Kuehnle, would see that he was paid; that he did not want the city to pay Cherry for the work and would guarantee payment himself. Kuehnle told Comiskey that he was through with Cherry.[113]

The Burns operation created a veritable feeding frenzy among the councilmen. John Murtland, holding out for more money, said: "I am as expensive as Kuehnle." But in the wake of the confessions, the worst that Thomas could say of Kuehnle was the following: "While Kuehnle had no part in the Boardwalk graft, it is not denied by the quartette who have just confessed that *he knew* [italics mine] of drainage graft. He did not discountenance graft in this instance."[114] Kuehnle was certainly no reformer, but if anything, Harris had Kuehnle in the role of safeguarding the interests of the city against a conniving and dissolute Cherry.

How deeply was graft embedded within the city government? A cornered Phoebus offered the following in his own defense:

> I only did what practically everybody did in council at one time or another and can honestly say that I never realized the enormity of the offense. . . . I blame my downfall and that of my colleagues in City Council on the fact that it has been generally understood that Councilmen who served without pay must "get theirs" out of the contracts and other jobs that were handed out to favor people. It seemed so easy to take this money that it was hard for any man to refuse. It got so that anybody who wanted anything "saw" somebody, but in many cases we Councilmen did not get a cent.[115]

Phoebus had served in council only since 1910, and, by his own account, pickings had been slim. Prior to the improvements begun in 1906 with the letting of the paving contracts there would have been little in municipal graft to begin with aside from gambling and liquor licenses, and even that appears to have been limited. Paving and storm drains created new opportunities for the local small-town politicos, but graft had never been an issue in the reform movement.

In June, Woodrow Wilson, visiting the city, pronounced the Burns operation and the entire reform movement "wholesome work." By the end of 1912 many results of reform in Atlantic City gladdened the hearts of Progressives in New Jersey. Kuehnle was destined for prison, and Wilson for the White House. Six of the councilmen had confessed to taking bribes and resigned in disgrace. The new administration kept the bars closed on Sunday and even suppressed gambling. Dutchy Muhlrad was finally corralled by a Burns detective, and his indictment ended his twenty-year career in Atlantic City. The "machine" was destroyed, and the city now had commission government. A Democrat defeated John Gardner for reelection to Congress in November; the sweep was thorough, or so it appeared, and little remained of the old order

The new order was signaled in *Atlantic City Commission Government*, a municipal journal published by the city.

> Ignorance and indifference has made possible the shame of the cities. Business and professional men took no interest nor part in politics because

they were too busy in the first place, and because it was "not respectable" in the second. Political rings, dominated by political Bosses, was the inevitable result. And these political rings and Bosses have controlled the cities. As political Bosses, any more than industrial Bosses, do not work from a love of it, they "got theirs" by looting the cities. That has been the old order. The dawn of a new era has broken.[116]

By 1913, a new era had indeed dawned in Atlantic City and in the United States. On March 3, Louis Kuehnle lost his final appeal before the New Jersey Supreme Court. On the following day, Wilson became president. What exactly was the relationship between these two events?

The movement which resulted in Kuehnle's downfall was, in one sense, a bizarre and isolated episode in the annals of Progressive reform. It began as a factional struggle within a Republican organization in a small American city and as a reaction to Fort's Saturnalia proclamation in 1908. Stoy's reelection that November meant that the Old Town interests, although not Kuehnle, controlled the organization. Sunday baseball and the riot further inflamed tensions between the two groups. In the fall of 1909, the Boardwalk faction formed the People's organization and mounted a political struggle for control of the city, framing the issues in terms of the national Progressive movement. The failure of that effort caused the beachfront to resort to more drastic measures.

Burns was hired in April 1910 to conduct what was essentially a fishing expedition. By Thomas's own account, a year's investigation produced no evidence of corruption on Kuehnle or anyone else. The Boardwalk faction then purchased the *Review* and placed it in the hands of Harvey Thomas. The Wilson campaign and the corrupt election of 1910 were windfalls for the movement. Wilson's great success in 1910, and in 1912, lay in his ability to articulate the issues in terms of the Progressive groundswell that was sweeping the state and the nation. Thomas wrote the assembly resolution that brought the Macksey Commission to Atlantic City. It is doubtful that anyone could have been more adept at maximizing the effects of its revelations.

Up to this point, Wilson had no role in the events in Atlantic City. In a letter written to the governor-elect on January 10, 1911, Thomas practically introduced himself to Wilson and laid out in brief the whole story of the reform movement.[117] The Wilson intervention took the form of the elisor grand jury, an innovation apparently devised by his attorney general, Edmund Wilson. This took place in the spring and summer of 1911 and became the decisive measure in bringing down Kuehnle and the "machine." Throughout that year, Wilson lent his growing prestige to the movement, and, in November, spoke vigorously on behalf of the Boardwalk fusion ticket. That effort came to naught, as the beachfront was soundly defeated at the polls. Meanwhile, the Burns detectives were quietly conducting the Boardwalk sting put together by Burns, Thomas, and Assistant Attorney General Nelson B. Gaskill that June. This provided a sensational finale to the reform movement in 1912, but did no further damage to Kuehnle. There is no evidence that Thomas enjoyed Wilson's personal confidence, but throughout this period he worked closely with members of the administration and carefully orchestrated developments to the maximum benefit of both Wilson and the reform movement.

By the spring of 1912, the Wilson presidential boom was well under way, but the nomination campaign was in trouble. By the eve of the Baltimore convention in June, Wilson's chief rival, Speaker of the House of Representatives Champ Clark of Missouri, had twice as many delegates as Wilson, and campaign funds were running low. James Kerney related that in May a worried William F. McCombs, Wilson's campaign manager, returning from an unsatisfactory canvas of national Democratic leaders, dispatched the candidate to Chicago to shore up the Wilson forces in the Illinois delegation. Desperate for funds, Wilson, on the train to Chicago, wired Harvey Thomas, who immediately gathered $6,000 from the Boardwalk hotelmen and turned it over to McCombs.[118] The Illinois delegation later turned the tables from Clark to Wilson on the forty-second ballot and paved the way for the nomination.[119]

Even if, as Kerney said, the funds came at a critical time for the Wilson campaign, this incident provides only an interesting sidelight to the story of Wilson's meteoric rise to the presidency. The symbiosis between Wilson and Thomas had to do with what Wilson later, in an international context, would call "moral suasion."

In addition to the quarter of a million dollars spent by McCombs to secure the triumph at Baltimore, he spent large sums to keep afloat the failing *Trenton True American* for the purpose of booming the Wilson candidacy. Its publisher, Harry Alexander, faithfully chronicled Wilson's political and legislative achievements in New Jersey and each week sent from five to ten thousand copies to "good Democrats" all over the country.[120] The lurid copy that appeared on the pages of the *Review* was picked up, almost to the letter, by the *True American* and by other Wilson organs, with the result that the Atlantic City affair was trumpeted throughout the nation.

As Governor Fort had found in 1908, the issues dividing Kuehnle from the beachfront would not carry a reform movement in a cosmopolitan city or an urbanized state like New Jersey. By painting the picture of a city in the thrall of gamblers, prostitutes, and saloon keepers, of a machine sustained by black votes, and of a hotbed of corruption in the process of redemption by a fearless and crusading governor, he struck the most responsive chords of the swelling Progressive refrain.

But we should not overestimate his success. Thomas was but one of a great chorus of voices that propelled Wilson to the White House. He was brought to Atlantic City and given a newspaper, not to boom Wilson, but to conduct a political movement within the city, an effort that was not successful. This is not surprising. The journalism of exposure and the symbiotic relationship Thomas created between the beachfront and the Wilson campaign may have been the best chance for a political movement mounted by a wealthy minority in a small American city during the Progressive era. But he alienated large segments of the voting population, particularly the Northside. Thomas harmonized well with the national Progressive movement, but he did not tell the whole truth.

CHAPTER SEVEN

Pharisees and Hypocrites

"I would rather see the people happy, tangoing on the beach," said Mayor William Riddle in January 1915, "than to take a certificate from the ministers and the hotelkeepers' association that I had a passport to Heaven for being a hypocrite."[1] "Riddleism" was now the enemy in the great American resort. A year later, the embattled mayor went down to defeat at the hands of a coalition consisting of the beachfront, the evangelicals, the regular Republican organization, including Louis Kuehnle and the black Northside, a combination that would have been unthinkable only four years earlier. The municipal election of 1916 ended Riddle's thirty-year political career in Atlantic City and marked the resort's final effort to come to terms with its image during the Progressive era. Ironically, Riddle's defeat brought about a political realignment within the city that paved the way for the rise of Enoch L. Johnson and the eventual realization of the worst fears of the reformers.

By 1916, Atlantic City had gone through its third season with the "lid down." The bars remained closed on Sunday, censorship was stricter on the Boardwalk, and local police were now working closely with the county prosecutor to eliminate gambling. Liquor licenses were curtailed, and the commission had given the city efficient and scandal-free government. More importantly, Progressive reform left in its wake a new consensus among the contending factions within the city that promised an end to the bitter conflict between the beachfront and the Old Town interests and the restoration of the resort's tarnished image. The resort emerged from its recent ordeal as Caesar's wife, a city that needed to be beyond reproach.

In 1913, the Methodist Conference rejoiced that Atlantic County now had a sheriff who was willing to enforce the laws of the state. The rigid enforcement of the Sunday liquor laws caused no falling off in the numbers of visitors. But in December, Mayor Riddle estimated the aggregate loss of revenue to resort business people at over a million dollars. Commissioner Joseph B. Thompson of the Chelsea Hotel, one of twelve large houses on the Boardwalk, estimated his own loss for the year at $15,000, and others reported declines in revenue from the previous year as high as $30,000. "Scores of cottagers," said Thompson, "have gone to Cape May and other resorts where the Sunday laws are not enforced."[2]

Many in the city, particularly the Boardwalk hotelmen, found the benefits of Sunday closing well worth the price. The dire predictions of economic disaster made by John J. White to the Excise Commission in 1908 had not come to pass, except in the excursion district. For many of the working-class cabarets and saloons, the denial of the Sunday excursion trade meant failure; two notorious saloons were renovated into ice cream parlors. Within four years, a Philadelphia corporation had secretly purchased a five-block section along the beachfront from Arkansas to Florida avenues, and plans were afoot to raze "the Bowery" to make way for luxury hotels and apartment houses.[3] Compliance with the law meant welcome relief from the perennial Sunday wars that had plagued the resort since 1890. Reluctant converts to the cause of dry Sundays, both the beachfront and the Republican organization now embraced it as a matter of public policy.

But the issue was far from settled. After a year in office, Mayor Riddle was determined to submit the Sunday question to the voters. The municipal elections were three years away, but by the end of 1913 Riddle was already laying the groundwork for his campaign. With Kuehnle in prison, the way appeared clear to revive the old Republican organization under his own leadership by exploiting the bitter divisions of the reform movement. For fifty years, said Riddle, the city had kept faith with the working classes under the liberal policy. The practice was condoned "even by the church element, . . . except for the few who constituted themselves the keepers of their brothers' conscience. . . . This was the condition when a political war broke out—a war of sordid, selfish, political vengeance, reprisal, and self-seeking. It was successful to the point of bringing about a closed Sunday and jeopardizing the future prosperity of the resort."[4] Standing squarely with the masses, Riddle declared that the majority should rule. But there could be "no return to the old order. . . . The remedy must be found in legislation, and the times are propitious to seek it."

More articulate but less cautious than Kuehnle, Riddle had essentially staked out the same territory as Kuehnle had in 1909 with the introduction of Sunday baseball. But by 1914, the state legislature was no more disposed toward liberalizing the Sunday laws than it was in 1909. As the session opened in January, the Essex and Hudson delegations, backed by the New Jersey Liquor Dealers Association, introduced a number of bills easing or repealing Sunday restrictions. Taken together, the bills for a "liberal Sunday," six in all, proposed to legalize baseball and other "clean sports," motion pictures and theatricals, and the sale of liquor after 1 P.M. under local option. Legislators also introduced the perennial Raines Law bill which allowed hotels to serve liquor to guests on Sunday with meals. Protestant churches from Camden to Jersey City mobilized to fight the measures, and the hearings on Sunday closing promised to be as contentious as they were in 1909.[5]

"The forces of good government will be represented in the State House by Atlantic City," wrote Harvey Thomas, as Boardwalk hotelmen Henry Leeds and Albert T. Bell, and the Reverend Birney Hudson of the Lord's Day Alliance, left for Trenton in March to testify against the Sunday bills. Hudson announced, and Leeds and Bell agreed, that the fifty-year reign of anarchy in Atlantic City was over. A new policy was now in effect, and Sunday closing had "hurt no business but the saloon business." Mayor Riddle was not a party to the new policy. Like Stoy in 1908, he testified that Sunday laws amounted to no more than class legislation and were destroying the boardinghouse and small hotel keepers who were the "bone and sinew" of Atlantic City.[6]

Riddle's testimony was a futile gesture. Of the Sunday bills, only the baseball measure was reported out of committee, but it never reached a vote in the senate. The county delegation, Senator Edge and Assemblymen Carlton Godfrey and Emerson Richards, were noncommittal. Yet Richards, a protégé of Kuehnle, had to admit that "it was odd, to say the least, that in view of the strenuous efforts of former years to procure 'liberal legislation,' the license forces of Atlantic City are . . . making no move at this time." The legislature was filled with hypocrites, said Riddle: "The members come down to Atlantic City and drink with me and then come back here and are afraid to vote for personal liberty." Riddle later added: "If Christ came to Atlantic City, he would be in favor of an open Sunday. After all, he was a good fellow who turned water into wine."[7]

A new compact was indeed in effect in Atlantic City in 1914, and it reflected the reform agenda of the Boardwalk interests. Even the *Press* "cheerfully and enthusiastically" subscribed to the "new Atlantic City policy," which was probably the strictest in the state, at least among the urban centers in terms of the enforcement of gambling and liquor laws. The brothels on North Carolina Avenue continued to operate discreetly, but an incident in January 1914 rekindled the prostitution issue and brought into sharper focus the conflicts and anxieties that lay at the heart of Progressive reform in Atlantic City.

A guest at the Marlboro-Blenheim Hotel had spent an evening at Minnie Wilson's establishment in the tenderloin and ran up a liquor bill of $27.50. The proprietress complained to Detective Herbert, who went to the hotel and attempted to collect the bill. When the affair became public on January 3, Reverend Hudson formed the "Ministerial Union" and announced a "war against the tenderloin." Herbert, who in 1912 had earned for himself and the city a federal commendation for his management of prostitution, was fired. Most in the city probably agreed with Mayor Riddle, who pointed out that "there have been women of that character since the beginning of time. Close them up and they scatter." But Hudson declared that segregation was a failure, and Public Safety Commissioner Bartlett and Chief Woodruff reluctantly closed the tenderloin.[8]

The reform initiative was now in the hands of the evangelicals. On January 14, Hudson and the Ministerial Union announced the formation of the Vice Commission, which would act in concert with city officials in "suppressing immoral houses and all crimes against morality and decency, including questionable amusements." The president of the commission, the Reverend Newton Cadwell, declared: "We will see that the lid is kept on the city's moral cesspool." Judge John J. White, smarting from the recent embarrassment at his Marlboro-Blenheim Hotel, in a much celebrated speech to the local YMCA declared that the sporting element was not necessary to Atlantic City. "Vice ruined Long Branch and Saratoga, and it may be fairly said that wherever it has become dominant, it has brought ruin."[9]

Between 1900 and 1912, the Boardwalk hotelmen had kept a prudent distance between themselves and the evangelicals, often ridiculing their efforts. Now both factions spoke in unison. William F. Hanstein, the president of the Atlantic City Hotel Men's Association, clarified the new reform agenda. "Now that we have stopped Sunday liquor sales, abated gambling, and closed our red light district, . . . it is time we started on a constructive program." The task at hand was to "get rid of tangoism . . . and improve the class and character of resort amusements." This would be accomplished by an Amusement Board operating under the following guidelines: "High grade music along the lines of the Philadelphia Orchestra, frequent recitals and concerts, educational entertainment in the way of the Chautauqua, lectures by well-known speakers, religious features, and a fine arts exhibition where good paintings and sculpture could be shown by the artists."[10] The elimination of working-class amusements had always been a thinly disguised objective of the beachfront interests, and part of that program was already in effect. Police were routing palmists and fakirs from the Boardwalk. Commissioner Bartlett now censured motion pictures, and a theater manager who advertised a "sacred concert," but added that nothing was sacred to him, was summarily shut down. But more remained to be done. The conduct of the bathers on the beach, said Hanstein, was "worse than the tango."[11]

Neither the Vice Commission nor the Amusement Board was ever formalized. The former reflected the morality-oriented campaign of the evangelicals, and the latter the class-oriented goals of the beachfront. But Harvey Thomas skillfully merged the two into a stringent and coherent reform policy. On January 19, in a front-page exposé, he listed the thirty-two known disorderly houses in the city, along with the names and addresses of the owners and mortgage holders of the properties.[12] He followed editorially with a stinging biblical rebuke of the profiteers and concluded with "A Mother's Appeal," a letter culled from many on file. The letter, composed of equal parts of racism and religion, urged Thomas to take a stand against the "Tango" and the "Turkey Trot" and concluded: "Help us, Mr. Thomas, and you will have the prayers of hundreds of mothers who are almost crazy with the awful outlook for their daughters. Such disgraceful afternoons and evenings as the Nigger Gink dance brings is beyond understanding. . . . God give you strength to help us."[13] More fallen girls had graduated from the cafes and piers than the "Shady District" ever saw, wrote another concerned citizen. "North Carolina Avenue collected them, but the cafes are manufacturing them."

Thomas made no apology for the "Mother's Appeal," instead describing the correspondent as a businesswoman who was "well known socially." Signed "One Who Has Suffered," the letter was chosen because it rang with "sincerity" and "vital feeling." On this point, Thomas was correct. If he recognized few rules, Thomas was adept at plumbing the depths of race and class anxiety that fueled reform in Atlantic City and infusing these feelings with the moral fervor and secular respectability that Progressivism required.

An objective observer of Atlantic City in 1914 may have briefly wondered who the Progressives really were. The year before, with the advent of commission government, Riddle accompanied Rudolf Blankenburg of Philadelphia and a number of other reform mayors to the "shrine of the Wisconsin idea," the university at Madison. He returned much impressed with the state's educational system and limited franchise laws. He had appointed James T. Bourne, a black druggist, to the Board of Education. In February he made a statement endorsing women's suffrage and published a letter he had written to Booker T. Washington requesting a copy of the curriculum to be implemented at the "Indiana Avenue School for Colored Children." But in the same breath, he declared himself "unqualifiedly in favor of the liberal Sunday," and wanted it distinctly understood that "he was not in favor of having the Ministerial Union run the city."[14]

Riddle had also been to Monte Carlo. Later that month, he outlined his own vision for Atlantic City in an interview with the *Philadelphia Public Ledger*. "People come here to enjoy themselves, and they desire refreshments on Sunday." He noted that a grand jury in Hudson County had refused to indict saloon keepers because, as they publicly stated, "public sentiment was in favor of selling liquor on Sunday." As things stood now, Atlantic City was practically the only city in the state that was dry on the Sabbath. If the legislature would amend the Walsh Act to give the cities wider home rule, 90 percent of the residents would vote for an open Sunday. "And why shouldn't they? A closed Sunday means a loss of $500,000 a season."[15]

Puffing on a cigar, Riddle warmed to his topic: "Why not a Monte Carlo? I would love to see it . . . a fine place, with the tables tested every morning, would be great, and certainly not as bad as the stock market. I would be there every night." Having declared for legalized gambling, Riddle went on to endorse regulated prostitution. The city had closed the red light district only because Herbert, who was both a city detective and a government agent, tried to collect a bill in Judge White's hotel. In an obvious reference to the evangelicals and the beachfront, Riddle said the resort was now controlled by "fanatics" and "hypocrites."

Riddle was a whimsical character, but he was no buffoon. Wealthy, learned, and well-read, he was, from all accounts, a devoted family man of temperate habits and refined tastes. His views on reformers, Sunday closing, and prostitution amounted to nothing more than those openly or tacitly agreed to by resort politicians for more than twenty-five years. His Monte Carlo comment, probably unguarded, took up only four sentences of a lengthy interview, but when it was published, on February 24, the article featured a large picture of the mayor with the headline, "U.S. Monte Carlo Is Mayor's Dream For Atlantic City. Municipal Gaming Tables, Wide Open Sunday, and Plenty of Whoop-la to Attract Visitors Urged."

On the following day, a petition was circulated for Riddle's recall, and a delegation of nine Boardwalk hotelmen entrained for Philadelphia to assure the editor and the publisher of the *Ledger* that Riddle spoke only for himself. "We know Mayor Riddle here," said H. B. Cook of the Seaside Hotel, "and do not take him seriously." Both Reverend Cadwell of The Vice Commission and Harvey Thomas saw Riddle as "the City's Arch Enemy." "The moral depravity of the mayor," proclaimed the *Review*, "has been revealed to its fullest." Riddle was "insane for publicity," a "misfit in City Hall," and his attitude toward decency "had always been a recognized shame."[16]

Such comments from the beachfront, the clergy, and the *Review* were to be expected, but support for Riddle's recall also came from other quarters. Bank president Sigmund Ojserkis, who had for a time managed Kuehnle's hotel, stated: "We are for sanity and consistency . . . and cannot for a minute sanction such statements as are credited to the Mayor." Samuel Comely, president of the Fourth Ward Businessmen's Association (the Fourth was Riddle's ward), was leading the recall movement, and Joseph McNamee, another Kuehnle associate and president of the Chamber of Commerce, declared that body unanimous in repudiating Riddle's utterances.[17] Each of these protests came from members of the Old Town faction of the Republican organization.

Interviewed in Trenton, Assemblyman Richards characterized the Riddle proposal as "assininity, pure and simple." Senator Edge, already maneuvering for the Republican gubernatorial nomination, said it was "absolutely ridiculous," but declined to comment on its specifics. "It is outbursts of this type," said Edge, "which interfere with the city's progress and desire to become a meeting place for clean, law-abiding, health-seeking people." In the city, special prayer services were held for Riddle, one clergyman stating: "If the Mayor worked as hard for God as he worked for the devil, there would be wonderful developments for better things here."[18] "The progress of the city," so long the bone of contention between the beachfront and the Old Town interests, had come to mean the same thing to both factions. The evangelicals as well had become civic boosters, as Progressive reform found both meaning and unity in opposition to Riddle.

Perhaps purposefully, but probably unwittingly, Riddle had made himself the issue. In doing so, he tapped feelings that ran as deeply among the working-class voters as the middle-class anxieties so cleverly exploited by Harvey Thomas. But the press reported no outpouring of public sentiment in support of Riddle. In a carefully prepared statement, he toned down his position on gambling.

> Of course, there are some things in the *Ledger* article that I did say, but I never expressed the desire that Atlantic City should become like Monte Carlo because I do not think that the American people want universal gambling the same as obtains in some European resorts. I think it is wrong to interfere with people who want to play an innocent game of pinochle and gather at a cigar store to have this innocent amusement. I think it is hopeless to expect that we shall ever cause the negro to lose his love for crap.[19]

If the statement assuaged some of the white voters, it no doubt nullified the gestures that Riddle had made to the Northside.

The *Ledger* article set the tone for another intense political conflict in Atlantic City, but initially both sides were dealing in impossibilities. Riddle knew full well that the legislature would not amend the Walsh Act to permit Sunday liquor sales, much less legalized gambling, and the anti-Riddle forces were aware that the recall petition had no basis in law. "Recall? I should worry," said Riddle, "most of these people didn't vote for me anyhow, and I don't owe them anything but good will."[20] But the Boardwalk hotelmen were indeed worried. The Riddle movement, though seeming to consist only of Riddle himself, threatened to undo the previous reform movement and return the city to the stormy and unsavory conflicts that occurred under the liberal policy. The Old Town interests had no desire to see their old political enemy construct a new organization on the ruins of the old one. The likelihood of the city again besieged by the evangelicals did not bode well for Edge's gubernatorial ambitions. As he later noted in a rare moment of candor, the previous reform movement was a "lesson in pressure politics; when you are assailed by the forces of organized righteousness, always roll with the punch."[21] To the evangelicals, the mayor was "Riddle the Apostate" and "Pontius Pilate," a man who would pander to the worst instincts of the people to achieve political power.

Louis Kuehnle spent the winter and spring of 1914 in prison, and he must have viewed developments in the city with satisfaction. In charge of a convict gang at the prison gate, he maintained a cheerful disposition and was popular with the deputies and the inmates. In January he was unanimously reelected to the board of directors of the Atlantic City Fire Insurance Company. In April the *Trenton Times* reported that Kuehnle was scheduled for release in June, after serving six months of his sentence, and noted that he would return to a city made "cleaner and drier" by his absence. Supporters made plans for a triumphal reentry for the Commodore, complete with a parade and a banquet. But Kuehnle declared, "I am out of politics," and canceled the tribute. When he was released on June 5, his dog Jerry was quietly bundled onto a boat and went into temporary seclusion with Kuehnle at his cabin on the meadows at Little Beach.[22]

During Kuehnle's stay in prison, most of Atlantic City was indeed drier, at least on Sundays, but it was apparently no cleaner. In August, the Ministerial Union complained that the behavior of the bathers on the beach on Sundays was disgusting. Indecently clad, they "dance the tango on the sands when sacred music is being played." Closed for a two-month period, the tenderloin establishments began to reopen as "lodging houses," and the *Review* reported: "The old time procession of cabs and autos bearing noisy males to the Red Light territory is nightly assuming an extent that provokes one conclusion."[23] Unlicensed, the tenderloin establishments were the easiest places to obtain drinks after midnight on Saturday and must have reaped a Sabbath bonanza.

In 1915, the Ministerial Union threatened the mayor and Commissioner Bartlett with criminal prosecution for failing to close the disorderly houses. Riddle replied: "How strange it is that I have heard no criticism at all on this subject, except from you. . . . It is mine to laugh when you threaten me with criminal prosecution, for I have as much regard for Pharisees and hypocrites as it is possible to have when one tries to follow the teachings of Christ and is charitable. Christ suffered much and had a very poor opinion of this sort."[24] The Ministerial Union declared that prostitutes had become "bolder than ever," but that is doubtful. Throughout 1914 and 1915, the Democratic county prosecutor, Charles S. Moore, assisted by local police, continued to harry gamblers from the resort but raided the tenderloin only once. Prostitutes operating outside of the district were summarily arrested, and during the war police conducted raids within the district in response to isolated outrages. But apparently all of the factions in the city, with the exception of the evangelicals, agreed with Riddle that segregation remained the best solution to the problem of prostitution. The Reverend Newton Cadwell of the Vice Commission blamed the "supporters of Sunday baseball" and complained that "the better element of citizenhood," blind to the evil, had "tossed another wrap of decency to the winds."[25] The two-block section of North Carolina Avenue served as the red-light district of Atlantic City for at least another decade.

Neither reform nor the war in Europe had much effect on the number of visitors. The summer crowds became larger, and the city began doing a brisk year-round convention trade. Already there was talk of building a large municipal convention hall. John J. White saw the war as a "great opportunity." Atlantic City had no rival in the United States. The only real competitor was Europe, but "that is impossible now, and may remain so for years to come." The time had come to make Atlantic City the entertainment capital of the world by offering the attractions suggested by Hanstein the year before. When asked if finer entertainment could compete with ragtime and "other crazes of the moment," he said that this was no problem. There was a taste for better things, such as Caruso, but since people came for relaxation, "grand opera may be a little too heavy." Said Riddle, "The middle class is no longer welcome here."[26] As the election of 1916 drew nearer, news of the war and of impending American involvement did not diminish the city's preoccupation with "Riddleism."

In March 1915 and January 1916, the Boardwalk hotelmen sponsored religious revivals on the Boardwalk, and hundreds prayed for the soul of the errant mayor. Riddle responded by saying that he would "pray for those who attack me," and the revivals encouraged only further apostasy from the mayor. "Morality," said Riddle, "is vice tired out," and at one point suggested that what the city needed was "50 gambling places, 50 pugilists, and 250 chorus girls."[27] In 1916, the evangelist Henry F.

Stough met privately with Riddle, and the mayor contributed $100 to the crusade. But Stough was not reassured when Riddle took him on a tour of the tenderloin, where the two observed a man being pitched from a window.[28]

Riddleism and revivalism represented the extremes of the social conflict in Atlantic City. Riddle was portrayed as a joke and an embarrassment by the *Review* and was largely ignored by the other papers. But, in fact, Riddle posed more of a threat to the reformers than Kuehnle had. In a speech to the Sane Sunday Amusement League, Riddle lampooned reformers and crusaders, but this appeal, and others for the liberalization of the city, also contained scholarly and reasoned appeals on behalf of the working classes.[29] At the beginning of 1916, the voters of Atlantic City could ponder many important issues. President Wilson was desperately trying to mediate the European conflict and to gain reelection, and Walter Evans Edge was equally desperate to become governor of New Jersey. But the attention of city residents turned to the upcoming municipal elections in May, and they promised a referendum on Riddleism.

Commission elections were supposed to be nonpartisan, but as the *Review* sized up the contest in January, it was to be "Riddle and Bartlett against the field." Twenty-five candidates had filed for the five commission seats, but the field included a "Citizens' Ticket" composed of Boardwalk hotelmen Charles D. White and J. B. Thompson, and regular organization Republicans Harry Bacharach, W. F. Sooy, and Albert Beyer.

In April, Bacharach's brother, Congressman Isaac Bacharach, bought the *Gazette* and the *Review*. Harvey Thomas departed the city to head the Public Relations Department of the Prudential Insurance Company in Newark. Edge had purchased the *Union* in 1905 and still controlled the *Press*. Riddle attempted to start his own weekly, offering the editorship to Alfred M. Heston. Heston, in a long letter criticizing Riddle's record, accused the mayor of not taking the campaign seriously and refused the offer.[30] Local Democrats also rebuffed Riddle's overtures. Bartlett, an organization Republican who was denied a spot on the citizens' ticket, became the only local politician to throw in with Riddle.

With the entire political establishment of the city and the local press arrayed against him, Riddle took his candidacy to the people, waging a class-oriented campaign. Riddle had no hope of continuing as mayor, but he had the support of a large bloc of city employees, and a good chance of reelection to the commission. As in 1908 and in 1911, the black vote became crucial, and Riddle and Bartlett campaigned extensively in the Northside. The year before, Bartlett had banned the showing of *The Birth of a Nation* on the Boardwalk, but that decision was based less on his sensitivity to feelings of the black community than on the prospect of the film drawing blacks to the Boardwalk and inciting racial violence.[31] To Riddle, the citizens' ticket was the "silk stocking ticket," and he pointed out that the Boardwalk hotelmen had removed the public seating in front of their hotels because of the presence of "Negro loungers."[32] Not surprisingly, his speeches went largely unreported in the local press, except for the intemperate parts, and his appeal to the Northside was blunted by an incident the year before when he prevented black youths from playing baseball on the Chelsea Field near his home.[33]

To the *Review*, Riddle was a demagogue and a fomenter of racial hatred. Harry Bacharach stated that he knew of nothing more contemptible in a community than to raise class against class, "unless it was to raise race against race, creed against creed, and color against color." "We are all hosts here," said Bacharach, "and it matters little whether we live on the North Side or the South Side." Headwaiters were again brought in to remind black males that the beachfront was their livelihood, and the point could not be missed when Bacharach stated: "They say we represent the hotel interests. Well, what are the hotel interests but the industries of Atlantic City without which you couldn't live."[34] Isaac Nutter, aligned with Bacharach since 1909, led the organization in the Northside and campaigned tirelessly for the citizens' ticket.

For the Northside community, Progressive reform had meant only demoralization and an increased police presence. But a vote for Riddle would be interpreted as a vote for vice and confirm the negative racial stereotypes. The black clergy unanimously denounced Riddle, one saying, "The dives have not helped our people." But the meaning of Riddleism to black people was more pointedly expressed by black speakers brought in from Baltimore and Chicago to address Northside voters. Harry S. Cummins was a member of Baltimore's city council, and Dr. A. J. Carey was one of three civil service examiners of the state of Illinois. The reelection of Riddle would be "an endorsement of the sentiments to which he has given utterance," they said, and bring disgrace to the city. "This election is not purely a local issue. Atlantic City belongs to the nation, and they eyes of the nation are focused here."[35] The message was clear. At stake for black voters in the election of 1916 was nothing less than the dignity and integrity of the race.

With the Northside leaders supporting the citizens' ticket, the closing of the political ranks against Riddle was almost complete. But consigning the mayor to political oblivion required the election of all five candidates, a formidable task in any case, but a task made more difficult by the nature of his campaign. Riddle was indeed an embarrassment, but, by 1915, not the only embarrassment in the city. From the beginning, he attempted to make the beachfront the issue and to exploit the bitter hostilities of the reform movement. In an article in the municipal journal, the only print media to which he had access, he described the reform movement as an effort of the "Beachfront Bund" to grab control of the amusements and exclude the common people from the Boardwalk: As part of their program a newspaper was subsidized to become the mouthpiece of the 'Reformers,' and what that organ published to the world and what it did to the fair fame of the people and of individuals of Atlantic City will never be forgotten, at least by this generation."[36] Earlier, of course, Riddle had hailed the reform movement as the dawn of a new day. But Thomas's vitriolic pen had cut a wide swath among the local population. By 1915 he had become the most hated man in the city. By contrast, Louis Kuehnle returned from prison a bigger man than when he left. Before his incarceration, he made arrangements for the continuance of his charitable donations in the poor sections of the city. To many, he was a scapegoat and a martyr, a view only reinforced by his continued pillorying by Thomas.

Kuehnle accomplished his political comeback in stages. In 1914, he supported his friend, Emerson Richards, against Isaac Bacharach in an unsuccessful primary race for a congressional seat. According to an account in the *Newark Evening News*, the Boardwalk hotelmen were "incensed": "It is no secret that the big hotel men who put up the money for the investigation of Atlantic City affairs which resulted in his indictment and conviction were willing that he should be let off with a fine. Nor is it any secret that they aided in securing his pardon."[37] The condition was Kuehnle's "solemn promise" that he would not engage in politics for a period of five years. It was unlike Kuehnle to break his word, but he was a stickler on the fine points. He was not pardoned; his sentence was commuted. He remained a convicted felon, as Thomas never tired of reminding his readers.

Burns, Thomas, Wilson, and the courts, but especially Thomas, had given the Boardwalk faction more reform than they had bargained for. Kuehnle's stoic silence in the face of his ordeal lends further confirmation to the story. But that situation changed with the Riddle movement.

Throughout 1915, there were rumors that Kuehnle was active behind the scenes. In January 1916, he appeared quietly with Edge at the annual Republican Club dinner. By April, Thomas was gone, and suddenly the "Citizens' Ticket" had become the "Kuehnle-Bacharach Ticket" in both the *Review* and the *Press*. Later that month, he was the featured speaker at a campaign rally with all five candidates, including Daniel S. White, the principal backer of the reform movement. Mounting the platform, the Commodore received a standing ovation as he declared:

> I am here in the interests of this ticket to which I give my endorsement, heart and soul, because I am interested in Atlantic City. I love Atlantic City because I have grown and prospered with it. But a change in the administration of executive affairs is necessary. Since you placed the man who occupies this position in office, he has done everything in his power to lower the dignity and standard of the city.[38]

Long speeches from Kuehnle were a rarity. He carefully instructed the faithful on the dangers of "cutting the ticket" and made but one reference to the reform movement. Recalling Fort's Saturnalia proclamation, he said that the mayor's statements in favor of "chorus girls, gamblers, and flubdubs" was "giving life" to the former governor's accusations. Bacharach followed by declaring that those conditions "never existed," and former prosecutor Goldenberg concluded by saying that Kuehnle was the foundation upon which the political success of the city had been built. "It is the Commodore's ticket you have endorsed this evening."

A week later, Kuehnle accompanied the candidates on a tour of the fortresses of his former adversaries, making a series of "plain talks to the white and colored help" of the Boardwalk hotels.[39] On the eve of the election, the *Review* featured a front-page letter entitled "Where The Commodore Stands." Above all, he stood for progress. "With the election of every man on the citizens' ticket, Atlantic City will enter the greatest era of prosperity the resort has ever known." He also stood for decency and rectitude, and perhaps even "Progressivism," but that word was not used. "It means for you and me, and for all of us, success, happiness, and contentment with freedom from slander and false representation." The *Newark Evening News* commended the Commodore's efforts, but could not help but wonder how Atlantic City had reached such a sorry state as to have to choose between Kuehnle and Riddle.[40]

The voters elected the entire slate, barely defeating Riddle by 362 votes.[41] On the following day, the victors staged a parade on Atlantic Avenue consisting of two hundred automobiles and over six thousand people. Carrying a black coffin with a picture of the mayor, they proclaimed "The Death of Riddleism." Passing Riddle headquarters on Texas Avenue, the celebration was marred by violence. According to the *Press*, the coffin angered the crowd, as a mob of protesters led by off-duty police attacked the paraders with clubs and stones. The *Review* reported: "Especially bitter were the taunts against the colored paraders. Flags were torn from the hands of the colored men and used to hit them over the head. One burly Leaguer got hold of a fragment of a political standard and whipped a horse a colored man was riding until it reared and pranced dangerously through the mob which surged about it."[42] The meaning of Progressive reform in Atlantic City may have eluded the editor of the *Newark Evening News*, but for black citizens it remained unchanged no matter which side they supported.

"Atlantic City Turns Over A New Leaf," proclaimed an article in *The Survey*, but, in the light of Kuehnle's role in the campaign, the author was at a loss to explain the results in terms of civic reform. Riddle's defeat was a boost for Edge's gubernatorial campaign, but a revived Kuehnle would have the opposite effect.[43] During the rest of 1916, the Commodore remained in the background. However, after Edge's successful gubernatorial campaign, the Edge Marching Club tendered Kuehnle a banquet and presented him with a live fox in appreciation for his efforts on behalf of the party. By 1917 Kuehnle was in serious financial trouble. Later that year, his assets, estimated to be worth $625,000, were placed in receivership.[44]

In 1918, pleading poverty, Kuehnle made a bid for the county clerkship, but Edge was now running for the United States Senate. During the campaign, one H. L. Johnson, "a noted colored orator" and "former Recorder of the Deeds of Washington," warned a Northside audience that Kuehnle's candidacy was "a political trap" laid by Democrats. Were Kuehnle to be nominated, "the newspapers from coast to coast would be filled with cartoons to show that the party of Edge had been camouflaging and gone back to Kuehnle and the old order of things." The *Sunday Gazette* named Edward L. Bader and Enoch L. Johnson as the leaders in the city and county, and Daniel S. White was back in the organization, declaring that it now represented "the new Republican Party." "This is not the time to slip Kuehnle back into power," said White, "the people will not brook it."[45]

In 1919, Kuehnle closed the bar at his hotel. He later sold the property and the landmark was razed to make way for a new bank. Ironically, "The Corner" was a victim of Wilson's wartime prohibition measures, which had actually begun in 1917. But already the city abounded with speakeasies, and fleets of swift speedboats were eluding Coast Guard launches off the coast of Atlantic City. Well before the passage of the Eighteenth Amendment, the bays and inlets of Absecon Island had become a major port of entry for illegal liquor. By 1920 the city was awash with indictments for liquor violations, gambling, and prostitution.[46]

The Boardwalk hotelmen formed the Committee of One-Hundred to eliminate vice and lawlessness. The commission elections, held in May 1920, found the beachfront and the reformers again arrayed against the Republican organization. The organization, now controlled by Bacharach, Edward Bader, and Enoch L. Johnson, offered Kuehnle a spot on the ticket. Kuehnle refused, saying, "I'll run on my own hitch." He campaigned little, but won handily, coming in fifth among eighteen candidates.[47]

Kuehnle was now a commissioner, along with Bacharach, Bader, and two other organization figures. Bader became mayor, and the other commissioners moved swiftly to strip Kuehnle of patronage. He was placed in charge of parks and playgrounds but shorn of real power, was a commissioner in name only.[48] In 1924 he won reelection, and in 1928 he received organization support and served continually as director of Parks and Public Property and controlled the city's waterworks until his death in 1934.

Kuehnle's body lay in state at city hall, and thousands filed past the coffin to pay their last respects to the beloved Commodore. By this time, the memories of Kuehnle were almost all fond ones and the legend of the "former boss" had taken firm root. Actually, the local version of the Kuehnle myth was established by 1926, as the *Press* marveled at the excellent condition of the parks and playgrounds. But what else could be expected of a "genius of Kuehnle's calibre?" "Under his able guidance," Atlantic City had become the greatest resort in the world. He was "the originator of the Boardwalk," the founder of the city's utilities, and the man who "brought the railroads to reason," and he also paved Atlantic

Avenue.[49] As with most legends, there are some truths in this one, and Kuehnle did nothing to discourage it.

By 1926 a different kind of legend was already in the making. At the time of Kuehnle's death, United States Treasury agents were investigating the affairs of Enoch L. Johnson, who they said presided over an empire of vice and crime that rivaled Alphonse Capone's regime in Chicago. According to their reports, Johnson and Prohibition had turned Atlantic City into a wide-open town with brothels, gambling dens, and speakeasies on practically every block. Liquor and commercial vice in the city reportedly grossed $10 million a year, and Johnson's yearly take from these sources and from patronage was variously estimated at from $300,000 to $500,000. During the summer of 1929, Johnson hosted Capone and a convention of organized gangdom. The picture of suited and vested mobsters dangling their toes in the surf or of Johnson and Capone strolling arm in arm on the Boardwalk complete a nostalgic and symbolic portrait of Atlantic City during the 1920s.[50]

In 1939, former Democratic prosecutor Charles S. Moore pronounced a severe judgment on Johnson by saying he was "worse than Kuehnle."[51] Moore was understandably bitter. Thirty years earlier he had worked closely with the Wilson administration to rid the city of the Republican machine only to see it reappear in a more powerful and corrupt form under Johnson. Johnson proved to be an elusive quarry. He was finally jailed in 1941 for income tax evasion after a five-year investigation in which federal agents resorted to such methods as counting the towels that brothels sent to laundries in order to determine his take from prostitution.[52]

With Johnson's conviction, the mantle of leadership fell to Frank S. "Hap" Farley. Farley's dominance of the city and county was said to be as great as that of Kuehnle and Johnson. In 1951, the Kefauver Crime Commission concluded that Atlantic City was "an important way station in the national highway of crime," controlled by a "secret government" composed of "hoodlums and key officials . . . making common cause in plundering the taxpayers." Farley escaped indictment and endured for twenty more years. He was defeated for state senator in the midst of a federal grand jury investigation that resulted in the conviction, in 1972, of seven city officials, including two former mayors, for bribery, extortion, and conspiracy.[53] So ended the "Republican Boss Era of Atlantic City." Johnson, Farley, and their successors are subjects for other studies. They are of interest here only in the sense that their careers further attached the Kuehnle myth to the political history of Atlantic City.

The Kuehnle myth is important to our understanding of Louis Kuehnle and of Atlantic City, but what importance does it have for our understanding of Progressive reform and of the broader scheme of social and political reform during the Industrial Era? A "friendly critic" of the reform tradition in American society saw the period after 1900 as "affected by a sort of spiritual hunger," a yearning to apply the principles of Christian morality to social problems. Progressivism was then, in part—and in large part—"a phase in the Protestant conscience, a latter day Protestant revival."[54] Atlantic City, of course, stood for something quite different in American society, but between 1854 and 1920, and even within the two decades of Progressivism, resort elites either resisted or succumbed to many phases in the Protestant conscience, and they responded to a number of revivals.

During the first twenty years, the residents and promoters built hotels, beer gardens, and saloons, but they also built churches. In the 1880s, they provided shows and mechanical amusements, and they closed them on Sundays. After 1890, reformers attacked gambling, prostitution, and the liquor traffic, as well as the liberal Sunday, and caused bitter divisions among the residents. But in truth, the liberal policy was never as liberal as its critics charged. Geared primarily toward profits and prosperity, it was also, especially after 1901, severely tempered by the Protestant conscience.

Between 1901 and 1908, Walter Evans Edge and the Boardwalk hotelmen ridiculed evangelical reformers, but in 1916 the elites and the clergy aligned in solemn partnership in the struggle against Riddleism. In 1909, a Sunday baseball game began a reform movement, but on Sunday, June 9, 1918, two games were played without protest.[55] The supreme irony of reform in Atlantic City is that, between 1909 and 1912, Progressives portrayed Kuehnle and the Northside as a detriment to the city and a menace to public decency, yet enlisted precisely these forces in 1916 to defeat Riddle, who posed as the champion of democracy and the working classes as against the entrenchment of wealth and privilege. Small wonder that *The Survey*, while applauding the results of that election, could find in it no meaning in terms of civic reform. Indeed, extracting the essence of Progressive reform from the tumult of social and political conflict in Atlantic City would seem a daunting task.

A good place to begin is at the end of the Kuehnle era. Explaining the march of Prohibition in the immediate prewar years, one historian asserted that the vast disorder of American life justified "keen moral anxieties": "Thus the 'search for order' was quite naturally directed toward the official and national validation of values which could sustain the family as the vital social institution. The configuration of individual responsibilities implied by these values—duty, restraint, self-discipline—were, in open society, often violently at odds with any tolerance for personal indulgences or moral pluralisms."[56] These were hardly new issues by 1913. But a decade of Progressive reform had focused constant publicity on the ills of industrial society, particularly in the cities, and created an increased urgency among middle-class Americans for the preservation of the family and traditional values. The war in Europe and the increasing prospect of American involvement further accentuated these anxieties.

Returning to the *Survey* article, we find the author baffled by resort politics but confident that election of 1916 was "significant from the standpoint of the psychology of public recreation. It means that in the view of the great amusement and hotel enterprises along the Boardwalk, their prosperity hangs on not catering to the tough and sporting element, but in their appeal to the vast bulk of every-day Americans who want a clean place to go for refreshment." This was "not repressive moralism," but "the same verdict which came with the cleaning out of the worst joints on Coney Island."[57] A more likely explanation for the demise of Coney Island is that it was the victim of its own success. Having accomplished a cultural revolution, commercial recreation lost its capacity to titillate and excite the masses. Coney Island, and by extension, commercial recreation, stirred an ambivalence that went to the heart of Progressive reform. Increasingly, progressives came to believe that the social environment decisively shaped the lives of the people. Thus, real reform required nothing less than the complete restructuring of the social order and the extension of controls into every sphere of American life.[58]

"The movement for organized play," as historians have labeled the impulse to reform recreational environments, found both public and private expression and long predated the Progressive era. Frederick Law Olmstead pioneered the movement when he created New York's Central Park in 1859, and it was carried on by a host of evangelical and secular reformers who sought to wrest control of the amusements from private entrepreneurs.[59] Evangelicals sought to beat commercial resorts at their own game by the creation of Ocean Grove and such things as Christian Endeavor, the YMCA, the YWCA, and other church-sponsored youth groups. Progressives responded to the challenge of commercial recreation by building municipal dance halls and sponsoring municipal athletic leagues. Jane Addams was in the forefront of that effort. In 1916, investigators of the Juvenile Protective Association of Chicago made six visits to nearby Riverview Park and discovered "vulgar and suggestive advertisements" and a number of other indecencies. Boys and girls were drinking and gambling, and a Cook County judge said that the prairie adjacent to the park was "the largest house of assignation in Chicago." Said Addams, "When commercialized recreation is left to its own devices, social neglect and lax enforcement of the law go hand in hand."[60]

Atlantic City and, more especially, Coney Island were, of course, the very antithesis of the municipal recreation movement, but the concerns addressed by reformers such as Jane Addams and the deeper anxieties of evangelicals were the forces to which the political elites in Atlantic City responded. This could prove to be a perplexing process. Jane Addams wrote: "Since the soldiers of Cromwell shut up the people's playhouses and destroyed their pleasure fields, the Anglo-Saxon city has turned over the provision for public recreation to the most evil-minded and most unscrupulous members of the community."[61] In 1917, James Peyton Sizer, a teacher of civics and manual training in Indianapolis, wrote *The Commercialization of Leisure*, advocating nothing less than the complete overthrow of the commerce in recreation in favor of municipal control. Sizer was a follower of Addams, and this obscure book of but ninety-one pages probably contains the purest expression of the secular Progressive response to commercialized recreation. It reads, in part, like a litany of social abuses created by the private purveyors of amusement. But Sizer was equally condemnatory of the YMCA:

> So they condescend to establish a swimming pool or a gymnasium, or even allow a club of boys to meet, providing it is thoroughly supervised. Then they try to present religion to him while he is off his guard by requiring him to attend Sunday school or by establishing a prayer meeting next door. . . . These places are always closed on Sunday and do not remain open late at night, thus forcing people out at the very time when they have the most leisure.[62]

An avid reader, William Riddle would have found much to commend in Sizer's book. He had advocated the creation of a municipal band so that the bathers could tango on the beach. Reform in Atlantic City followed the lines of Progressivism, but that message was often confused.

To elevate Sabbatarians to the legitimate ranks of Progressive reformers is to further muddy the historians' debate over the nature of Progressive reform. In 1915, in a protest highly typical of secular urban Progressives, Cleveland mayor Newton D. Baker said that state-enacted Sunday restrictions and "other dead-letter laws" were the source of "more trouble and confusion than all other aspects of social control combined."[63] One historian has proposed that a good way to make sense of the Progressive mosaic is to acknowledge the distinction between the moral-coercive crusades for Social Purity and Prohibition (to this category I would obviously add Sabbatarianism) and the more positive and humane aspects of the movement that liberal secular historians felt alone deserved the term "Progressive." But underlying the diverse strands of reform lay a "moral substratum" grounded in American Protestantism that reformers across the broad spectrum of Progressivism had imbibed in their youth and which was manifest in "an infinite capacity for moral indignation." Their shared reliance on statistics and technical expertise gave the "moral dimension" "scientific legitimacy" and provided further links among Progressives.[64] To these we might add, as cementing and common characteristics, their common resort to law, politics, and government as a means for effecting reforms, and a shared fundamental hostility toward the culture of the underclass, particularly blacks. Northern Republicans might wax indignant over lynching and race riots, and a few white Progressives, most notably Ray Stannard Baker and Oswald Garrison Villard, attempted to stir the nation's conscience over the systematic injustice of the color line. In fact, a recent study documents the efforts of members of the Social Gospel Movement on behalf of racial reform.[65] But a majority of Northern liberals either remained indifferent to the enormities of racial injustice or blamed blacks themselves for the squalor and vice of urban slums. It is doubtful that anything could quicken the moral indignation of either a coercive or a Progressive as an account of an interracial brothel. On the one hand, we find much to imply a unity of social outlook among Progressives.

On the other hand, the experience of Atlantic City more clearly illustrates the divisions within the ranks of reform and might suggest that historians should abandon the search for the essence of Progressivism and treat the movement for what it was: "ambiguous," "inconsistent," and devoid of central meaning.[66] Running for governer in 1916, Walter Evans Edge posed as a "Business Man With a Business Plan," but "Progressives could be found who admired the efficiency of the big corporation and who detested the trusts, who lauded the 'people' and who yearned for an electorate confined to white and educated voters, who spoke the language of social engineering and the language of moral uplift, or (to make matters worse) did all of these things at once."[67]

Edge, Harvey Thomas, the Boardwalk hotelmen, the evangelicals, Woodrow Wilson, and even Kuehnle and Riddle, all made good use of the rhetoric of Progressive reform, a language "thick with straw men."[68] Although often at war with itself, Progressivism was more than just words. Perhaps it is best understood as an often cynical, but mostly genuine reaction to the agonies of social change, a process that, in the words of one historian, "wrenched American society from the moorings of familiar values," long predated the Progressive Era, and was seen most deeply at the level of culture.[69]

The Progressive movement washed over Atlantic City, leaving nothing of enduring significance but more than just footprints in the sand. The tides of reform had swelled many times over tiny Absecon Island, and as they receded, their high-water marks left successive indices of the limits of reform and of changing social values. Beneath the rumbling waters surged powerful crosscurrents of intense human emotion, and each time, as we survey the wreckage, we find evidence of the increasing intensity of social conflict during the industrial era. Coming to terms with this conflict, successive generations of local elites forged the liberal policy— an expression, like reform itself, of the human need to preserve social and moral order in the face of rapid and profound change.

In 1920, with tongue in cheek, the *New Republic* hailed Atlantic City as "The American Utopia." There were no good books to be bought on the Boardwalk, but family life was intact.

> For Atlantic City is the American Utopia, as truly as though it had been planned by a congress representing our sturdy middle class millions, assembled to lay down the groundwork of the millennium. Atlantic City exists but to please; the men who built it beside the ocean's cool sands gambled on their knowledge of What The Public Wants. Those who guessed rightly were enriched beyond the dreams of yesterday's avarice. Those who guessed incorrectly, "went broke," and the place has seen them no more.[70]

As Enoch L. Johnson once explained: "We always gave the people what they wanted."

Notes

ONE The Kuehnle Myth

1. *Atlantic City Press*, July 28, 1989, 1, B1–8.
2. Charles Yeager, "The Republican Boss Era of Atlantic City: *1900–1971*" (unpublished manuscript held in the Heston Room, Atlantic City Public Library, Atlantic City, N.J.; Ovid Demaris, *The Boardwalk Jungle* (New York: Bantam Books, 1986), 21.
3. *Philadelphia Evening Times*, January 26, 1912, 4; *Philadelphia North American*, January 26, 1912, 6.
4. "Kuehnle, Arch Boss, to Prison," *New York Sun*, December 8, 1913, 1, 4.
5. Arthur S. Link, ed., *The Papers of Woodrow Wilson*, vol. 23: *1911–1912* (Princeton, N.J.: Princeton University Press, 1977), 522–531.
6. *Philadelphia North American*, September 21, 1909, 6.
7. James E. Wright, "The Ethnocultural Model of Voting," *American Behaviorial Scientist* 16 (June 1973): 653–673; Richard L. McCormick, "Ethno-Cultural Interpretations of Nineteenth-Century American Voting Behavior," *Political Science Quarterly* (June 1974): 351–377.
8. Foster Rhea Dulles, *A History of Recreation: America Learns to Play* (New York: Appleton Century Crofts, 1965), chaps. 11, 12, and 13.
9. John Higham, "The Reorientation of American Culture in the 1890s," in John Weiss, ed., *The Origins of Modern Consciousness* (Detroit: Wayne State University Press, 1965), 62.
10. "The Summer Problem," *Scribner's Magazine*, 18, (July-December 1895): 56–57.
11. Josiah Strong, *Our Country* (Cambridge, Mass.: Harvard University Press, 1963), 55.
12. Ibid., 104.
13. Stanley Weintraub, *Victoria: An Intimate Biography* (New York: E. P. Dutton, 1987), 212–213.

14. Daniel T. Rogers, *The Work Ethic in Industrial America, 1850–1920* (Chicago: University of Chicago Press, 1978), 106–107.

15. Winton Solberg, *Redeem the Time: The Puritan Sabbath in Early America* (Cambridge, Mass.: Harvard University Press, 1977), ix.

16. Ibid., xi.

17. *Newark Evening Call*, November 11, 1911, 4.

18. *Atlantic City Press*, July 11, 1912, 1.

19. John D'Emilio and Estelle B. Freedman, *Intimate Matters: A History of Sexuality in America* (New York: Harper and Row, 1988), 202–203.

20. New Jersey Dependency and Crimes Commission, *Report* (Trenton, N.J.: MacCrellish, State Printers, 1909), 20–21, 26–27. Boom was not given the funds to conduct studies of his own. He therefore relied on European studies done principally in Germany and France.

21. Jed Dannenbaum, *Drink and Disorder* (Chicago: University of Illinois Press, 1984), x–xi. See also Mark Edward Lender and James Kirby Martin, *Drinking in America: A History* (New York: The Free Press, 1982), chap. 3.

22. I have used the term "popular resort" as opposed to "mass resort" to characterize Atlantic City because it seems to fall neatly between the latter and the term "exclusive resort." "Popular resort" was a term continually used by the city in promotional literature during and after the 1880s, and its use reflects an intention to put a genteel gloss on the majority of its patrons who were of the middle and lower classes. Charles Funnell preferred to style the city as a mass resort because of its large-scale reliance on mass transportation and advertising as well as the extensive efforts the city made to attract the excursion trade. See Funnell, *By the Beautiful Sea*, 163n. My use of the term is intended to distinguish Atlantic City from, for example, Coney Island, which was almost exclusively dedicated to a working-class clientele, and Cape May, a resort that made comparatively little efforts to promote the working-class trade.

23. Harrison Rhodes, "Atlantic City, Seeing America At Last," *Saturday Evening Post*, February 20, 1915, 11–12.

TWO   *From Pitney's Folly to World's Playground*

1. Alfred M. Heston, ed., *South Jersey. A History: 1664–1924*, 5 vols. (New York: Lewis Historical Publishing Co., Inc., 1924), 754–755.

2. Lewis M. Haupt, "Changes Along the New Jersey Coast," *New Jersey Geological Survey, 1860–1915* (Trenton, N.J., 1905), 32.

3. [Albert Hand, ed.], *A Book of Cape May* (Cape May, N.J.: Albert Hand Co., 1937), 67–68.; Haupt, "Changes Along the New Jersey Coast," 32; William McMahon, *South Jersey Towns: History and Legend* (New Brunswick, N.J.: Rutgers University Press, 1983), 14–15.

4. Federal Writers Project, Works Progress Administration, *Entertaining a Nation: The Career of Long Branch* (Bayonne, N.J.: Jersey Printing Company, 1940), 28; Haupt, "Changes Along the New Jersey Coast," 32.

TWO   *From Pitney's Folly to World's Playground* • 203

5. Haupt, "Changes Along the New Jersey Coast," 32.

6. Robert C. Alexander, *Ho! For Cape Island* (Cape May, N.J.: By the Author, 1956), 27–24, 108; *Entertaining a Nation*, 29.

7. Haupt, "Changes Along the New Jersey Coast," 32.

8. A. L. English, *History of Atlantic City* (Philadelphia: Dickson and Gilling Publishers, 1884), 44–45. Pitney's life has been sketched in a number of local histories. The most complete account appears in Sarah W. R. Ewing and Robert McMullin, *Along Absecon Creek* (Bridgeton, N.J.: C.O.W.A.N. Printing, 1965), 225–245. See also Allen H. Brown, *Fifty Years of Progress on the Coast of New Jersey* (Newark, N.J.: Daily Advertiser Printing House, 1886), 14 (a paper prepared for the New Jersey Historical Society).

9. Carnesworth [pseud.], *Atlantic City: Its Early and Modern History* Philadelphia: William C. Harris and Co., 1868), 36; Ewing and McMullin, *Along Absecon Creek*, 139–140; Alfred M. Heston, *Absegami: Annals of Eyren Haven and Atlantic City* (Camden, N.J.: Sinnickson Chew and Sons Company, 1904), 10n; Arthur D. Pierce, *Family Empire in Jersey Iron* (New Brunswick, N.J.: Rutgers University Press, 1964), 230.

10. Charles Funnell, *By the Beautiful Sea: The Rise and High Times of That Great American Resort, Atlantic City* (New York: Alfred A. Knopf, 1975), 4.

11. Ewing and McMullin, *Along Absecon Creek*, 137–138.

12. Heston, *South Jersey*, vol. 2, 755.

13. "Atlantic City," *The Pennsy*, vol. 3, no. 6, June 1954 (Philadelphia: Pennsylvania Railroad Company, Inc.), 4.

14. Camden and Atlantic Railroad, *Atlantic City, N.J.* (Philadelphia: J. B. Lippincott and Co., 1873), 4.

15. Harold Wilson, *The Jersey Shore* (New York: Lewis Historical Publishing, 1953), 527.

16. Heston, *South Jersey*, vol. 2, 722.

17. "Atlantic City," *The Pennsy*, 4; Wilson, *The Jersey Shore*, 529.

18. Undated press clipping in file, "Atlantic City Hotels," Camden County Historical Society, Camden, N.J.

19. Heston, *South Jersey*, 724.

20. Pierce, *Family Empire in Jersey Iron*, 233; Sarah Thompson Smith, *A History of Ventnor City, N.J.* (n.p, 1963), 13.

21. *Presbyterian*, January 8, 1856, 1.

22. John Hall, *The Daily Union History* of Atlantic City and County, New Jersey (Atlantic City, N.J.: Daily Union, 1900), 345; Alfred Heston, *South Jersey*, vol. 2, 722.

23. Camden and Atlantic Railroad, *Atlantic City*, 11–15.

24. Edward Strahan, *Some Highways and Byways of American Travel* (Philadelphia: J. B. Lippincott and Company, 1878), 102.

25. "The Seaside," *The Lady's Friend*, 5 (January-December 1868): 640.

26. Heston, *Annals*, 161.

27. Camden and Atlantic Railroad, *Annual Report 1872*, 19; *Annual Report 1873*, 10. The assumption here is that the railroad passenger figures include both

leaving and return trips. These statistics comport with local newspaper accounts which estimate, for example, the number of excursionists alone for 1872 at 140,000. See *Atlantic City Daily Review*, August 20, 1872, 4.

28. Camden and Atlantic Railroad, *Atlantic City*, 5.
29. *Atlantic City Review*, August 18, 1873, 5; August 20, 1873.
30. Heston, *Annals*, 327.
31. *Atlantic City Commission Government Journal* 1, no. 4 (July 1913): 2–7.
32. Ibid.
33. W. George Cook and William J. Coxey, Atlantic City Railroad: The Royal Route to the Sea (Ambler, Pa.: Crusader Press, 1980), 6; Camden and Atlantic Railroad, *Annual Report 1882*, 8.
34. Pierce, *Family Empire in Jersey Iron*, 234–235.
35. Wilson, *The Jersey Shore*, 528; Miriam V. Studley, *Historic New Jersey through Visitors' Eyes* (Princeton, N.J.: D. Van Nostrand Company, Inc., 1964), 158–159.
36. Wilson, *The Jersey Shore*, 473.
37. *New Jersey State Census*, Volume for Atlantic County, 1885, 4; U.S. Department of Commerce, Bureau of the Census, *Thirteenth Census of the United States, 1910*, (Supplement for New Jersey), 594.
38. Funnell, *By the Beautiful Sea*, chapter 3.
39. *Atlantic City Daily Union*, August 18, 1890, 1.
40. Between 1860 and 1875 the average work week in all industries declined from 65 hours per week to just under 62, while the average weekly wage rose from $7.08 to $11.20 during the same period. See Robert E. Snow and David E. Wright, "Coney Island: A Case Study in Popular Culture and Technical Change," *Journal of Popular Culture*, September 1980, 974. (Data extracted from *The Statistical History of the United States from the Colonial Times to the Present* (Stamford, Conn.: Fairfield Publishers, Inc., 1965).
41. Alfred M. Heston, *Illustrated Hand-Book of Atlantic City* (Philadelphia: Franklin Printing House, 1887), 83–85; "Atlantic City Hotel-Keepers." (pamphlet located in clipping file entitled "Atlantic City," in New Jersey State Archives, Trenton, N.J.).
42. "A Complete Guide to Atlantic City" (Philadelphia: Burk and McFetridge, 1885), 19.
43. Ibid., 15.
44. *Weekly Herald* (Atlantic City), March 12, 1889, (Scattered copies located in Atlantic County Historical Society, Somers Point, N.J.).
45. *Atlantic City Press*, July 28, 1895, 6.
46. *New York Times*, July 6, 1897, 10.
47. *Philadelphia Press*, April 5, 1903, 7.
48. *Souvenir Program of the Semi-Centennial Celebration of Atlantic City, N.J.* (Heston Room, Atlantic City Public Library, Atlantic City, N.J.).
49. Ibid., June 12, 1904 (Special Resort Section); see also the *Press*, the *Union*, and the *Review*, June 16, 17, 18, 19, 20, 1904.
50. Katherine Busby, *Home Life in America* (New York: The Macmillan Company, 1910), 325.

TWO   *From Pitney's Folly to World's Playground* • 205

51. *Atlantic City, New Jersey: The World's Greatest Resort* (Atlantic City Publicity Bureau, 1912), 23. While sources such as this can be expected to exaggerate in estimating the volume of tourists, the crowds were undoubtedly huge, particularly in July and August. In June 1914, George Lenhart, the director of the Atlantic City Publicity Bureau, estimated that the one thousand hotels and boardinghouses in the city could shelter well over a quarter million guests at one time, and that for "weeks at a stretch" the population of the city exceeded 300,000. See Atlantic City, N.J., *Atlantic City Commission Government*, vol. I, No. 11, June, 1914, 4. On July 4, 1909, it was reported that "one hundred thousand new arrivals have been discharged into the resort during the last three days. Added to the 150,000 who were here before the recent inflow, it gives a total of 250,000 strangers." During this period the city's capacity was stretched to the limit. "It required the use of cots and billiard tables to stow away the throngs who demanded accommodations." See *Philadelphia Inquirer*, July 4, 1909, 1.

52. *Philadelphia Press* , June 12, 1904 (Resort Section), 1.

53. Population figures for Atlantic City are as follows: 1890 - 13,055; 1900 - 27,838; 1905 - 37,593; 1910 - 46,150; 1915 - 51,667. U.S. Department of Commerce, Bureau of the Census, *Thirteenth Census of the United States, 1910* (Supplement for New Jersey), 594; *New Jersey State Census, 1905, 1915*. A summary of the New Jersey census of 1905 indicates that of the 24,615 residents over the age of 21, 4,283 were engaged in "commercial pursuits." This represented 17.4 percent of the adult population; *New Jersey State Census, 1905, Supervisor's Report*. In 1915, of the 35,778 adult residents, 6,304 or 17.6 percent were so engaged. *New Jersey State Census, 1915, Supervisor's Report*.

54. *Philadelphia Evening Times*, August 29, 1909, 3.

55. In 1906, the *Trenton Times* lamented: "Most of the resorts that were dear to the hearts of our fathers are now deserted and well nigh forgotten." Except during the racing season, Saratoga was frequented only by "a few shirt waist women, . . . some invalids, and a handful of politicians who wish to meet in a quiet spot." It also reported that plans were afoot to transform it into primarily a winter resort. Atlantic City had "robbed both Cape May and Long Branch of their glory." Long Branch was a "banquet hall deserted," and its decline was attributed to the state prohibition of gambling in 1900 (the Vorhees Act). Cape May enjoyed all the advantages of Atlantic City, but according to the report, its natives "lacked enterprise." See *Trenton Times*, September 11, 1906, 4. In 1894, the *New York Times* reported that Cape May had given notice that it proposed to "overthrow the lethargy of a dozen years" in an effort to regain "some of her lost prestige as the most fashionable seaside resort in America." See "Cape May's New Aspirations," *New York Times*, May 23, 1894, 21.

56. Hall, *Daily Union History*, 175.

57. *Atlantic City Commission Government*, vol. 2, no. 8, March 1915, 1.

58. Ibid.

59. Tova Novarra, *The New Jersey Shore: A Vanishing Splendor* (Philadelphia: The Art Alliance Press, 1985), 15.

60. Herbert Foster, "The Urban Experience of Blacks in Atlantic City, New Jersey: 1850–1915" (Ph.D. diss., Rutgers University, 1981), 21.

61. *Ibid.*, 28. Two New Jersey studies explain the compelling attraction of Atlantic City for black workers and their extremely weak bargaining position in the hotel industry. A survey of 398 manufacturing firms in New Jersey "representing all fields of industry" revealed the following: The aggregate number of persons employed in these establishments was 128,412, a number considerably in excess of 50 percent of the total employed in all kinds of manufacturing in New Jersey. It was found that only eighty-three establishments out of the total number reporting (questionnaires were sent to 475 places) employed Negro labor in any capacity. Two hundred and ninety-two reported no Negroes at work in any branch of their business. The aggregate number of persons of both races employed in the eighty-three establishments reporting Negro labor is 38,364. There were 963 Negroes among these, of whom only 234 were either skilled or semi-skilled workers. The remaining 729 were common laborers, stablemen or team drivers. See W. C. Garrison, Chief of the Bureau of Statistics, *The Negro in Manufacturing and Mechanical Industries* (Somerville, N.J.: Unionist Gazette Association, State Printers, 1903), 72. (Copy in Governor Edward Stokes Correspondence, Archives, New Jersey State Library, Trenton, N.J.). A study of the occupational distribution of black workers done in 1935 revealed that in 1910, 66 percent of all blacks employed in New Jersey were in the fields of Agriculture and Personal and Domestic Service, 55.9 percent in the latter category. Only 16.9 percent were employed in Manufacturing and Mechanical Industries. This process was disrupted by the First World War, and by 1920 the percentage of blacks in Personal and Domestic Service declined to 42.9 percent and those employed in Manufacturing and Mechanical Industries almost doubled to 31.2 percent. See Edgarton Elliot Hall, *The Negro Wage Earner in New Jersey* (New Brunswick, N.J.: Rutgers University School of Education, 1935), 27.

62. Charles Henry Cope, *Reminiscences of Charles West Cope R. A.* (London: Richard Bentley and Son., 1891), 289.

63. Data derived from the United States Census of 1890 revealed that 52.1 percent of black men in Atlantic City were Southern-born. The percentage of black men in hotel work was much higher, or 68.6 percent. See Foster, "The Black Experience," 76, 81.

64. *Atlantic City Daily Union*, June 14, 1893, 1.

65. Ibid., August 11, 1899, 1.

66. Foster, "The Black Experience," 39. After 1906, hotels also hired white women as cooks and for other jobs traditionally held by black males. In some instances, blacks were replaced by an entirely white staff. The trend was accelerated by the war, which not only siphoned off black males into the armed services, but also presented opportunities in industrial work that had heretofore been unavailable. See Federal Writers Project, Works Progress Administration, "Earning a Living in Atlantic City," *New Jersey Ethnic Survey* (Atlantic City), Box WK2, New Jersey State Library, Trenton, N.J., 1–2. Apparently, the dominance of blacks in hotel employment in the North was in serious jeopardy earlier in the century. This was evident at the annual convention of the United States Headwaiters Association meeting in Atlantic City in 1903. President F. Johnson of

From Pitney's Folly to World's Playground • 207

New York addressed over one hundred delegates from fifteen states in Fitzgerald's Auditorium (in the Northside) and deplored the increasing reluctance of hotels to hire black men, saying: "The race question does not enter into the employment or non-employment of the colored man, but the fault lies with the rank and file of young men of this generation who, without any training, are entering the field seeking work." See *Atlantic City Press*, October 14, 1903, 1.

67. "Earning a Living in Atlantic City," 2.

68. William M. Ashby, *Tales Without Hate* (Newark, N.J.: Newark Landmarks and Preservation Committee, 1980), 36–37.

69. *Philadelphia Inquirer*, July 23, 1893, 10.

70. *Atlantic City Daily Union*, August 1, 1893, 4.

71. *Atlantic City Review*, August 21, 1884, 1.

72. *Atlantic City Press*, August 18, 1896, 1.

73. Federal Writers Project, Works Progress Administration, "Atlantic City Industrial Improvement Company," Atlantic County Historical Society, Somers Point, N.J., 1–3. For a brief account of the career of George Walls, see Foster, "The Black Experience," 66–68.; Federal Writers Project, New Jersey Ethnic Survey, "Recreation," 16.

74. Wynetta Devore, "The Education of Blacks in New Jersey, 1900–1930: An Exploration in Oral History" (Ph.D. diss., Rutgers University, 1980), 90–91.

75. *Atlantic City Sunday Gazette*, June 29, 1906, 4. Federal Writers Project, "Recreation," 16.

76. *Philadelphia Press*, August 24, 1904, 9.

77. *Atlantic City Review*, June 26, 1906, 1.

78. *Atlantic City Sunday Gazette*, June 29, 1906, 4.

79. Ibid., August 8, 1906, 4.

80. William Tuttle, Jr., *Race Riot: Chicago in the Red Summer of 1919* (New York: Atheneum, 1978), 3.

81. *Philadelphia Bulletin*, June 25, 1888, 4.

82. *New York Times*, August 19, 1906, 1.

83. *Philadelphia Inquirer*, September 6, 1896, 21.

84. *Atlantic City Daily Union*, September 1, 1892, 1.

85. Ibid., September 1, 1898, 1.

86. *Atlantic City Press*, September 8, 1900, 1.

87. Foster, "The Black Experience," 19; *New Jersey State Census, 1915, Supervisor's Report*, 1.

88. Foster, "The Black Experience," 144. In 1910 in the First Precinct of the First Ward which was in the Inlet section, the census listed only forty-two blacks in residence. Of these, all but four were listed as butlers, maids, gardeners or live-in help of some other kind. In Precinct Two the same pattern prevailed. Listed at one address were twenty-one blacks and twenty-nine whites in residence. This was a small hotel. Each of the blacks indicated that their family relationship was that of maid, cook, or some other service occupation. United States Department of Commerce, Bureau of the Census, *Thirteenth Census of the United States*, 1910 (Supplement for New Jersey), 572–575.

208 • TWO   *From Pitney's Folly to World's Playground*

89. Atlantic City Common Council, *Minutes*, October 5, 1881.

90. Alfred M. Heston, *Illustrated Handbook of Atlantic City* (Atlantic City, N.J.: A. M. Heston and Company, 1888), 124.

91. *Atlantic City Gazette Review*, January 29, 1905, 1.

92. Margaret Brett, "Atlantic City: A Study in Black and White," *Survey*, 28 (September 7, 1912): 723.

93. *Atlantic City Commission Government*, vol. 1, no. 9 (April 1914), 7–8.

94. *Atlantic City Commission Government*, vol. 1, no. 9 (April 1914), 8.

95. Foster, "The Black Experience," chap. 4. For an account of the school segregation controversy in Atlantic City, see Federal Writers Project, Works Progress Administration, "Education of Negroes in Atlantic City," *New Jersey Ethnic Survey*, Box WK2, New Jersey State Archives, Trenton, N.J., 1–4. Segregated schools became an issue at least as early as 1894 and raged within the black community, many blacks favoring separate schools. See *Atlantic City Daily Union*, December 12, 1894, 1. The issue became particularly heated in 1899. See *Atlantic City Press*, October 21, October 23, October 25, November 3, November 5, November 6, and November 7, 1899, 1. Blacks in favor of school integration brought suit, but in December a superior court judge ruled against them. See *Atlantic City Press*, December 24, 1899, 1.

96. Heston, *Absegami*, 231–234.

97. *Thirteenth Census of the United States, 1910* (Supplement for New Jersey), Statistics of Population for Cities of 25,000 or More, 594.

98. *Atlantic City Daily Union*, October 26, 1891, 1. See also Federal Writers Project, Box C2, "Atlantic City," New Jersey State Archives, Trenton, N.J.

99. "Election Returns for '90 and '91," *Atlantic City Daily Union*, November 4, 1891, 1.

100. Ibid., March 9, 1892, 1.

101. Michael H. Frisch, "The Community Elite and the Emergence of Urban Politics: Springfield, Massachusetts, 1840–1880," in *Nineteenth-Century Cities: Essays in the New Urban History*, ed. by Stephen Thernstrom and Richard Sennett (New Haven, Conn.: Yale University Press, 1976), 283–285.

102. John F. Hall, *Atlantic City and County Biographically Illustrated* (Philadelphia: Albert M. Slocum Co., 1899), 485.

103. *Atlantic City Daily Union*, February 19, 1890, 1; March 3, 1890, 1.

104. *Atlantic City Press*, April 27, 1900, 1.

105. *Atlantic City Daily Press*, April 26, 1900, 1; April 27, 1900, 1.

106. *Atlantic City Press*, February 8, 1901, 1.

107. *Atlantic City Daily Union*, April 21, 1901, 1.

108. *Atlantic City Press*, June 26, 1931, 8.

109. Ibid., August 12, 1934, 1.

110. The major conflict within Republican ranks in 1901 was over political appointments given to former Democrats, which rankled some party veterans. Complained one: "The only way to get an office is to be a former Democrat." See *Atlantic City Gazette Review*, July 9, 1901, 1. During the previous year when the Democrats did not field a candidate for mayor, this paper accused the Democrats of a plot to promote factional infighting so that when the dust settled they could

TWO   *From Pitney's Folly to World's Playground* • 209

take over the city. In 1903 the Democrats fielded only two candidates in an election where eight seats were contested and nominated no candidates for the Democratic County Convention. See "Demoralization of Democrats Leaves Republicans a Clear Field," *Atlantic City Sunday Gazette*, August 30, 1903, 1. By 1905, Clarence Cole was still struggling to keep the organization intact, but their prospects were limited, as indicated by the following quote attributed to a Cole supporter: "The Democrats have a duty to perform if they are in the minority. They want to keep alive and fight on simply to let the opposition know that they have a minority which is on the watch and aggressive." See *Atlantic City Sunday Gazette*, January 29, 1905, 1.

111. The history of the old city charter was sketched by local historian Frank Butler. See *Atlantic City Press*, April 28, 1957, 12; *Atlantic City Daily Union*, April 3, 1902, 1; *Atlantic City Daily Press*, April 4, 1902, 1. See also Franklin W. Kemp, *Firefighting by the Seashore* (Egg Harbor City, N.J.: The Laureate Press, 1972), 169–170.

112. *Atlantic City Daily Press*, April 8, 1902, 1.

113. Untitled twelve-page summary of Riddle's tenure as councilman from 1902 to 1910, probably prepared as a campaign document prior to the election of 1916 and found among his effects. Original in the possession of his son, Graeme Riddle of Ventnor, N.J., and hereafter referred to as Riddle Document.

114. See, for example, *Atlantic City Daily Union*, October 26, 1891, 1, November 27, 1891, 1, and November 30, 1891, 1.

115. *Atlantic City Sunday Gazette*, September 9, 1906, 1.

116. *Atlantic City Press*, December 14, 1903, 4.

117. *Atlantic City Sunday Gazette*, September 14, 1907, 4.

118. *Atlantic City Daily Union*, March 9, 1892, 1; November 12, 1892, 1.

119. *Philadelphia Bulletin*, March 3, 1892, 4.

120. *Atlantic City Daily Union*, February 12, 1892, 1.

121. *Philadelphia Bulletin*, March 7, 1892, 4.

122. Ibid.

123. *Atlantic City Daily Union*, March 9, 1892, 1.

124. *Philadelphia Bulletin*, March 7, 1892, 6.

125. *Atlantic City Daily Union*, March 9, 1892, 1.

126. New Jersey State Senate, *Protest, Testimony Taken before the Committee on Elections, and Reports of Committee in the Matter of the Contest for State Senator of Atlantic County, New Jersey between William Riddle, Contestant and Samuel D. Hoffman, Incumbent* (Trenton, N.J.: MacCrellish and Quigley, State Printers, 1893), 2.

127. *Riddle v. Hoffman*, 144–149.

128. Ibid. 82–85, 126–134, 24–25 (Minority Report).

129. Ibid. (Minority Report), 24.

130. Ibid. (Majority Report), 5.

131. *Atlantic City Daily Union*, November 21, 1892, 1.

132. *Riddle v. Hoffman*, 151, 422.

133. Council Minutes, December 5, 1881; *Atlantic City Daily Union*, March 5, 1898, 1.

210 • THREE *The Robbery of the Sabbath*

134. Riddle Document, 5; *Atlantic City Press*, September 9, 1906, 1.

135. The histories, in the order of their publication, were Carnesworth, *Atlantic City: Its Early and Modern History* (1868); A. L. English, *History of Atlantic City* (1884); John F. Hall, *Daily Union History of Atlantic City* (1900); and Alfred M. Heston, *Absegami: Annals of Eyren Haven and Atlantic City* (1904).

THREE   *The Robbery of the Sabbath*

1. Sidney E. Ahlstrom, *A Religious History of the American People*, vol. 2, (Garden City, N.Y.: Doubleday and Company, Inc., 1975), 404.

2. New Jersey Excise Commission, *Public Hearings* (Trenton, N.J.: New Jersey State Legislature, 1908), 1730–1731.

3. William E. Sackett, *Modern Battles of Trenton*, vol. 2: *From Werts to Wilson* (New York: Neale Publishing Company, 1914), 116, 277.

4. James M. King, General Secretary, National League for the Protection of American Institutions, *Facing the Twentieth Century—Our Country: Its Power and Peril* (New York: American Union League Society, 1899), 94.

5. New Jersey Methodist Conference, *Minutes* (1914), 104–105. Complete collection found in the Archives of the Methodist Conference of Southern New Jersey, Pennington School, Pennington, New Jersey; Hereafter cited as N.J.M.C., *Minutes*.

6. Letter, Wilbur T. Crafts to John F. Fort, September 5, 1908, Governor John F. Fort Correspondence, New Jersey State Archives, Trenton, N.J.

7. See Charles A. Fecher, *Mencken: A Study of His Thought* (New York: Alfred A. Knopf, 1978), 106–107. As late as the 1960s, the following Hofstadter comment was standard fare for college undergraduates: "For Prohibition, in the twenties, was the skeleton at the feast, a grim reminder of the moral frenzy that so many wished to forget, a ludicrous caricature of the reforming impulse, of the Yankee-Protestant notion that it is both possible and desirable to moralize private life through public action." See Richard Hofstadter, *The Age of Reform* (New York: Random House, 1955), 289. Of course, Hofstadter's point that Prohibition deserved a share of the blame for the decline of Progressivism in the 1920s is more substantive than his analysis of the movement itself.

8. King, *Facing the Twentieth Century*, 92.

9. Winton Solberg, *Redeem the Time* (Cambridge, Mass.: Harvard University Press, 1977), 51.

10. John Timberlake, *Prohibition and the Progressive Movement* (New York: Atheneum, 1970), 110–111; Norman Clark, *Deliver Us From Evil* (New York: W. W. Norton Company, 1976), 57. Said Andrew Sinclair: "The saloon is the church of the poor. While the churches supplied a meeting place for the respectable, the saloons were the rendezvous of the workers." See Andrew Sinclair, *Era of Excess: A Social History of the Prohibition Movement* (New York: Harper and Row, 1962), 75.

11. Perry Duis, *Public Drinking in Chicago and Boston* (Chicago: University of

THREE *The Robbery of the Sabbath* • 211

Illinois Press, 1983), 234, 254, 286–288; S. H. Popper, "Newark, N.J., Chapters in the Evolution of an American Metropolis" (Ph.D diss., New York University, 1971), chap. 4; Edmund Morris, *The Rise of Theodore Roosevelt* (New York: Coward, McCann and Geoghegan, Inc., 1979), 496–514.

12. William Addison Blakely, ed., *American State Papers Bearing on Sunday Legislation* (New York: National Religious Liberty Association, 1890), 272–323.

13. William Addison Blakely, ed., *American State Papers on Freedom in Religion* (Washington, D.C.: National Religious Liberty Association, 1943), 231–232, 243.

14. Blakely, *American State Papers on Sunday Legislation*, 10. The "ordained minister" was a Seventh Day Adventist, a Christian sect that celebrates the seventh day as the Sabbath.

15. Blakely, *American State Papers on Freedom in Religion*, 245–260. Eighty of the Sunday bills related to Sunday closing or work prohibition in the District of Columbia. Three bills that were passed set Sunday closing as conditions to appropriations for the Chicago Exposition in 1892, the St. Louis Exposition in 1901, and the Jamestown Exposition in 1907. The National Sunday Rest Bill of 1888, which Blakely regarded as the first shot in the national campaign of the National Reform Movement, was prefaced as follows: "Bill to Secure to the People the Enjoyment of the First Day of the Week, Commonly Known as the Lord's Day, as a Day of Rest, and to Promote Its Observance as a Day of Religious Worship."

16. Blakely, *American State Papers on Freedom in Religion*, 235–236. Article II of their constitution read as follows: "The object of this Society shall be to maintain existing Christian features in the American Government; to promote needed reforms in the action of the government touching the Sabbath, the institution of the Family, the religious element in Education, the oath, and public morality as affected by the liquor traffic and other kindred evils; and to secure such an amendment to the Constitution of the United States as will declare the nation's allegiance to Jesus Christ and its acceptance of the moral laws of the Christian religion, and so indicate that this is a Christian nation, and place all Christian laws, institutions, and usages of our government on an undeniably fundamental basis in the fundamental laws of the land."

17. (Mrs.) E. G. White, *The Great Controversy between Christ and Satan* (Oakland, Calif.: The Pacific Press Publishing Company, 1892), 689n.

18. Ruth Bordin, *Frances Willard: A Biography* (Chapel Hill, N.C.: University of North Carolina Press, 1986), 98.

19. White, *The Great Controversy*, 689.

20. Although Jews were frequent defendants in Sabbatarian cases, one is struck by the relative silence of American Jewish intellectuals on the subject throughout this period. One can only conclude that their position within American society was particularly vulnerable, and that agitation was impolitic. Walter Lippmann, for example, had grown up in an exclusive Jewish world and by the 1920s had cracked all but the pinnacles of social barriers posed for American Jewry. According to Ronald Steel, he dealt with instances of discrimination and his Jewish identity by ignoring it, and in doing so, "was hardly unique among

people of his class and generation." See Ronald Steel, *Walter Lippmann and the American Century* (Boston: Little, Brown and Company, 1980), 186, and chap. 15, "A Conspicuous Race."

21. Church of the Holy Trinity v. United States, 143 U.S. 457 (1892).

22. According to statistics gathered by the American Union League Society in 1899 when the nation's population barely reached 75 million, religious communicants of all denominations totaled 26,054,385. This included six sects of Seventh Day Adventists that totaled 81,945 members, and two bodies of Jews totaling 143,000. See King, *Facing the Twentieth Century*, 94.

23. See Soon Hing v. Crowley, 113 U.S. 703 (1885); Hennington v. Georgia, 163 U.S. 209 (1896); Petit v. Minnesota, 177 U.S. 164 (1900); McGowan v. Maryland, 366 U.S. 420 (1961).

24. An 1893 revision decriminalized Sunday newspapers and allowed the sale and delivery of milk as well as walking, riding or driving for recreation. George Labarre, "History of the Observance of Sunday" (reprint of six articles appearing in *Trenton Times*, November and December, 1923), 20. New Jersey State Archives, Trenton, N.J.

25. For case law on the Sunday issue in New Jersey, see Reeves v. Butcher, 2 Vroom 224 (1865); McMillan v. Kuehnle, 76 N.J. Equity 256 (1909); Singer v. Criminal Court of Newark, 79 N.J. Law 386 (1910); and especially Sherman v. Paterson, 82 N.J. Law 345 (1912). In the Paterson case, Justice James Mintern gave municipalities sweeping power to make and enforce Sunday restrictions. See also Paulsson, "Politics and Progressivism in Atlantic City: A Brief Hour of Reform" (Ph.D. diss., Rutgers University, 1991), 42–43.

26. Blakely, *American State Papers on Freedom in Religion*, 479–481, 565; David N. Laband and Deborah Hendry Heinbuch, *Blue Laws: The History, Economics, and Politics of Sunday Closing Laws* (Lexington, Mass.: D. C. Heath and Company, 1987), 49.

27. Blakely, *American State Papers on Freedom in Religion*, 12.

28. S. C. Breyfogel, *Landmarks of the Evangelical Association* (Reading, Pa.: Eagle Book Print, 1898), 202, 312.

29. G. C. Knobel, ed., *The Congress of the Evangelical Association* (Cleveland, Ohio: Thomas and Matill, 1894), 220–225. Single copy found in the archives of the Methodist Conference of Southern New Jersey, Pennington, N.J.

30. N.J.M.C. *Minutes*, (1871), 20; (1880), 36–37.

31. Ibid. (1893), 59.

32. Lord's Day Alliance of the United States, *Twenty Third Annual Report*, November 14, 1910, to November 13, 1911, 8. Single copy found in Presbyterian Historical Society, Philadelphia.

33. A. Nelson Hollifield, *Shall We Legalize Sabbath Desecration, and Races and Gambling on Race Courses?* (Newark, N.J.: Advertiser Printing House, 1891), 13. Hollifield's sermon grew out of a meeting of Newark clergymen to oppose the efforts of the State Liquor Dealers Association to legalize Sunday selling. Sunday, January 25, 1891, was designated as a day of general protest when every Presbyterian minister in the state was to preach on the subject.

34. *Newark Evening News*, January 26, 1891, 1.

THREE *The Robbery of the Sabbath* • 213

35. Throughout the summer of 1901, the *Newark Evening News* gave a running front-page account of Black's crusade against saloons. See June 24, July 15, July 20, August 14, August 15, and August 16, 1901, 1.

36. Steelman, *What God Has Wrought*, 133.

37. N.J.M.C., *Minutes* (1900), 76; (1901), 31.

38. See *Newark Evening News*, February 6, 16, 1901, 1; March 20, 1901, 1; March 21, l901, 4; May 17, 1901, 1. By 1901 the protection of commercial vice and Sunday selling by local grand juries had become an issue throughout the state. The problem was most acute in Newark, Jersey City, and Long Branch, where private reform groups had succeeded in having offenders arrested only to have them released by sheriff-picked grand juries. Even when police were cooperative, their efforts were nullified. Dr. John D. McGill, president of the Jersey City Police Board, complained: "There is not much use of the police department making strenuous efforts to abate the evils of policy (gambling) and poolrooms if the prisoners who are arrested on evidence absolutely complete and convincing escape indictment by the grand jury. We had been after Sullivan for some time. He had been under the aegis of political protection. It was a difficult matter to get him. By good police work, however, he was finally caught. According to the police vernacular, he was caught 'dead right.' The police department had done its duty in ferreting out this case, but it seems the grand jury failed to do its share. This is one of those cases that discredit our system of government and offer a sad commentary on our grand jury system. If justice is thus to be defeated, you might as well abolish the police department, let off the rogues, and stop your efforts to eradicate evils." See *Newark Evening News*, March 20, 1901, 4.

39. *Newark Evening News*, March 20, 1901, 1; March 21, 1901, 4.

40. *Atlantic City Press*, June 25, 1901, 1; June 25, 1901, 1; June 28, 1901, 1; *New York Times*, June 29, 1901, 1; July 15, 1901; July 22, 1901, 1; July 28, 1901, 1; August 12, 1901, 1; *Newark Evening News*, August 14, 1901, 1.

41. *Newark Evening News*, July 6, 1901, 4.

42. T. T. Mutchler to Franklin Murphy, February 25, 1902; Franklin Murphy to William Stanhope, July 2, 1902, Governor Franklin Murphy Correspondence (1902–1905) New Jersey State Archives, Trenton, N.J.

43. N.J.M.C., *Minutes* (1902), 76.

44. *Trenton Times*, January 19, 1906, 1; January 20, 1906, 4; January 23, 1906, 1; January 27, 1906, 1; New Jersey Dependency and Crimes Commission (1908), *Stenographic Minutes*, 208–209.

45. Sackett, *Modern Battles of Trenton*, vol. 2, 217–222.

46. Stenographic copy of unsigned and undated letter to Frank O. Briggs found in Stokes files; Governor Casper Stokes Correspondence (1905–1907), New Jersey State Archives, Trenton, N.J.

47. Stenographic copy of unsigned letter to Stokes dated September 21, 1906, Stokes Correspondence.

48. John F. Dodd to Governor Stokes, April 6, 1907, Stokes Correspondence.

49. Ransom E. Noble, Jr., *New Jersey Progressivism before Wilson* (Princeton, N.J.: Princeton University Press, 1946), 75–76.

50. Ibid., 90–91n. Although Fort deftly avoided a firm commitment to the

214 • THREE *The Robbery of the Sabbath*

Bishops' Law during the election of 1907, once in office he moved in stages into the camps of the evangelicals and the New Idea contingent of his party denouncing the liquor interests and Republican party bosses. See, for example, text of a speech to Camden Methodists in *Trenton Times*, October, 9, 1909, 2, and "Fort Flays Party Bosses," *Trenton True American*, September 23, 1909, 1. He was caused considerable embarrassment by a story unearthed by the *Newark Evening News* that previous August, which held that despite his campaign posture, he privately assured Atlantic City Republicans that he would seek immunity for the resort from Sunday closing laws. See "Atlantic City Accuses Governor," *Trenton True American*, August 21, 1908, 1.

51. Samuel Wilson to Otto Wittpenn, August 9, 1908, New Jersey Excise Commission, *Public Hearings*, Appendix.

52. *Trenton True American*, August 4, 1908, 4.

53. New Jersey Excise Commission, *Public Hearings*, 1535–1544, 1717–1722, 1715–1716.

54. Ibid., 1572–1583, 1637–1640, 1623–1625.

55. New Jersey Crimes Commission, *Report*, 22–23.

56. New Jersey Excise Commission, *Public Hearings*, 1739–1740.

57. *Trenton True American*, August 28, 1908, 1.

58. Ibid.

59. *New York Times*, August 26, 1908, 7.

60. *Philadelphia Bulletin*, August 28, 1908, 6; *New York Times*, August 30, 1908, 8.

61. Nelson Gaskill to Franklin Fort, August 27, 1908, Fort Correspondence. This was a telegram which read: "Grand jury discharged. No excise indictments. Foreman defended action practically challenging you to enforce law."

62. Petition, John J. Ryan to Casper Stokes, February 26, 1906, Stokes Correspondence.

63. John Kelly to Franklin Fort, September 16, 1908; Josiah Strong to Franklin Fort, September 1, 1908; Oswald Garrison Villard to Franklin Fort, August 31, 1908, Fort Correspondence.

64. Hoffman, Burlington County Local Option League to Franklin Fort, August 28, 1908; E. S. Black to Franklin Fort, August 28, 1908, Fort Correspondence.

65. Franklin Fort to Mahlon Pitney, September 8, 1908, Fort Correspondence.

66. Christian Fischer to Franklin Fort, September 7, 1908, Fort Correspondence.

67. New Jersey Excise Commission, *Public Hearings*, 3529–3533.

68. Undated copy of press release from Samuel Wilson, Fort Correspondence.

69. Nelson Gaskill to Franklin Fort, August 31, 1908, Fort Correspondence.

70. William Winter to Franklin Fort, October 20, 1908, Fort Correspondence.

71. Petition, Anna Steelman to Franklin Fort, January 19, 1909, Fort Correspondence.

72. "Easter Sunday at Atlantic City," *Trenton True American*, April 9, 1909, 4. See also editorial, March 1, 1909, 4, August 24, 1909, 1; August 25, 1909, 5.

FOUR *Low Resorts* • 215

73. New Jersey Excise Commission, *Report*, 85.
74. Ibid., *Minority Report*, 3.
75. New Jersey Crimes Commission, *Report*, 21–23.
76. Ibid., 21.
77. Ibid., *Minority Report, Recommendations, and Supplementary Statement*, 62–67.
78. *Atlantic City Review*, January 29, 1909, 1; February 2, 1909, 1; February 16, 1909, 1; February 17, 1909, 1; *Trenton Times*, February 8, 1909, 1; February 16, 1909, 1; February 26, 1909, 14.
79. *Atlantic City Review*, March 2, 1909, 1; *Trenton Times*, March 1, 1909, 1, 12; March 2, 1909, 1.
80. *Trenton Times*, March 13, 1909, 1; April 1, 1909, 1.
81. Steelman, *What God Has Wrought*, 135–136.
82. *Address of Hon. James F. Mintern Delivered before the Committee to Consider Legislation Affecting Sunday Observance* October 10, 1919 (n.p.) New Jersey State Archives, Trenton, N.J., 3–4.
83. E. Thompson, *The Making of the English Working Class* (New York: Random House, 1963). My use of the term "moral economy" is meant only to describe a defined set of practices and expectations built up over a long period of time which explain extreme reactions to a new set of conditions imposed by an external force. Essential to a moral economy is the belief that the old practices are grounded in righteousness or at least represent a commitment agreed to by authorities which is violated by the new conditions. Thompson used the term to explain workers' attitudes as well as frame breaking in early nineteenth-century England. See Thompson's chap. 14, "An Army of Redressers." For Atlantic City, the moral economy was the liberal policy, a citywide compact which in the eyes of the locals was given tacit approbation by the courts and state authorities for fifty years. Reform broke that compact, and this explains in part the defiance of the city and much of the violence and vituperation that attended the reform movement.

FOUR *Low Resorts*

1. Brown was the synodical missionary of the presbytery of West Jersey. He was born in 1820 in New York City, graduated from Columbia College in 1839, did graduate and postgraduate work at Princeton Theological Seminary, and was licensed to preach in 1843. Perhaps foresaking the prospect of a prosperous parsonage, he spent the next thirty years in southern New Jersey. The *Presbyterian* said of him in 1856: "Though accustomed to all the comforts and luxuries which affluent circumstances and his native city, New York, could provide, when he entered the ministry he made up his mind to count all but loss for Christ. He might readily have found a settlement in some old established congregation, but he chose the then greatly neglected field of the pines of New Jersey. Here, for some eight years he has labored with a zeal and fidelity which has won for him the universal respect and esteem of the population." His diary, though sparsely

216 • FOUR *Low Resorts*

kept and personally unrevealing, contains references to Pitney, Doughty, Richards, Bell, and other local capitalists who aided his work. He was one of the dignitaries on the first train, and his brief biography of Jonathan Pitney was laudatory of Pitney's role in the development of South Jersey and of the creation of Atlantic City in particular. See the *Presbyterian*, August 30, 1856, 3; William D. Aikman, D.D., "Historical Discourse Delivered on the Fiftieth Anniversary of the First Presbyterian Church, Atlantic City, N.J.," delivered October 28, 1906 (pamphlet file, Atlantic County Historical Society); Allen H. Brown Diary, Brown Collection (Atlantic County Historical Society); Brown, *Fifty Years of Progress*.

2. Brown Diary, entry for June 5, 1854.
3. Aikman, *Historical Discourse*, 6.
4. (Philadelphia) *Presbyterian*, July 28, 1855, 1.
5. Ibid., February 6, 1875, 1.
6. S. W. Lauderbach, *A Century After* (Philadelphia: Allen, Lane, and Scott, 1885), 142–143.
7. *South Jersey Republican*, March 12, 1866, 1.
8. *Atlantic City Daily Review*, July 7, 1873, 2.
9. *Atlantic City Review*, August 4, 1884, 1; August 12, 1884, 1.
10. Atlantic City Common Council, *Public Ordinances of Atlantic City from September 8, 1854 to August 25, 1903* (reprinted by Board of Commissioners, 1924), 206–207.
11. *Atlantic City Review*, August 10, 1885, 1.
12. Ibid., August 27, 1885, 1.
13. "Site Used Here 75 Years Ago in Whiskey License Racket," *Atlantic City Press*, July 24, 1966, 18; *Atlantic City Review*, July 14, 1884, 1.
14. A. L. English, *History of Atlantic City* (Philadelphia: Dickson and Gilling Publishers, 1884), 82–83.
15. Ibid., 175.
16. *Atlantic City Press*, June 29, 1895, 1; Henry Adams, *The Education of Henry Adams* (Boston: Houghton Mifflin Company, 1961), 304.
17. *Atlantic City Review*, July 11, 1885, 1.
18. Ibid., August 20, 1884, 1.
19. Ibid., July 19, 1881, 1; July 31, 1886, 1.
20. Atlantic City Common Council, *Minutes*, August 4, 1890.
21. *Philadelphia Bulletin*, August 5, 1890, 2.
22. *Philadelphia Inquirer*, June 1, 1890, 7.
23. *Atlantic City Daily Union*, July 30, 1890, 1.
24. *Philadelphia Bulletin*, August 5, 1890, 1.
25. Ibid., August 7, 1890, 1.
26. Ibid., August 18, 1890, 1.
27. Ibid., August 19, 1890, 1.
28. Ibid.
29. Ibid., August 16, 1890, 1.
30. David J. Pivar, *Purity Crusade: Sexual Morality and Social Control, 1868–1900* (Westport, Conn.: Greenwood Press, 1973), 131–139.

FOUR *Low Resorts* • 217

31. *Philadephia Bulletin*, August 9, 1890, 1.
32. Ibid., August 16, 1890, 1.
33. Ibid., August 30, 1890, 1.
34. Ibid., August 14, 1890, 1.
35. Ibid., August 16, 1890, 1.
36. Ibid., August 23, 1890, 1.
37. Ibid., August 11, 1890, 1.
38. Ibid., August 22, 1890, 1.
39. Ibid., August 12, 1890, 1, August 23, 1890, 1.
40. *Atlantic City Daily Union*, August 23, 1892, 1; August 24, 1892, 1, 4; August 30, 1892, 1.
41. *Philadelphia Bulletin*, April 30, 1889, 6; May 14, 1888, 7.
42. Ibid., August 8, 1890, 1.
43. Ibid., August 11, 1890, 1.
44. Ibid., June 8, 1891, 6; June 23, 1891, 2.
45. *Atlantic City Daily Union*, November 14, 1891, 1.
46. A. J. Corocoran, *The History of Gloucester City, New Jersey* (Gloucester City, N.J.: Gloucester City Historical Society, 1973), 11–12.; William E. Sackett, *Modern Battles of Trenton, 1868–1894* (Trenton, N.J.: John L. Murphy [Printer], 1895), 384–=385.
47. *Atlantic City Daily Union*, August 15, 1892, 1, 4.
48. *Philadelphia Bulletin*, July 24, 1895, 1, August 26, 1895, 1.
49. *Atlantic City Press*, August 10, 1895, 1.
50. Ibid., August 19, 1895, 1; *Philadelphia Inquirer*, August 12, 1895, 2; August 13, 1895, 2; August 14, 1895, 2; August 19, 1895, 2; August 20, 1895, 2; August 26, 1895, 2; *Atlantic City Daily Union*, August 19, 1895, 1.
51. *Philadelphia Inquirer*, August 4, 1895, 21.
52. *Philadelphia Bulletin*, August 5, 1895, 3.
53. *Philadelphia Press*, August 5, 1895, 4.
54. *Trenton Times*, July 25, 1895, 1.
55. *New York World*, August 7, 1895,
56. *Atlantic City Daily Union*, December 20, 1894, 1.
57. *Philadelphia Inquirer*, August 4, 1895, 22.
58. See, for example, Ruth Rosen, *The Lost Sisterhood: Prostitution in America, 1900–1918* (Baltimore: Johns Hopkins University Press, 1982), 5–6.
59. *Philadelphia Inquirer*, August 4, 1895, 22.
60. *New York Journal*, June 27, 1897 (Resort Section), 1; *Atlantic City Press*, September 13, 1897, 1.
61. *Atlantic City Daily Union*, July 30, 1898, 1.
62. *Atlantic City Press*, October 31, 1899, 1.
63. Ibid., November 3, 1899, 1–2.
64. *Atlantic City Press*, December 5, 1899, 2.
65. Ibid., December 6, 1899, 1.
66. Ibid., December 8, 1899, 1.
67. *Atlantic City Sunday Gazette*, February 18, 1900, 1.
68. *Atlantic City Daily Review*, February 20, 1900, 1.

218 • FIVE *A Saturnalia of Vice*

69. *Atlantic City Daily Union*, July 23, 1900, 1.
70. Quoted in *Atlantic City Daily Union*, July 23, 1900, 1.
71. *Atlantic City Daily Union*, July 20, 1900, 1 (quoting *Review;* copies of *Review* not extant for this period).
72. *Atlantic City Sunday Gazette*, July 22, 1900, 1.
73. Quoted in *Sunday Gazette*, July 22, 1900, 1.
74. *Atlantic City Daily Union*, July 25, 1900, l, August 24, 1900, 1; *Philadelphia Bulletin*, August 28, 1900, 2.
75. *Atlantic City Sunday Gazette*, July 29, 1900, 4.
76. *Atlantic City Daily Union*, August 24, 1900, 1; September 15, 1900, 1.
77. *Philadelphia Public Ledger*, August 29, 1900, 5.

FIVE *A Saturnalia of Vice*

1. *Atlantic City Sunday Gazette*, February 9, 1908, 8.
2. *Atlantic Review*, November 5, 1908, 1.
3. *Trenton True American*, August 31, 1908, 1, 5.
4. *Atlantic Review*, September 8, 1908, 1, 4.
5. New Jersey Excise Commission, *Public Hearings* (Trenton, N.J.: New Jersey State Legislature, 1908), 1675–1686.
6. *Atlantic City Press*, May 24, 1891, 1.
7. *Atlantic City Sunday Gazette*, June 30, 1901, 1. The *Gazette* also noted that Sea Isle City, "a resort patronized principally by Philadelphia beer drinkers," was "startled" by the order and that "consternation reigned" among hotel keepers who stood to lose hugely by the edict. But, as the mayor was out of town, no order came down to close.
8. *Atlantic City Daily Union*, June 29, 1901, 1.
9. *New York Times*, July 1, 1901, 1; *Atlantic City Daily Union*, July 1, 1901, 1; *Atlantic City Press*, July 1, 1901, 1.
10. *Atlantic City Press*, April, 9, 1901, 1.
11. Although contemporary press reports continually indicate a strong majority feeling against Sunday amusements, council was loathe to legislate on the subject. For example, following the 1895 *Inquirer* probe, a stringent Sunday amusement ordinance was introduced but did not pass. See *Atlantic City Daily Union*, September 3, 1895, 4. Council debates are not extant, but one can only surmise that members felt that the less said on the subject, the better. To raise the amusement question was inevitably to poke a hornet's nest of Sabbath controversy as the experiences of 1890 and 1895 had shown.
12. *Atlantic City Daily Union*, July 8, 1901, 1.
13. *Atlantic City Sunday Gazette*, July 14, 1901, 1.
14. *Atlantic City Press*, July 17, 1901, 1; July 22, 1901, 1; July 29, 1901, 1; August 1, 1901, 1; August 5, 1901, 1; August 14, 1901, 1. For text, see "An Ordinance for the Suppression of Vice and Immorality" dated August 13, 1901, in Atlantic City Common Council, *Public Ordinances of Atlantic City from September*

8, *1854 to August 25, 1903* (reprinted by Board of Commissioners, 1924), 206–207.

15. *Newark Evening News*, July 15, 1901, 1; July 20, 1901, 1; August 14, 1901, 1; August 15, 1901, 1; *Atlantic City Sunday Gazette*, August 15, 1901, 1.

16. *Atlantic City Press*, August 19, 1901, 1.

17. Ibid., August 26, 1901, 1.

18. The local movement against Sunday violators grew out of a meeting of the "Ministerial Association," a group of local clergy who arranged for Hann's agents and became the nucleus of the Citizens' League. See *Atlantic City Daily Union*, July 18, 1901, 1. The lawyer who processed the complaints was Clarence Cole, who was also the county Democratic chairman, but it was not a tactic calculated to improve the fortunes of his party. The Democratic *Union* ignored his activities, but Edge's *Press* summarized them with the sarcastic headline, "Crusader Cole is Saving the City." See *Atlantic City Press*, August 16, 1901, 1. Hann's role in the movement did not surface publicly until September 6, when he felt constrained to defend himself against charges that he was a carpetbagger. See *Atlantic City Daily Union*, September 6, 1901, 1.

19. *Atlantic City Press*, September 6, 1901, 1. Edge prefaced the announcement with the following: "Public Stand Taken by Citizens no Longer Leaves the Movement Under the Veil That Has Been Overhanging it Since Its Inception—To Be Successful From a Practical Standpoint Must Be Handled With Moderation and Consideration of All."

20. *Atlantic City Sunday Gazette*, September 15, 1901, 1.

21. *Atlantic City Daily Union*, September 17, 1901, 1. From the list of grand jurors published in the *Union* on September 10, it appears highly unlikely that Sheriff Johnson in this instance stacked the panel for the purpose of foiling Hendrickson. Members included John F. Hall, publisher of the *Union*, William A. Faunce, and Dr. J. B. Thompson, all prominent Democrats. Republicans included Lewis Evans, John L. Young, and Edward S. Lee, all of whom while having little sympathy for Sunday laws had even less for saloons. Moreover, it was widely reported in the press that an unofficial deal had been struck with Hendrickson which provided that he would not press for indictments as long as the saloons remained closed on Sunday. While there is no solid evidence of this arrangement, the presence of the above-named members of the grand jury corroborates this view. While from the viewpoint of the liquor interests they could not be considered "safe," they would be considered by the community as "reasonable." See *Atlantic City Daily Union*, September 14, 1901, 1, 4; *Atlantic City Press*, September 9, 1901, 1.

22. *Atlantic City Sunday Gazette*, November 24, 1901, 10, December 1, 1901, 10; *Atlantic City Daily Union*, November 22, 1901, 1; January 18, 20, 1902, 1.

23. *Atlantic City Daily Union*, January 27, 1902, 1; *Atlantic City Sunday Gazette*, January 19, 1902, 1; March 2, 1902, 1.

24. Ed Davis, *Atlantic City Diary: A Century of Memories, 1880–1980* (Egg Harbor City, N.J.: The Laureate Press, 1980), 26–28. By 1900 vaudeville had separated into two classes, "high class" and "variety," which was more bawdy and vigorous. In the hotel district, shows of the more refined type were featured

on, for example, Young's Pier and on the Iron Pier Music Pavilion, but in the excursion district, shows tended toward burlesque and were often risqué. See Charles Funnell, *By the Beautiful Sea*, (New York: Alfred B. Knopf, 1975), 50–52. The advent of vaudeville and other mediums of popular culture made the task of censorship increasingly difficult for city officials, delineating, as it were, between the "respectable" and the "vulgar." Sunday banning of these shows was also a means of assuaging Protestant clergy who were highly suspicious of all forms of popular culture to begin with.

25. *Atlantic City Sunday Gazette*, July 13, 1902, 1.

26. *Atlantic City Press*, April 12, 1902, 1.

27. Ibid.

28. Ibid., July 22, 1902, 1.

29. Ibid., August 11, 1902, 1.

30. *Atlantic City Sunday Gazette*, December 1, 1901, 1.

31. Ibid., August 2, 1903, 1; April 2, 1905, 1; April 28, 1906, 4; June 17, 1906, 1.

32. *Atlantic City Sunday Gazette*, July 16, 1905, 1; August 6, 1905, 1; August 13, 1905, 4.

33. *Atlantic Review*, March 22, 1906, 4; March 21, 1906, 1; *Atlantic City Sunday Gazette*, March 18, 1906, 4; *Atlantic City Daily Union*, July 10, 1906, 1; *Atlantic Review*, July 11, 1906, 1.

34. *Atlantic Review*, July 12, 1906, 1.

35. Ibid., May 12, 1906, 1; May 22, 1906, 1; June 29, 1906, 4; *Atlantic City Daily Union*, April 5, 1906, 1; May 3, 1906, 1. As for the "secrecy" of the Citizens' League, its nature surfaced in a published report of council hearings on the license renewal of Robert Delaney, the proprietor of the Dunlop Hotel at Ocean Avenue and the Boardwalk, widely known as a "Boardwalk Monte Carlo," for its reputed gambling operations. One W. L. Carter, a Camden detective who had worked for Samuel Hann, was hired in 1902 by Henry W. Leeds, proprietor of Chalfonte-Haddon Hall, and William H. Wahl, another beachfront property owner, to investigate Delaney. When he was asked, "Who is the Citizens' League?" his counsel objected, saying that "council could not discover the identity of the Citizens' League by the witness." Leeds, who was a member of the council, said that the body need "not know who the Citizens' League is." William Riddle replied with the question, "Is the Citizens' League ashamed of itself?" Later it surfaced that Leeds, along with Buzby and the Whites, were the core of the League and that Wahl was its president. But League members never spoke as League members, their pronouncements and warnings coming from their attorneys, Clarence Cole and Clarence Goldenberg. See *Atlantic Review*, June 27, 1906, 1; August 20, 1906, 1.

36. *Atlantic City Daily Union*, May 4, 1906, 4; *Atlantic City Sunday Gazette*, May 6, 1906, 4. *Atlantic Review*, June 29, 1906, 4.

37. *Atlantic City Daily Union*, August 11, 1906, 1. In 1907 the city budget included a $500 donation to the Florence Crittendon Home. See *Atlantic City Review*, August 13, 1907, 1.

38. *Atlantic Review*, December 12, 1910, 1.

FIVE   *A Saturnalia of Vice* • 221

39. Although this edict did not come from the Citizens' League as such, it came from the Boardwalk hotelmen who by this time controlled that organization. It was signed by, among others, the Whites, Walter Buzby, and Councilman Henry Leeds. Like the Citizens' League memorial of 1901, it read like a *Who's Who* of wealthy beachfront interests. See *Atlantic City Daily Union*, July 26, 1906, 1, 4.

40. *Atlantic City Daily Union*, January 15, 1907, 1; *Atlantic City Sunday Gazette*, May 19, 1907, l; *Atlantic City Daily Union*, April 18, 19, 20, 22, 1907, 1.

41. *Atlantic Review*, April 23, 1907, 1.

42. *Atlantic City Daily Union*, April 23, 1907, 2; *Atlantic City Sunday Gazette*, April 28, 1907, 4.

43. *Atlantic Review*, May 13, 1907, 1.

44. Ibid., May 29, 1907, 1.

45. The "Regulations Agreed To, To Take Effect June 1, 1907" were published in full in New Jersey Dependency and Crimes Commission, *Report*, 22–23.

46. *Atlantic Review*, July 25, 1907, 1; July 29, 1907, 1; *Atlantic City Daily Union*, May 2, July 29, August 25, 1907, 1.

47. *Atlantic Review*, July 25, August 1, 1907, 1.

48. Ibid., June 27, August 20, 1906, 1; *Trenton Times*, August 3, 1906, 4; *Trenton True American*, August 12, 1908, 1. Commenting on Delaney's political aspirations, the *Sunday Gazette* offered the following: "If Delaney had been trusted with political power, any citizen can draw conclusions as to what would likely have happened. Robert Delaney socially is a good companion. Politically he was a danger to Atlantic City." Of course the *Gazette* was Kuehnle's organ. Delaney was largely ignored by the other three papers between 1901 and 1908.

49. *Trenton True American*, August 12, 1908, 1.

50. *Philadelphia Bulletin*, August 12, 1908, 1–2.

51. *Atlantic City Daily Union*, July 25, 26, 1907, 1.

52. Ibid., February 5, 1908, 1.

53. Ibid., March 28, April 10, 16, 22, 24, August 22, 1908, 1.

54. *Trenton True American*, August 13, 1908, 1, 7.

55. Ibid., August 28, 1908, 1, 5.

56. *Atlantic City Daily Union*, April 22, August 22, 1908, 1.

57. Ibid., June 19, 1908, 1. In a sweep of the Northside in September, Goldenberg's detectives arrested sixty men, "most of them colored," and most of whom were playing poker. See *Atlantic Review*, September 14, 1908, 1. By this time Goldenberg employed at least twenty-six private detectives, some of whom were paid by Boardwalk hotelmen. A year later, Daniel S. White, president of the Hotel Men's Association, referred to Goldenberg's detectives as "our detectives." See *Atlantic Review*, September 19, 1909, 1.

58. *Atlantic Review*, July 25, 1907, 1; *Trenton True American*, August 13, 1908, 1, 7. These were Warner Crowley, 23 S. Kentucky Avenue; The Illinois Club, 18 S. Illinois Avenue; "a palatial cottage" run by A. S. Rally on Montpelier Avenue; and one other run by "Harris and Sweeny," which apparently floated. Any or all of these could have been run by Delaney, but there is no solid evidence on this point.

59. *Atlantic Review*, July 6, 1908, 1; *Atlantic City Daily Union*, July 13, 1909, 1; July 14, 1909, 4.
60. *Atlantic City Daily Union*, January 9, 1908, 1.
61. *Atlantic Review*, March 9, 1910, 1.
62. Quoted in *Atlantic City Evening Union*, August 29, 1908, 4.
63. A. Maurice Low, *America at Home* (London: George Newnes, Ltd., 1908), 176–177.
64. Atlantic City's use of the allure of the forbidden received an excellent treatment in Funnell, *By the Beautiful Sea*, chap. 4, "The Perspectives of Janus," especially 76–88.
65. Quoted in *Atlantic Review*, August 26, 1908, 4.
66. New Jersey Crimes Commission, *The Report of the Secretary*, 2002. New Jersey State Archives, Trenton, N.J.
67. New Jersey Crimes Commission, *Stenographic Minutes*, "Atlantic City, General Conditions," 1696–1700.
68. Ibid., "Asbury Park, Conditions," 1821–1826.
69. New Jersey Crimes Commission, *The Report of the Secretary*, 2001.
70. William Riddle, "Killing the Goose that Laid the Golden Egg," *Atlantic City Commission Government*, vol. 2, no. 6 (January 1915), 1.
71. *Atlantic Review*, September 14, 1907, 4.
72. John F. Hall to Franklin Fort, August 27, 1908, Fort Correspondence. New Jersey State Archives, Trenton, N.J.

SIX *The Reason: The Rise and Fall of Boss Kuehnle*

1. *Atlantic Review*, May 13, 1909, 4; May 15, 1909, 1.
2. Ibid., May 25, 1909, 1. Under the city charter an ordinance needed to pass three readings to become law. Voting against the ordinance were councilmen White and Buzby, Boardwalk hotelmen, and councilmen Bacharach, Gale, and Parker, who represented the First Ward where the field was located. Riddle's bill would have eliminated the mandatory $200 fine in the Vice and Immorality ordinance allowing the city recorder, an elected magistrate, to assess whatever fine he thought appropriate for Sunday infractions. This in effect would have conferred censorship status on the recorder, instead of on the mayor and the police.
3. Ibid., June 3, 1909, 1, 3.
4. Ibid., May 31, June 5, 1909, 1.
5. For a lengthy exposition of Riddle's view on Sunday closing, see William Riddle, "Travesties of the Law—The Puritans Had Little on Atlantic City in Controlling Personal Liberty," in *Atlantic City Commission Government*, vol. 2, no. 12 (July 1914), 5.
6. *Atlantic City Sunday Gazette*, June 6, 1909, 1.
7. *Atlantic Review*, June 3, 1909, 4.
8. The Crimes Commission reported a number of almost farcical confrontations between evangelicals and participants in Sunday baseball games, particu-

SIX   *The Reason: The Rise and Fall of Boss Kuehnle* • 223

larly in Jersey City, and gave an account of their devastating effects on the poor and working classes. See New Jersey Crimes Commission, *Secretary's Report*, 1998–2001.

9. *Atlantic Review*, June 7, 8, 1909, 1.
10. *Atlantic City Evening Union*, June 8, 1909, 1.
11. *Atlantic Review*, June 9, 1909, 1.
12. Ibid., June 17, 1909, 1; *Philadelphia Evening Times*, September 1, 1909, 2; *Atlantic City Press*, June 9, 1909, 1.
13. *Atlantic Review*, July 3, 5, 27, 1909, 1.
14. Ibid., July 26, August 13, 14, 1909, 1; *Atlantic City Evening Union*, August 14, 15, 1901, 1; *Trenton Times*, August 14, 1909, 1, 11; *Trenton True American*, August 16, 24, 25, 26, 1909, 1; August 27, 1909, 2; August 31, 1909, 1.
15. *Trenton True American*, August 23, 1909, 1; August 26, 1909, 5; August 31, 1909, 1, 5.
16. *Newark Evening News*, August 31, 1909, 4.
17. *Trenton Times*, August 16, 1909, 11.
18. Quoted in *Atlantic City Press*, August 23, 1909, 5.
19. *Atlantic City Press*, August 17, 1909, 5.
20. *Atlantic Review*, August 26, 1909, 4; *Trenton Times*, August 21, 1909, 1.
21. *Trenton True American*, August 24, 1909, 1; *Trenton Times*, September 1, 5, 1909, 1.
22. *Philadelphia Evening Times*, September 5, 1909, 1, 2.
23. McMillan v. Kuehnle, 76 N.J. Equity 256 (1909). The incident was described in some detail on September 15 in front-page articles by the *Press*, the *Union*, and the *Review*, by the Philadelphia papers, and by the *Trenton True American* and the *Trenton Times*. These facts represent the only points upon which all of the sources agreed. Hearings held on September 17 disclosed nothing materially different. See *Atlantic Review* and *Trenton Times*, September 18, 1909, 1. My account is based on the *Review*, which blamed Stoy, Kuehnle, and the police; the *Press*, which blamed Goldenberg and the detectives; the *True American* and the *Philadelphia North American*, which most severely condemned the "Kuehnle-Stoy gang"; and the *Trenton Times*, which, although critical of Stoy, tended to be more careful with the facts.
24. *Atlantic Review*, September 16, 1909, 2.
25. Ibid., September 16, 1909, 4; September 15, 1909, 1.
26. *Trenton True American*, September 15, 1909, 1.
27. *Atlantic City Evening Union*, September 15, 1909, 4.
28. *Atlantic City Press*, September 15, 1909, 1, 3.
29. *Atlantic Review*, May 19, 1909, 1; *Baltimore Sun*, September 5, 1909, 2.
30. *Trenton True American*, September 6, 1909, 1. This account was corroborated by the *Trenton Times* and the *Sunday Gazette*, which described the incident as a "tiny raid in a small negro joint on Surf Avenue." See *Trenton Sunday Advertiser*, September 5, 1909, 1; *Atlantic City Sunday Gazette*, September 5, 1909, 1. See also *Trenton True American*, September 22, 1909, 1, 10, and the account of subsequent hearings on the riot in *Atlantic Review* and *Trenton Times*, September 18, 1909, 1.

224 • SIX *The Reason: The Rise and Fall of Boss Kuehnle*

31. G. Howard Fletcher to Casper Stokes, July 7, 1909, Stokes Correspondence. New Jersey State Historical Archives, Trenton, N.J.

32. *Atlantic City Sunday Gazette*, September 19, 1909, 1.

33. *Atlantic Review*, September, 18, 1909, 1,3 5; *Trenton Times*, September 18, 1909, 6; *Atlantic City Sunday Gazette*, September 19, 1909, 1.

34. *Philadelphia North American*, September 21, 1909, 1, 4.

35. *Atlantic Review*, September 20, 1909, 1.

36. *Atlantic City Sunday Gazette*, March 22, 1908, 1; March 29, 1908, 4.

37. Joseph Salus to Franklin Fort, August 28, 1909, no. 97, Fort Correspondence; *Trenton True American*, September 1, 1908, 1. New Jersey State Archives, Trenton, N.J. Apparently Salus made a strategic error in denouncing the governor. Having cast his lot with the Boardwalk faction, his outburst would not have gone well with a group anxious to placate the governor and mute the clamor of the press. Hence his candidacy did not go far.

38. *Trenton True American*, August 20, 1908, 1; September 5, 1908, 5; *Atlantic Review*, September 1, 2, 1908, 1; *Atlantic City Sunday Gazette*, July 12, 1908, 1. Walter Evans Edge presents a curious figure in Atlantic City politics during this period. In 1906 in his first attempt at elective office, he ran in the county primary for the state senate. He was defeated by incumbent Edward S. Lee, a setback which he attributed to the "Scott machine." After that the *Press* supported that organization faithfully until he ceased active involvement with the paper in 1908, when he was elected to the assembly. The *Press* remained a staunch supporter of the city against outside critics, but remained aloof from internal conflicts. All of Edge's personal and business contacts were on the beachfront. His closest friends were Henry Leeds and J. Haines Lippincott who in 1907 traveled with him to Memphis as members of his wedding party. By 1910, the conflict between the beachfront and the Old Town had become bitter. There were few places to hide, and Edge, running for the senate, campaigned with Kuehnle against Woodrow Wilson who was supported by the Boardwalk faction. All that can be said of Edge during this period is that he managed to ride out the storm without antagonizing either faction. It is characteristic of Edge that his autobiography contains absolutely no mention of the bitter conflict in his native city between 1909 and 1914, no mention of Louis Kuehnle, nor, for that matter, any reference to Enoch L. Johnson, who, along with Frank Hague, is widely credited with his election to the governor's chair in 1916. See Walter Evans Edge, *A Jerseyman's Journa*, (Princeton, N.J.: Princeton University Press, 1948), 31ff, 62–65.

39. *Atlantic Review*, September 24, 1908, 4; November 5, 1908, 1; *Atlantic City Sunday Gazette*, September 6, 1908, 4; September 13, 1908, 1; *New York Times*, January 2, 1909, 6.

40. *Atlantic City Evening Union*, May 26, 1909, 1.

41. Ibid., January 23, February 29, 1908, 1; *Atlantic City Sunday Gazette*, March 22, 1908, 1. Although the ward and precinct lines were changed from what they were in 1892, they still ran from the beach to the meadows, and this prevents a precise determination of the black influence in the primary and general elections that year. However, the greatest concentration of black votes were in

SIX *The Reason: The Rise and Fall of Boss Kuehnle* • 225

the Second and Third wards from which Stoy received majorities in November of 382 and 486, respectively. See *Atlantic City Press*, November 5, 1908, 1.

42. *Atlantic Review*, August 26, 27, 30, 1909, 1; September 20, 24, 1909, 1; *Atlantic City Press*, August 26, 27, 1909, 1; September 1, 21, 22, 23, 24, 28, 1909, 1; *Atlantic City Sunday Gazette*, September 12, 1909, 1; September 19, 1909, 1, 4; September 26, 1909, 1, 4.

43. *Trenton Times*, August 31, 1909, 1.

44. *Atlantic Review*, September 1, 21, 1909, 1.

45. Ibid., September 9, 13, 23, 25, 1909, 1.

46. *Atlantic City Sunday Gazette*, September 19, 1909, 6. The discrepancy between White's and Murray's statistics on black employment in the city was that Murray included fifteen black teachers who taught in the city system.

47. *Atlantic City Press*, September 30, 1909, 1.

48. *Atlantic Review*, October 26, November 3, 1909, 1.

49. Ransom Noble, *New Jersey Progressivism before Wilson*, (Princeton, N.J.: Princeton University Press, 1946), 146–150.

50. *Atlantic City Evening Union*, November 12, 1909, 1.

51. *Atlantic Review*, July 4, 20, 30, 1910, 1, August 2, 1910, 1.

52. Ibid., January 19, 25, 1910, 1; February 15, 1910, 4; August 2, September 10, 1910, 1.

53. Ibid., September 1, 1910, 1.

54. James Kerney, *The Political Education of Woodrow Wilson*, (New York: The Century Co., 1926), 157–158. See also *Atlantic City Press*, February 21, 1943, 5. Thomas owned all but two shares of the Review Publishing Company, and indications are that the paper was placed in his hands on liberal terms by a coalition of Boardwalk hotelmen and local and state Democrats. Thomas went bankrupt in 1926, listing a total of $50,839 in liabilities and no assets. Among his liabilities were $15,050 in "unsecured notes" owed to, among others, Charles D. White ($1,000), Daniel S. White ($3,700), and Henry Leeds ($1,500). Local Democratic creditors included Clarence Cole ($2,100). Another creditor was Wilson supporter James Kerney of the *Trenton Times* ($500). See "Examine Thomas to Find Assets," *Atlantic City Press*, June 10, 1926, 1.

55. Joseph Tumulty, *Woodrow Wilson As I Know Him* (Garden City, N.Y.: Garden City Publishing Company, 1927), 14–22; Kerney, *The Political Education of Woodrow Wilson*, 36–37; Ray Stannard Baker, *Woodrow Wilson: Life and Letters* (Garden City, N.Y.: Doubleday, Duran, and Company, 1931), 74–75; Arthur Link, ed., *The Papers of Woodrow Wilson*, vol. 21 (Princeton, N.J.: Princeton University Press, 1977), 310–320.

56. Kerney, *The Political Education of Woodrow Wilson*, 185–190. As governor, Wilson wrote the following to the Reverend Thomas B. Shannon, superintendent of the Anti-Saloon League: "They [temperance and local option] have thrown every other question, however important, into the background and have made constructive party action impossible for long years together. . . . I can never consent to having the question of local option made an issue between political parties in this state. My judgement is very clear in this matter. I do not believe

226 • SIX *The Reason: The Rise and Fall of Boss Kuehnle*

that party programmes of the highest consequence to the political life of the State and of the Nation ought to be thrust on one side and hopelessly embarrassed for long periods together by making a political issue of a great question which is essentially non-political, non-partisan, moral and social in its nature." See Link, *The Papers of Woodrow Wilson*, vol. 22, 598–599.

57. *Atlantic Review*, October 29, 1910, 1; November 3, 4, 1910, 1.

58. New Jersey State Assembly Investigation of the General Election of 1910 in Atlantic City, *Testimony* (Trenton, N.J., 1911), 1324, 1433–1434 (hereafter referred to as Macksey Commission); *Atlantic Review*, October 26, November 1, 1910, 1; William Sackett, *Modern Battles of Trenton*, vol. 2 (New York: Neale Publishing, 1914), 350.

59. Macksey Commission, *Report*, 1–9.

60. The bulk of the 1,439-page testimony centered about illegal registration which existed throughout the city and in equal proportions in both the white and black communities. See, for example, Ben Allen's hotel, ibid., 605–615, Notter's Hotel, a boardinghouse for white construction workers, 740–746. For local firemen, see 135–139.

61. Ibid., 1386.

62. Ibid., 1385.

63. Ibid., 97–103, 404–410, 676–679, 1025–1038.

64. Ibid., 162, 1249–1254.

65. Ibid., 54–58, 201–206, 497–507.

66. For Murtland, see ibid., 943–950; for Majane, 528–529, 918–919, 976–977, 1170–1171; for McDevitt, 176–182; for Griffin and Allen, 909–914; for Mahoney, 997–1002; and for Gillison, see 497–507, 1199–1200.

67. Ibid., 1432–1433.

68. Ibid., 1321–1323.

69. Of election officers, Kuehnle said to Clarence Cole, "I don't control the election officers. You know that as well as I do. I don't bother with them." See ibid., 1322. Simon Faber, among private local citizens, was the most active against organization efforts to pad the lists and import repeaters going as far as employing detectives and offering rewards for information leading to proof of irregularities. His testimony indicates his belief that Alfred Gillison directed the scheme. By his account Kuehnle "handled no money," and Isaac Bacharach, with whom Kuehnle by now was closely associated, made an honest effort to curb the worst of the abuses. See ibid., 960–963. But my assessment of Kuehnle as not being active in vote stealing is based more on the nature of the organization, Kuehnle's role in it, Kuehnle's character and reputation, and on subsequent statements by people such as Joseph Salus and William Riddle made after Kuehnle was indicted. See, for example, *Atlantic City Sunday Gazette*, March 24, 1912, 1, 6. In the election of 1910, Riddle was a candidate for Congress on the "Progressive Labor" ticket. It was only a token candidacy undertaken at the request of Samuel Gompers. On the night before the election, Riddle's office was broken into and all of the ballots with his stickers were stolen. His assessment of the election and, by extension, of Kuehnle was as follows: "No one denies that there was a large number of repeaters from Philadelphia; everyone admits that.

SIX *The Reason: The Rise and Fall of Boss Kuehnle* • 227

... The people of Atlantic City want a fair election, everybody wants that—even the people in power want it." See Macksey Commission, *Hearings*, 601. All of the evidence points to a corrupt election over which the leaders of the organization had little control.

70. Ibid., 1384, 962–963.
71. *Atlantic City Sunday Gazette*, November 13, 1910, 4; February 5, 19, 26, 1911, 4; March 5, 1911, 4; *Trenton True American*, January 6, 11, 1910, 4; *Trenton Times*, February 9, 25, 1911, 1; March 10, 1911, 6; *New York Times*, January 21, 1911, 1; February 5, 1911, 4.
72. *Atlantic City Review*, January 13, 14, 16, 21, 1911, 1.
73. Ibid., January 31, 1911, 1; March 6, 1911, 1; *Trenton Times*, March 6, 1911, 1.
74. *Atlantic City Press*, August 14, 1981, 7.
75. *Trenton Times*, March 10, 1911, 6; June 6, 1911, 6.
76. *Atlantic City Review*, June 5, 1911, 4.
77. *Trenton Times*, June 6, 1911, 6.
78. Sackett, *Modern Battles of Trenton*, vol. 2, 369–378.
79. *New York Times*, July 2, 1911, 10; July 8, 1911, 2; July 10, 1911, 4; *Atlantic City Press*, July 2, 9, 1911, 1. A complete account of the elisor grand jury was given by the *Trenton Times*, July 1, 18, 27, 1911, 1. For lengthy editorial comment, see July 3, 5, 8, 17, 1911, 6.
80. *Atlantic City Press*, July 20, 1911, 1.
81. *New York Times*, August 6, 1911, 10; August 10, 1911, 4; September 7, 1911, 1; September 29, 1911, 4; October 11, 1911, 4; October 12, 1911, 18; *Atlantic City Review*, September 29, 1911, 1; *Atlantic City Press*, September 29, 1911, 1.
82. *Atlantic City Press*, July 3, 21, 1911, 1; October 16, 1911, 1; *Atlantic City Sunday Gazette*, October 15, 1911, 1.
83. *New York Times*, July 31, 1911, 2.
84. *Atlantic City Sunday Gazette*, July 23, 1911, 1; *Atlantic City Press*, July 24, 25, 1911, 1.
85. *Philadelphia Public Ledger*, July 30, 1911, quoted in *Atlantic City Press*, July 31, 6.
86. Arthur Link, *Wilson: The Road to the White House* (Princeton, N.J.: Princeton University Press, 1965), 292–294.
87. *Atlantic City Review*, August 4, 1911, 4.
88. *Newark Evening News*, September 1, 1911, 4.
89. *Atlantic City Review*, August 14, 15, 17, 18, 19, 21, 23, 1911, 1.
90. Ibid., November 4, 1911, 4.
91. *Atlantic City Sunday Gazette*, November 5, 1911, 4.
92. *Atlantic City Review*, November 4, 1911, 2.
93. Ibid., October 31, 1911, 1.
94. Ibid., October 26, 1911, 1; *Atlantic City Press*, October 26, 1911, 1; *Atlantic City Sunday Gazette*, August 6, October 29, 1911, 1.
95. The speech is reprinted in full in Link, *The Papers of Woodrow Wilson*, vol. 23, 522–531.

228 • SIX *The Reason: The Rise and Fall of Boss Kuehnle*

96. Bacharach won by 1,414 votes, 5,087 to 3,673. Fusion candidates for sheriff and assembly were also defeated. For results, see *Atlantic City Press*, November 8, 1911, 1.

97. *Atlantic City Review*, November 8, 1911, 4.

98. *Newark Evening Call*, November 12, 1911, 4.

99. Transcripts of the Kuehnle trial were printed verbatim in the *Atlantic City Review*, December 20, 21, 22, 23, 1911. For a brief history of the United Paving Company, see *Atlantic City Press*, April 15, 1911, special section. During 1911 the company was granted $670,000 in paving contracts. For hostile comment, see *Atlantic City Review*, February 28, March 11, June 15, June 20, August 5, 1911. In January 1912 the new administration voided all city contracts with the company. See *Atlantic City Review*, January 9, 1912, 1.

100. *Atlantic City Sunday Gazette*, January 28, 1912, 4.

101. Ibid., March 25, 1912, 1, 2.

102. *Atlantic City Review*, January 13, 1912, 1; February 1, 1912, 1; *Atlantic City Press*, July 14, 1912, 1.

103. *Atlantic City Sunday Gazette*, January 21, 1912, 1.

104. *Atlantic City Review*, March 8, 1911, 1; *Atlantic City Press*, August 16, 17, 1911, 1.

105. *Atlantic City Review*, April 23, 24, 1912, 1; May 3, 15, 1912, 1; *Atlantic City Sunday Gazette*, May 19, 1912, 4.

106. *Atlantic City Review*, June 28, 1912, 1.

107. While it is doubtful that Thomas published everything that he received from Burns, the particulars of the operation were laid out in detail in the *Review* between May 31 and July 27, 1912, including verbatim printings of recorded conversations between Burns detectives and the principals in the case as well as transcripts of reports made by the detectives to Burns. Both Kessler and Phoebus admitted that everything that the *Review* printed was "essentially correct." See *Atlantic City Review*, May 31, June 1, 2, 3, 1912.

108. Ibid., May 31, 1912, 1.

109. The plan called for each of the participating members of council to receive $5,000 upon the completion of the project. The money was to be paid in stages, each man getting $500 for introducing and voting for the required ordinance. See ibid., June 14, 1912, 1.

110. Palmer was quickly shunted aside by Phoebus, but he treated the deal as he would have any real estate transaction, later demanding a $500 "commission" for setting up the transaction. See ibid., June 27, 1912, 1.

111. Ibid., June 14, 1912, 1; June 5, 1912, 1, 2; June 7, 1912, 1, 5.

112. Ibid., June 6, 1912, 1, 5; June 7, 1912, 1, 5.

113. Ibid., June 8, 1912, 1, 2.

114. Ibid., June 7, 1912, 4; June 1, 1912, 1.

115. Ibid., June 1, 1912, 2.

116. *Atlantic City Commission Government*, vol. 1, no. 1 (March 1913), 2.

117. Link, *The Papers of Woodrow Wilson*, vol. 23 (1911–1912), 309–310.

118. Kerney, *The Political Education of Woodrow Wilson*, 157–158.

SEVEN *Pharisees and Hypocrites* • 229

119. Arthur Link, *Woodrow Wilson and the Progressive Era: 1910–1917* (New York: Harper and Row, 1954), 13.
120. Kerney, *The Political Education of Woodrow Wilson*, 157–159.

SEVEN *Pharisees and Hypocrites*

1. *Atlantic City Review*, January 22, 1915, 1.
2. Robert B. Steelman, *What God Has Wrought: A History of the Southern New Jersey Conference of the United Methodist Church* (Rutland, Vt.: Academy Books, 1986), 133; City of Atlantic City, *Atlantic City Commission Government*, vol. 1, no. 5 (December 1913), 1–2.
3. *Atlantic City Review*, April 7, 1917, 8.
4. *Atlantic City Commission Government*, vol. 1, no. 5 (December 1913), 2.
5. *Trenton Times*, February 2, 1914, 1; February 3, 1914, 4; February 6, 1914, 1; February 17, 1914, 3.
6. *Atlantic City Review*, March 16, 1914, 1, 4; March 24, 1914, 1.
7. *Trenton Times*, March 17, 1914, 3; April 9, 1914, 7; April 10, 1914, 1; *Atlantic City Review*, March 24, 1914, 1; April 3, 1914, 1.
8. *Atlantic City Review*, January 2, 1914, 1; January 3, 1914, 1; January 6, 1914, 1; January 7, 1914, 1, 6; January 8, 1914, 4; January 12, 1914, 1; January 20, 1914, 1; January 21, 1914, 1.
9. Ibid., January 14, 1914, 1; January 15, 1914, 1; January 17, 1914, 1.
10. Ibid., February 18, 1914, 1; February 20, 1914, 1.
11. William H. Bartlett, "So Called 'Amusement War' Is a Myth," *Atlantic City Commission Government*, vol. 2, no. 7 (February 1915), 1–2.
12. Of the thirty-two properties listed by Thomas as disorderly houses, seventeen were white-owned establishments between 111 North Carolina Avenue and 213 North Carolina Avenue, or between Arctic and Mediterranean avenues. Properties located at 215, 219, and 219 were classified as "negro dives," and the mortgages were held by the Delaware Avenue Investment Company in which Harry Bacharach had an interest. They were not licensed to sell liquor, an almost sure indication that they were indeed brothels. But the Bacharachs owned many properties in the city, and Thomas's article, while no doubt an embarrassment to the owners and mortgagors, made no connection between prostitution and city officialdom. These properties, seventeen white and three black, constituted the tenderloin as it existed in Atlantic City in 1914. The remaining twelve, except one white-owned establishment on Mediterranean Avenue, were located on Natter's Alley, an interracial slum district within the Northside. Two were occupied by whites, and nine by blacks, but this area had never enjoyed police protection and was the continual target of raids by both city and county officials. See *Atlantic City Review*, January 19, 1914, 1.
13. Ibid., January 20, 1914, 4.
14. "The Wisconsin Idea," *Atlantic City Commission Government*, vol 1, no. 3 (June 1913), 8; *Atlantic City Review*, January 16, 1914, 1; February 16, 1914, 1.

230 • SEVEN *Pharisees and Hypocrites*

15. *Philadelphia Public Ledger*, February 24, 1914, 2.
16. Ibid., February 25, 1914, 1; *Atlantic City Review*, February 25, 1914, 1, 4.
17. *Philadelphia Public Ledger*, February 25, 1914, 1.
18. Ibid., February 26, 1914, 1.
19. *Atlantic City Press*, February 26, 1914, 1.
20. *Atlantic City Review*, February 26, 1914, 1.
21. Walter Evans Edge, *A Jerseyman's Journal* (Princeton, N.J.: Princeton University Press, 1948), 68.
22. *Atlantic City Review*, January 2, 1914, 1; January 13, 1914, 1; *Trenton Times*, April 15, 1914, 6; *Philadelphia Public Ledger*, June 5, 1914, 1; *Newark Evening News*, June 2, 1914, 10; June 4, 1914, 4.
23. *Atlantic City Review*, August 29, 1914, 1; August 31, 1914, 1.
24. *Atlantic City Review*, September 2, 1915, 1.
25. Ibid., August 31, 1914. Riddle's view of prostitution was stated at length in a municipal journal article entitled, "The Problem of the Ages, the Social Evil, Will Not Be Solved By Public Clamor." See *Atlantic City Commission Government*, vol. 1, no. 6 (January 1913), 4–5.
26. *Atlantic City Review*, July 3, 1915, 1; January 22, 1915, 1.
27. Ibid., June 22, 1915, 1.
28. Ibid., January 3, 1916, 1; January 4, 1916, 1; January 10, 1916, 1.
29. *Atlantic City Press*, May 21, 1915, 1. See also William Riddle, "Travesties of the Law—The Puritans Had Little On Atlantic City In Curtailing Personal Liberty," *Atlantic City Commission Government*, vol. 1, no. 12 (July 1914), 5.
30. Alfred M. Heston to William Riddle, January 18, 1916, Heston Collection, Atlantic City Public Library, Atlantic City, N.J.
31. *Atlantic City Press*, August 14, 1915, 1.
32. *Ibid.*, May 4, 1916, 3.
33. Heston to Riddle, January 18, 1916.
34. *Atlantic City Review*, May 8, 1916, 4; *Atlantic City Press*, April 27, 1916, 1; April 29, 1916, 1.
35. *Atlantic City Review*, May 8, 1916, 1.
36. William Riddle, "Killing the Goose That Laid the Golden Egg," *Atlantic City Commission Government*, vol. 2, no. 6 (January 1915), 1–2.
37. *Newark Evening News*, September 17, 1914, 10.
38. *Atlantic City Press*, April 10, 1916, 1, 3.
39. Ibid., April 15, 1916, 1.
40. *Atlantic City Review*, May 9, 1916, 1; *Newark Evening News*, April 11, 1916, 6.
41. *Atlantic City Press*, May 10, 1916, 1.
42. Ibid., May 11, 1916, 1; *Atlantic City Review*, May 11, 1916, 1.
43. "Atlantic City Turns Over a New Leaf," *The Survey* 44 (May 27, 1916): 216.
44. *Atlantic City Press*, January 28, 1917, 1; November 15, 1917, 1, 8; November 18, 1917, 1.
45. *Atlantic City Sunday Gazette*, September 22, 1918, 1, 2; September 8, 1918, 1, 4.

46. Ibid., July 27, 1919, 1; August 10, 1919, 1; September 7, 1919, 1; November 30, 1919, 1; February 22, 1920, 1; February 29, 1920, 1; *Atlantic City Press*, April 20, 1920, 1; May 1, 1920, 1; Herbert Asbury, *The Great Illusion: An Informal History of Prohibition* (Westport, Conn.: Greenwood Press, 1968), 243.

47. *Atlantic City Press*, January 27, 1920, 1; April 17, 1920, 1; April 26, 1920, 1; April 27, 1920, 1; April 30, 1920, 1; May 8, 1920, 1; May 10, 1920, 1; May 12, 1920, 1.

48. Ibid., May 19, 1920, 1.

49. Ibid., August 31, 1926, 7.

50. William E. Frank, Special Agent, Intelligence Unit, United States Treasury Department, and Joseph E. Burns, Special Assistant to the United States Attorney for the District of New Jersey, *The Case of Enoch L. Johnson* (special report detailing five-year investigation of Johnson under above auspices, 1941. Complete report held by New Jersey State Archives, Trenton, N.J.). See also Jack Alexander, "Boss on the Spot," *Saturday Evening Post*, August 26, 1939, 5–7, 52–53.

51. *Atlantic City Press*, May 19, 1939, 7.

52. Frank and Burns, *The Case of Enoch L. Johnson*, 1–2.

53. U.S. Congress, Senate, *Subcommittee of the Special Committee to Investigate Organized Crime in Interstate Commerce, Hearings* before the Special Committee to Investigate Organized Crime in New York and New Jersey, on S. Res. 202 (81st Congress), Washington, D.C., July 19, 1951, 989.

54. Richard Hofstadter, *Anti-Intellectualism in American Life* (New York: Alfred A. Knopf, 1962), 197; idem, *The Age of Reform* (New York: Random House, 1955), 152.

55. *Atlantic City Sunday Gazette*, June 9, 1918, 1.

56. Norman Clark, *Deliver Us From Evil: An Interpretation of American Prohibition* (New York: W. W. Norton and Company, 1976), 120–121.

57. "Atlantic City Turns Over A New Leaf," 217.

58. John Kasson, *Amusing the Million: Coney Island at the Turn of the Century* (New York: Hill and Wang, 1978), 104–112.

59. Melvin Kalfus, *Frederick Law Olmsted: The Passion of a Public Artist* (New York: New York University Press, 1990).

60. *The Survey*, May 6, 1916, 163–164.

61. James Peyton Sizer, *The Commercialization of Leisure* (Boston: Richard G. Badger, 1917), 37.

62. Ibid., 23–24.

63. Newton D. Baker, "Law, Police, and Social Problems," *Atlantic Monthly* 195 (July 1915): 12–20.

64. Paul Boyer, *Urban Masses and Moral Order in America, 1820–1920* (Cambridge, Mass.: Harvard University Press, 1978), 195–198.

65. Ronald C. White, Jr., *Liberty and Justice for All: Racial Reform and the Social Gospel* (New York: Harper and Row, 1990).

66. Peter G. Filene, "An Obituary for 'The Progressive Movement,' " *American Quarterly*, 22 (1970): 20–34.

67. Daniel Rodgers, "In Search of Progressivism," *Reviews in American History* 10 (December 1982): 122.

68. Ibid.

69. Alan Trachtenberg, *The Incorporation of America: Culture and Society in the Gilded Age* (New York: Hill and Wang, 1982), 7. See also Hofstadter, *The Age of Reform*, 7.

70. "The American Utopia: Atlantic City," *The New Republic* 25 (December 29, 1920): 126–127.

Bibliography

DOCUMENTS AND REPORTS

"Address of Hon. James F. Mintern Delivered Before the Committee to Consider Legislation Affecting Sunday Observance." Trenton, N.J.: New Jersey State Legislature, 1923.
Atlantic City Commission Government Journal, 1913–1916.
Atlantic City Common Council. *Minutes*, 1854–1920.
Atlantic City Common Council. *Public Ordinances of Atlantic City from September 8, 1854, to August 25, 1903*. Reprinted by Board of Commissioners, 1924.
Atlantic City, New Jersey, The World's Greatest Resort. Atlantic City Publicity Bureau, 1912.
Burns, Joseph W., and Frank, William E. *The Case of Enoch L. Johnson*. Special report prepared for United States Treasury Department and United States Attorney for New Jersey, 1941.
Camden and Atlantic Railroad. Annual Reports, 1868–1886.
Federal Manuscript Schedules of the Census, 1860–1920.
Garrison, C. G. *Publication of the Results of the Investigations into the Affairs of Atlantic City, September 1, 1884*.
Garrison, W. C. *The Negro in Manufacturing and Mechanical Industries*. Somerville, N.J.: Unionist Gazette Association, State Printers, 1903.
Labarre, George. "History of the Observance of Sunday." Reprint by State Legislature of six articles appearing in the *Trenton Times*, November and December 1923.
Lord's Day Alliance of the United States. *Twenty-Third Annual Report*, 1911.
New Jersey Dependency and Crimes Commission. *Stenographic Minutes*. Trenton, N.J.: New Jersey State Legislature, 1908.
New Jersey Dependency and Crimes Commission. *Report*. Trenton, N.J.: MacCrellish, State Printers, 1909.

234 • *Bibliography*

New Jersey Excise Commission. *Public Hearings*. Trenton, N.J.: New Jersey State Legislature, 1908.

New Jersey Manuscript Schedules of the Census, 1885–1915.

New Jersey Methodist Conference. *Minutes*, 1860–1920. Methodist Conference of Southern New Jersey, Archives.

New Jersey State Assembly Investigation of the General Election of 1910 in Atlantic City. New Jersey State Assembly, 1910.

New Jersey State Senate. *Protest, Testimony Taken Before the Committee on Elections and Reports of Committee in the Matter of the Contest for State Senator of Atlantic County, New Jersey between William Riddle, Contestant and Samuel D. Hoffman, Incumbent*. Trenton, N.J.: MacCrellish and Quigley, State Printers, 1893.

U.S. Congress, Senate. *Subcommittee of the Special Committee to Investigate Organized Crime in Interstate Commerce*. Hearings before the Special Committee to Investigate Organized Crime in New York and New Jersey, on Sen. Res. 202, 81st Cong., 1950 and Sen. Res. 129, 82nd Cong., 1951.

Journals and Periodicals

Alexander, Jack. "Boss on the Spot." *Saturday Evening Post*, August 26, 1939, 5–6, 52–53.

"The American Utopia: Atlantic City." *The New Republic*, December 29, 1920, 126–127.

"Atlantic City." *The Pennsy*, June 1954, 4–6.

"Atlantic City Turns Over a New Leaf." *The Survey*, May 27, 1916, 214.

Baker, Newton D. "Law, Police, and Social Problems." *Atlantic Monthly*, July 1915, 12–20.

Brett, Margaret. "Atlantic City: A Study in Black and White." *Survey*, September 7, 1912, 723–726.

Brownell, W. C. "Newport." *Scribner's Magazine*, August 1894, 137–143.

Filene, Peter. "An Obituary for the 'Progressive Movement.'" *American Quarterly*, Vol. 22, 1970, 20–24.

Rhodes, Harrison. "Atlantic City, Seeing America At Last." *Saturday Evening Post*, February 20, 1915, 11–12.

Rogers, Daniel. "In Search of Progressivism." *Reviews in American History*, December 1982, 114–132.

Russell, Don. "Atlantic City Hustle: A Profile of Corruption in the World's Playground." *January Magazine*, January 30, 1985, 5–7, 18–19.

Sardella, Carlo M. "When 'The Organization' Ruled Atlantic City." *Atlantic City Press*, June 13, 1982, Section G, 1,6.

"The Seaside." *The Lady's Friend*, January-December 1868, 640.

Snow, Robert E., and Wright, David E. "Coney Island: A Case Study in Popular Culture and Technical Change." *Journal of Popular Culture*, September 1980, 966–974.

"The Summer Problem." *Scribner's Magazine*, July-December, 1895, 56–57.

Walker, Greg. "The Only Game in Town." *Philadelphia Magazine*, August 1971, 50–55, 88–92.

NEWSPAPERS

Atlantic City Daily Press, 1895–1920
Atlantic City Daily Union, 1888–1920
Atlantic City Review, 1873–1920
Atlantic City Sunday Gazette, 1900–1920
Baltimore Sun, September 5, 1909
Newark Evening Call, November 11, 1911
Newark Evening News, January 26, 1891, 1901–1914
New York Journal, June 27, 1897
New York Sun, December 8, 1913
New York Times, 1894–1914
Philadelphia Bulletin, 1888–1913
Philadelphia Evening Times, 1909–1912
Philadelphia Inquirer, 1895–1913
Philadelphia North American, 1909–1912
Philadelphia Press, 1904–1914
Philadelphia Public Ledger, 1904–1914
South Jersey Republican, March 12, 1866
Trenton Times, 1901–1914
Trenton True American, 1908–1909
Weekly Herald (Atlantic City), March 12, 1889

SECONDARY WORKS

Adams, Henry. *The Education of Henry Adams*. Boston, Mass.: Houghton Mifflin Company, 1961.
Ahlstrom, Sidney. *A Religious History of the American People*. New Haven, Conn.: Yale University Press, 1972.
Alexander, Robert C. *Ho! For Cape Island*. Cape May, N.J.: By the Author, 1956.
Asbury, Herbert. *The Great Illusion: An Informal History of Prohibition*. Westport, Conn.: Greenwood Press, 1968.
Ashby, William M. *Tales Without Hate*. Newark, N.J.: Newark Landmarks and Preservation Committee, 1980.
Baker, Ray Stannard. *Woodrow Wilson: Life and Letters*. Garden City, N.Y.: Doubleday, Duran, and Company, 1931.
Blakely, William Addison, ed. *American State Papers Bearing on Sunday Legislation*. New York: National Religious Liberty Association, 1890.
———. *American State Papers on Freedom in Religion*. New York: National Religious Liberty Association, 1943.

Bordin, Ruth. *Frances Willard: A Biography*. Chapel Hill, N.C.: University of North Carolina Press, 1986.
Boyer, Paul. *Urban Masses and Moral Order in America: 1820–1920*. Cambridge, Mass.: Harvard University Press, 1978.
Breyfogel, S. C. *Landmarks of the Evangelical Association*. Reading, Pa.: Eagle Book Print, 1898.
Busby, Katherine. *Home Life in America*. New York: The Macmillan Company, 1910.
Camden and Atlantic Railroad. *Atlantic City, N.J.* Philadelphia: J. B. Lippincott & Co., 1873.
Carnesworth [pseud.] *Atlantic City: Its Early and Modern History*. Philadelphia: Wm. C. Harris & Co., 1868.
Clark, Norman. *Deliver Us From Evil: An Interpretation of American Prohibition*. New York: W. W. Norton Company, 1976.
Cook, W. George, and Coxey, William J. *Atlantic City Railroad: The Royal Route to the Sea*. Ambler, Pa.: Crusader Press, 1980.
Cope, Charles Henry. *Reminiscences of Charles West Cope, R. A.* London: Richard Bentley & Son, 1891.
Corocoran, A. J. *The History of Gloucester City, New Jersey*. Gloucester City, N.J.: Gloucester City Historical Society, 1973.
Cunningham, Hugh. *Leisure in the Industrial Revolution*. New York: St. Martin's Press, 1980.
Dannenbaum, Jed. *Drink and Disorder*. Chicago: University of Illinois Press, 1984.
Demaris, Ovid. *The Boardwalk Jungle*. New York: Bantam Books, 1986.
D'Emilio, John, and Freedman, Estelle B. *Intimate Matters: A History of Sexuality in America*. New York: Harper and Row, 1988.
Duis, Perry. *Public Drinking in Chicago and Boston*. Chicago: University of Illinois Press, 1983.
Dulles, Foster Rhea. *A History of Recreation: America Learns to Play*. New York: Appleton Century Crofts, 1965.
Edge, Walter Evans. *A Jerseyman's Journal*. Princeton, N.J.: Princeton University Press, 1948.
English, A. L. *History of Atlantic City*. Philadelphia: Dickson and Gilling Publishers, 1884.
Ewing, Sarah W. R., and McMullin, Robert. *Along Absecon Creek*. Bridgeton, N.J.: C.O.W.A.N. Printing, 1965.
Fecher, Charles A. *Mencken: A Study of His Thought*. New York: Alfred A. Knopf, 1978.
Federal Writers Project, Works Progress Administration. *Entertaining a Nation: The Career of Long Branch*. Bayonne, N.J.: Jersey Printing Company, 1940.
Frisch, Michael H. "The Community Elite and the Emergence of Urban Politics: Springfield, Massachusetts, 1840–1880," in *Nineteenth Century Cities: Essays in the New Urban History*. Edited by Stephen Thernstrom and Richard Sennett. New Haven, Conn.: Yale University Press, 1976.
Funnell, Charles. *By the Beautiful Sea: The Rise and High Times of That Great American Resort*. New York: Alfred A. Knopf, 1975.

Hall, Edgar Elliot. *The Negro Wage Earner in New Jersey.* New Brunswick, N.J.: Rutgers University Press, 1935.
Hall, John F. *The Daily Union History of Atlantic City and County, New Jersey.* Atlantic City, N.J.: Daily Union Printing Company, 1900.
Hand, Albert, ed. *A Book of Cape May.* Cape May, N.J.: Albert Hand Co., 1937.
Haupt, Lewis M. "Changes Along the New Jersey Coast," in *New Jersey Geological Survey 1860–1915.* Trenton, N.J.: 1915.
Heston, Alfred M. *Illustrated Hand-Book of Atlantic City, New Jersey.* Philadelphia: Franklin Printing House, 1887.
———. *Illustrated Hand-Book of Atlantic City, New Jersey.* Atlantic City, N.J.: A. M. Heston and Company, 1888.
———. *Illustrated Hand-Book of Atlantic City, New Jersey.* Atlantic City, N.J.: A. M. Heston and Company, 1889.
———. *Heston's Hand-Book of Atlantic City.* Philadelphia: Franklin Printing Company, 1892.
———. *Heston's Hand-Book of Atlantic City.* Philadelphia: Franklin Printing Company, 1894.
———. *Heston's Hand-Book of Atlantic City.* Atlantic City, N.J.: A. M. Heston, 1899.
———. *Heston's Hand-Book of Atlantic City: Twentieth Century Souvenir Edition.* Atlantic City, N.J.: Alfred M. Heston, 1901.
———. *Absegami: Annals of Eyren Haven and Atlantic City, 1609 to 1904.* 2 vols. Camden, N.J.: Sinnickson Chew and Co., 1904.
———, ed. *South Jersey, A History: 1664–1924.* 5 vols. New York: Lewis Historical Publishing Co., Inc., 1924.
Higham, John. "The Reorientation of American Culture in the 1890s," in *The Origins of Modern Consciousness.* Edited by John Weiss. Detroit: Wayne State University Press, 1965.
Hofstadter, Richard. *The Age of Reform.* New York: Random House, 1955.
———. *Anti-Intellectualism in American Life.* New York: Alfred A. Knopf, 1962.
Hollifield, A. Nelson. *Shall We Legalize Sabbath Desecration, and Racing and Gambling on Race Courses?* Newark, N.J.: Advertiser Printing House, 1891.
Kasson, John. *Amusing the Million: Coney Island at the Turn of the Century.* New York: Hill and Wang, 1982.
Kerney, James. *The Political Education of Woodrow Wilson.* New York: The Century Co., 1926.
King, James M. *Facing the Twentieth Century—Our Country: Its Power and Peril.* New York: American Union League Society, 1899.
Knobel, G. C., ed. *The Congress of the Evangelical Association.* Cleveland, Ohio: Thomas and Matill, 1894.
Laband, David N., and Heinbuch, Deborah H. *Blue Laws: The History, Economics, and Politics of Sunday Closing Laws.* Lexington, Mass.: D. C. Heath and Company, 1987.
Lauderbach, S. W. *A Century After.* Philadelphia: Allen, Lane, and Scott, 1885.

Link, Arthur S. *Woodrow Wilson and the Progressive Era: 1910–1917.* New York: Harper and Row, 1954.

———, ed. *The Papers of Woodrow Wilson.* Vols. 21, 22, 23. Princeton, N.J.: Princeton University Press, 1977.

———. *Wilson: The Road to the White House.* Princeton, N.J.: Princeton University Press, 1965.

Low, A. Maurice. *America At Home.* London: George Newnes, Ltd., 1908.

McMahon, William. *South Jersey Towns: History and Legend.* New Brunswick, N.J.: Rutgers University Press, 1983.

Morris, Edmund. *The Rise of Theodore Roosevelt.* New York: Coward, McCann, and Geoghegan, Inc., 1979.

Muelder, Walter G. *Methodism and Society in the Twentieth Century.* Vol. II of *The Methodist Church in Thought and Action.* New York: The Abington Press, 1961.

Noble, Ransom E., Jr. *New Jersey Progressivism before Wilson.* Princeton, N.J.: Princeton University Press, 1946.

Novarra, Tova. *The New Jersey Shore: A Vanishing Splendor.* Philadelphia: The Art Alliance Press, 1985.

Pierce, Arthur D. *Family Empire in Jersey Iron.* New Brunswick, N.J.: Rutgers University Press, 1964.

Pivar, David J. *Purity Crusade: Sexual Morality and Social Control, 1868–1900.* Westport, Conn.: Greenwood Press, 1973.

Rogers, Daniel T. *The Work Ethic in Industrial America, 1850–1920.* Chicago: University of Chicago Press, 1978.

Rosen, Ruth. *The Lost Sisterhood: Prostitution in America, 1900–1918.* Baltimore: Johns Hopkins University Press, 1982.

Rosenzwieg, Roy. *Eight Hours for What We Will: Workers and Leisure in an Industrial City, 1870–1920.* London and New York: Cambridge University Press, 1983.

Sackett, William E. *Modern Battles of Trenton.* Vol. 2, *From Werts to Wilson.* New York: Neale Publishing Co., 1914.

Sinclair, Andrew. *Era of Excess: A Social History of the Prohibition Movement.* New York: Harper and Row, 1962.

Sizer, James Peyton. *The Commercialization of Leisure.* Boston: Richard G. Badger, 1917.

Solberg, Winton. *Redeem the Time: The Puritan Sabbath in Early America.* Cambridge, Mass.: Harvard University Press, 1977.

Steel, Ronald. *Walter Lippmann and the American Century.* Boston: Little, Brown and Company, 1980.

Steelman, Robert B. *What God Has Wrought: A History of the Southern New Jersey Conference of the United Methodist Church.* Pennington, N.J.: The United Methodist Conference, 1986.

Sternlieb, George, and Hughes, James W. *The Atlantic City Gamble.* Cambridge, Mass.: Harvard University Press, 1983.

Strahan, Edward. *Some Highways and Byways of American Travel.* Philadelphia: J. B. Lippincott & Co., 1878.

Strong, Josiah. *Our Country.* Revised ed. Cambridge, Mass.: Harvard University Press, 1963.

Studley, Miriam V. *Historic New Jersey through Visitors' Eyes.* Princeton, N.J.: D. Van Nostrand Company, 1964.
Thompson, E. *The Making of the English Working Class.* New York: Random House, 1963.
Timberlake, John. *Prohibition and the Progressive Movement.* New York: Atheneum, 1970.
Trachtenberg, Alan. *The Incorporation of America: Culture and Society in the Gilded Age.* New York: Hill and Wang, 1982.
Tumulty, Joseph. *Woodrow Wilson As I Knew Him.* Garden City, N.Y.: Garden City Publishing Co., 1927.
Tuttle, William, Jr. *Race Riot: Chicago in the Red Summer of 1919.* New York: Atheneum, 1978.
Weintraub, Stanley. *Victoria: An Intimate Biography.* New York: E. P. Dutton, 1987.
White, E. G. *The Great Controversy between Christ and Satan.* Oakland, Calif.: The Pacific Press Publishing Company, 1892.
White, Ronald C. *Liberty and Justice For All: Racial Reform and the Social Gospel.* New York: Harper and Row, 1990.
Williamson, Jefferson. *The American Hotel: An Anecdotal History.* New York: Alfred A. Knopf, 1930.
Wilson, Harold F. *The Jersey Shore.* 2 vols. New York: Lewis Historical Publishing Company, 1953.

UNPUBLISHED MATERIALS

Alfred M. Heston Collection. Heston Room, Atlantic City Public Library, Atlantic City, N.J.
Allen H. Brown Collection. Atlantic County Historical Society, Somers Point, N.J.
Atlantic City Hotels. Clipping File, Camden County Historical Society, Camden, N.J.
"Atlantic City Industrial Improvement Company." Federal Writers Project, Atlantic City. Atlantic County Historical Society, Somers Point, N.J.
Devore, Wynetta. "The Education of Blacks in New Jersey." Ph.D. diss., Rutgers University, 1980.
"Earning a Living in Atlantic City." Federal Writers Project, New Jersey Ethnic Survey. New Jersey State Archives, Trenton, N.J.
"The Education of Negroes in Atlantic City." Federal Writers Project, New Jersey Ethnic Survey. New Jersey State Library Archives, Trenton, N.J.
Foster, Herbert. "The Urban Experience of Blacks in Atlantic City, N.J.: 1850–1915." Ph.D. diss., Rutgers University, 1981.
Governor Casper Stokes Correspondence. New Jersey State Archives, Trenton, N.J.
Governor Franklin S. Fort Correspondence. New Jersey State Archives, Trenton, N.J.

Governor Franklin Murphy Correspondence. New Jersey State Archives, Trenton, N.J.
Popper, S. H. "Newark, N.J., Chapters in the Evolution of an American Metropolis." Ph.D. diss., New York University, 1971.
"Recreation." Federal Writers Project, Atlantic City. Atlantic County Historical Society, Somers Point, N.J.
Yeager, C. "The Republican Boss Era of Atlantic City: 1900–1971." Manuscript in Heston Room, Atlantic City Public Library, Atlantic City, N.J.

Index

Absecon Island, 1; as wilderness, 14–16
Adams, Henry, 93
Addams, Jane, 198
American Sabbath Union, 68
American State Papers Bearing on Sunday Legislation (Blakely), 61, 211 n.
American Union League Society, 60–61, 212 n.
"Amusement War of 1895," 103–6
Anti-Saloon League, 60, 72, 85, 129
Asbury Park, N.J., 12, 78, 137–38
Ashby, William M., 34–35
Atlantic City: amusement industry, 24–25, 89–91, 94–95, 103–5, 108–9, 112, 119, 123, 134, 182–83, 219–20 n.; beachfront, 31–32, 44; black community (*see* Black people; Northside); Chelsea, 43; churches, 87–88; commission government, 171–73, 175–76; Ducktown, 43; ethnicity, 43; excursion district, 43, 91, 96, 98, 101, 104–5, 109, 180; founding and early years, 14–21; gambling, 2–4, 93–94, 96–97, 106, 113–14, 123–25, 130–34, 136, 147–48, 195, 221 n.; German concert gardens, 92–93; Golden Jubilee, 28; as health resort, 11–12, 20; hotels, 25–26, 30–32; Inlet, 43; liquor traffic, 89, 91–93, 99–100, 116–17; municipal corruption, 1–4, 49, 58, 174–75, 194; "Old Town," 42–43, 45, 98, 119–20, 140, 149–50, 164, 185; organized crime, 175; politics, 43–56, 114–16, 139–40, 149–55; as popular resort, 11, 202 n.; population, 20, 21, 24, 29, 91–92, 205 n.; promotion, 18, 20–22, 26–28, 56; Quaker influence, 20–21, 25–26, 32; railroads, 15–18, 23–24; as reflection of American society, 10–11, 26–30, 105–6, 109, 134–36, 139–40, 200, 208–9 n.; resort economy, 40–42; tenderloin, 44, 78, 106–8, 112–13, 114, 128, 136, 144, 182–84, 187–88, 189, 229 n.; tourism, 17, 21, 25, 29–30, 102–3, 203–4 n, 205 n.

Bacharach, Harry, 160, 162, 192, 194; and Boardwalk bribery scandal, 173; elected mayor (1911), 167–69, 171; and election of 1916, 189–90, 229 n.
Bacharach, Isaac, 116, 156, 171, 189
Bader, Edward L., 49, 141, 143, 193, 194
Baker, Newton D., 199
Baker, Ray Stannard, 199
Belisle, D. W., 89, 102
Birth of a Nation, The, 190
Bishops' Law, 73–75, 79, 126–27
Black people, 22; associated with commercial vice, 52, 99, 130–31, 145–49, 176, 183–84, 186, 221 n., 223 n.; and city's image, 35–36; and liberal policy, 128; population, 40; and Progressive reform, 10, 199; and racial violence, 38–39; and resort economy, 32–35, 40–42, 54–55, 152–53, 205–6 n.; and segregation,

241

242 • *Index*

Black people (*Continued*)
  36–39, 207 n., 208 n.; September excursions, 22, 39–40; as voters, 4, 12, 43–44, 51–56, 151–53, 169, 172, 178, 190–93, 224–25 n. *See also* Ashby, William M.; Cope, Charles West; Walls, George
Blakely, William Addison, 62–63, 66, 211 n.
Boardwalk, 22–23, 93, 108
Boardwalk bribery scandal (1912), 172–75, 228 n.
Boardwalk hotelmen, 3, 31–32, 71–72, 82, 121–22, 130, 139–40, 141–42, 149–50, 152, 161, 164; and W. J. Burns, 173; and Committee of One-Hundred, 194; and evangelicals, 182–83; purchase *Atlantic City Review*, 155. *See also* Good Citizens' League
Boom, Rev. Ernest A., 10, 83
Brandeis, Louis, 9
Brewer, Justice David J., 64
Bridgeton, N.J., 73
Brown, Rev. Alan H., 87–88, 215–16 n.
Bryan, William Jennings, 9
Bulletin (Philadelphia) probe (1890), 94–103
Burlington, N.J., 138, 144
Burns, William J., 172–75, 177

Camden, N.J., 40, 58, 70
Camden and Atlantic Land Company, 17
Camden and Atlantic Railroad, 17–19, 23, 88
Cape May, N.J., 15, 19, 30, 38, 115, 202 n., 205 n.
Cherry, William, 170, 174–75
Chicago, 62
Christian Statesmen, 63–64
Church of the Holy Trinity v. U.S., 64
Colby, Everett, 152, 154
Cole, Clarence, 48, 100, 110, 156, 162, 209 n., 219 n.
Commercial recreation: and cultural change, 4–5, 86–87, 88–89, 115; and Progressive reform, 197–98; and Protestant clerics, 5–7, 57; and racial violence, 38–39; and Sunday laws, 83–84, 142
Comstock, Anthony, 134
Coney Island, 27, 103, 104, 120, 142, 197, 202 n.
Cope, Charles West, 33
Croly, Herbert, 9

Davis, Robert, 161–62
Debs, Eugene V., 9
Delaney, Robert, 123–24, 131, 139, 151, 160, 162, 171, 220 n.

Edge, Walter E., 39, 46, 49, 90, 108, 123–25, 139, 156, 171, 173, 181, 189, 196; and Atlantic City politics, 224 n.; as gubernatorial candidate, 185–86, 199–200
Eldridge, Harry, 100, 113, 127
Elisor grand jury, 161–63
Elwood, Rev. Robert A., 109–11
English, Albert L., 22, 90, 92
Evangelical United Brethren Church, 66
Extra Dry Cafe, 97, 106, 108

Farley, Frank S. (Hap), 1–3, 195
Fish, Charles J., 58, 75
Fitzwilliams, Rev. Charles H., 111–12, 118
Fletcher, Rev. G. Howard, 147–48
Florence Crittenden Circle, 10, 127–28
Foreman Joshua, 53–54, 106, 113
Fort, Gov. John Franklin, 8, 71, 74–75, 82, 132–33, 144–45, 151, 213–14 n.; and Saturnalia proclamation, 8, 78–81, 116–17, 140, 150
Furney, William H., 51, 53–54

Gardner, John, 17, 22, 45, 50, 122, 139–40, 175
Gloucester, N.J., 103, 105, 110
Goldenberg, Clarence, 75, 132–33, 145–49, 153, 192
Good Citizens' League, 75–76, 82, 112–14, 121–24, 127–29, 132–33, 163, 219 n., 220–21 n.
Good Citizenship League, 128–30, 133
Gouldy, "Squire" John, 102
Grand juries, 71, 76, 78, 110, 114, 121–22, 161–64, 213 n., 219 n.
Grundy, Mrs., 27, 135–36

Hall, John F., 30, 51, 52, 102–3, 108, 109, 112, 140
Hann, Rev. Samuel H., 70, 83, 121–25, 127–28, 133, 144–45, 219 n., 220 n.
Heston, Alfred M., 36, 90, 189
Heston's Handbook, 26–27, 37
Hoboken, N.J., 11, 58, 73, 75, 80
Hoffman, Samuel, 44, 51, 95, 100

Hofstadter, Richard, 60, 210 n.
Hollifield, Rev. A. Nelson, 68–69, 212 n.
Hudson, Rev. Birney S., 141, 143, 144–45, 181, 182

International Reform Bureau, 59–60
Inquirer (Philadelphia) probe (1895), 103–6

Jagmetty, Victor, 47–48
Jersey City, N.J., 70, 72–73, 80, 81, 141
Johnson, Enoch L., 1, 3, 13, 50, 140, 160–61, 162, 179, 193, 194, 195, 200, 231 n.
Johnson, Jack, 4, 34, 155
Johnson, Smith E., 44, 45, 122, 140, 219 n.

Kalisch, Justice Samuel, 162
Katzenbach, Frank S., Jr., 74
Kerney, James, 156, 177
Keyport, N.J., 39, 72
Knights Templar, 60, 70, 80
Kuehnle, Louis, Jr., 1–5, 117, 119–20, 121, 130, 145, 152, 153, 161, 200; and Boardwalk bribery scandal, 172–75; as city commissioner, 194; "Commodore," 46; conviction of, 170–71, 228; death of, 194; early career, 45–47; indictment of, 162–65; and Macksey Commission, 159, 226–27 n.; personal characteristics, 47; as political leader, 47–51, 154–57, 191–94; portrayed as boss, 149–50; prison term of, 187; and Progressive reform, 196–97; on Riddle, 192; and Sunday baseball, 141–44
Kuehnle, Louis, Sr., 44
Kuehnle's Hotel, 30, 44, 72, 120, 194

Law and Order Leagues, 10, 70, 72–76, 109–14, 112, 121–22, 124–26, 144
Lee, Edward S., 49, 150, 151, 219 n.
Leeds, Chalkley, 20
Leeds, Henry W., 25, 32, 139, 141, 155, 181, 220 n., 221 n.
Lewis, Irving, 134–35
Liberal policy, 3–4, 12, 13, 56, 86–87, 89–90, 100, 104, 106, 112, 114–15, 126, 129, 138–40, 200; and popular music, 122–23, 183; and Protestant conscience, 196; and racial segregation, 128; and vaudeville, 125–26
Lippincott, J. Haines, 25, 152

Lippmann, Walter, 9, 211–12 n.
Long Branch, N.J., 11, 15, 19, 30, 70, 115, 124, 182, 205 n.
Lord's Day Alliance, 60, 68, 74, 81–84; in Atlantic City, 141–42
Low, A. Maurice, 135–36

Macksey Commission, 157–60; on Delaney, 158, 159–60; on Kuehnle, 159
Marlboro-Blenheim Hotel, 31, 34, 182
Matthews, Michael, 1
Mencken, H. L., 60, 134, 210 n.
Moore, Charles S., 162, 168, 188, 195
Muhlrad, William (Dutchy), 96–97, 106, 113–14, 131–32, 171
Murray, Rev. A. L., 148–49, 151, 153

Nation, Carrie, 70, 120
National Evangelical Association, 66–67
National Reform League, 60, 63, 211 n.
New Idea Movement, 60, 74, 78–79, 151–52
New Jersey Dependency and Crimes Commission, 11, 82, 83, 138, 140; on Asbury Park, 137–38; on Atlantic City, 136–37, 138; on Paterson, 136; on prostitution, 136; on Sunday baseball, 143; on Sunday laws, 83
New Jersey Excise Commission, 13, 58, 116, 140; on Atlantic City, 75–79, 82–83; on Sunday laws, 82
New Jersey Methodist Conference, 59, 67–68, 70, 72, 74, 81, 84–85, 117, 180
New Jersey Sabbath Association, 83
Newark, N.J., 10, 62, 65, 69, 70, 73, 75
Northside, 3, 28, 32–44, 128; and commercial vice, 97, 99, 102, 130–31, 145–49, 167–68, 178, 189–91; and Republican organization, 52–56, 151–53. *See also* Black people; Fletcher, Rev. G. Howard; Murray, Rev. A. L.; Nutter, Isaac
Nugent, James R., 157, 161, 164
Nutter, Isaac, 150–51, 153, 167, 190

Ocean City, N.J., 124–25, 128
Ocean Grove, N.J., 65, 78, 197
Olmstead, Frederick Law, 197
Organized Charities, 41–42
Osborne, Richard, 16, 17, 25

244 • *Index*

Paterson, N.J., 11, 75, 80, 136, 138, 144
Pennsylvania Railroad, 24, 25, 45, 65
Philadelphia, 15, 20–21, 91, 101, 110–11, 160
Philadelphia Sabbath Association, 61, 68
Phoebus, Samuel, 173–75
Pitney, Jonathan, 16–17, 88, 149, 203 n.
Presbyterians, 68–69, 87–88
Progressive reform, 4, 8–11, 13, 49, 164–65, 196–200; in Atlantic City, 153–54, 156, 176–78, 179, 184; and black people, 4, 8–10, 145–49, 150–53, 167–68, 189–90, 193, 196, 199; and commerical recreation, 4–5, 197–98; and liberal policy, 200; in New Jersey, 153–54; and Protestant conscience, 196; and William Riddle, 185–86; and Sabbatarianism, 174–75, 198–99
Prohibition movement, 10–11, 68–72, 84, 112, 194, 195–96
Prostitution, 2, 3, 8, 10, 98–101, 106–8, 112–13, 114, 127–28, 136, 138, 171, 182, 187–88, 229 n.; and fornication laws, 138; and venereal disease, 11, 138, 187–88. *See also* Atlantic City, tenderloin.
Protestant establishment, 9, 10, 27; and commerical recreation, 5–6, 88–89; crisis of, 57, 59–61, 87, 212 n. *See also* New Jersey Methodist Conference; Sabbatarianism
Protestant hegemony, 10, 58–60, 115, 212 n. *See also* Law and order leagues; Protestant establishment; Sabbatarianism; Sunday closing laws

Quakers. *See* Atlantic City, hotels; Atlantic City, Quaker influence; Boardwalk hotelmen

Rauschenbusch, Walter, 59
Religious Liberty Association, 66
Richards, Samuel, 16, 23, 87, 88
Riddle, William, 44–45, 48, 49, 53, 55, 130, 139, 179, 198, 200; elected mayor, 172; and election of 1916, 180–81, 186–93; on gambling, 184–86; personal characteristics, 185; as Progressive, 184; on prostitution, 182, 230 n.; on Sunday baseball, 141–42
Roosevelt, Theodore, 5, 60, 106

Royal Arch, 76–77, 81–83, 116, 117, 128–29, 147

Sabbatarianism, 4–8, 10; and censorship, 65; decline in New Jersey, 84–85; and historians, 6–8, 57, 61–62, 85; and liberal policy, 117–18; origins of, 61; and Progressive reform, 57–58, 74–85, 179–82; and Prohibition, 68, 72, 84–85, 112; and Protestant churches, 59–61, 66–70; and Roman Catholic Church, 63–64; as social control, 61, 79–81; transformation from religious doctrine to public policy, 66–85. *See also* National Evangelical Association; National Reform League; New Jersey Methodist Conference; Sunday closing laws
Salus, Joseph S., 77–78, 133, 143, 149–51, 170–72
Saratoga, 30, 124, 130, 182, 205 n.
Sea Isle City, N.J., 218 n.
Schaufler, Alois, 92–93
Schaufler's Hotel, 92–93, 94
Scott, Lewis, 45, 140
Scribner's magazine, 5
Seaford, Del., 39
Seventh Day Adventists. *See* Sabbatarianism
Sizer, James Peyton (*The Commercialization of Leisure*), 198
Social Gospel movement, 199
Social purity movement, 97–98
Sousa, John Philip, 123
Stoy, Franklin P., 45, 71, 75, 77, 81, 118, 119–20, 125–27, 130; and Amusement War of 1895, 103–6, 108; death in 1911, 163; and election of 1908, 149–53
Stokes, Gov. Casper M., 72, 79, 147
Sunday baseball, 83–85, 141–45, 149, 150, 152, 176, 196, 222 n.
Sunday closing laws, 6, 61–66, 79, 103, 108, 145, 184; Crimes and Excise commissions on, 82–84; and federal courts, 64; and German-Americans, 62, 65; and grand juries, 65, 71, 73, 76, 121; and Jews, 64–65, 84, 211–12 n.; legislative hearings, 83–84, 179–82; municipal ordinances (Atlantic City), 90–91, 94–95, 119–20, 218 n., 222 n.; and New Jersey courts, 64–65, 212 n.; and New Jersey

politics, 71–75, 84; and working classes, 222 n.

Thomas, Harvey, 155, 161, 164, 181, 189, 200; and *Atlantic City Review*, 225 n.; on Kuehnle, 164–66; as Progressive journalist, 178, 183–84, 191; and Wilson's presidential campaign, 176–78
Thompson, E. P., 85–86, 215 n.
Thompson, James B., 103, 110
Thompson, Joseph B., 44, 48, 110, 145, 180, 189, 219 n.
Traymore Hotel, 25–26, 31–32
Tumulty, Joseph P., 156

United Paving Company, 170
Usry, James, 1

Villard, Oswald Garrison, 79, 199
Vorhees, Gov. Foster M., 71
Vorhees Act, 71, 118, 145, 162

Walls, George, 37
Walsh Act, 171–72
Washington, Booker T., 36, 134
West Jersey and Atlantic Railroad, 24

White, Charles D., 146, 189
White, Daniel S., 26, 31, 139, 142, 151, 152, 164, 194; and Harvey Thomas, 155; as mayoral candidate, 167–69
White, John J., 77–78, 117, 180, 182, 184, 188
Whitman, Walt, 23–24
Willard, Frances, 63
Wilson, Edmund, 161–62, 176
Wilson, Woodrow: on Atlantic City, 2, 4, 9, 168–69, 200; and election of 1910, 153–57; on Kuehnle, 156; presidential campaign of, 176–78; on Prohibition, 156, 225–26 n.; and reform movement in Atlantic City, 163, 164, 175
Winter, William, 75–76, 81
Wittpenn, Otto, 75
Women's Christian Temperance Movement (WCTU), 60, 81, 127, 134, 141
Woodruff, Malcomb, 75, 76, 127–28, 146, 158
Wright, Willard, 44, 51, 52, 100, 110

YMCA, 9, 127–28, 197
YWCA, 197
Young's Pier, 94, 124–25

www.ingramcontent.com/pod-product-compliance
Lightning Source LLC
Chambersburg PA
CBHW022041290426
44109CB00014B/942